Divine Design for Discipleship

Following God's Blueprint for Spiritual Development

By

Chad M. Craig

Divine Design for Discipleship
by Chad M. Craig

Printed in the United States of America

ISBN 978-1-60647-643-7

www.xulonpress.com

Reference Sources Used:

Astronomical League (2008). Retrieved July 6, 2008, from http://www.astroleague.org/al/astrnote/astnot19.html

Barnhouse, Donald. *The KJV New Testament Greek Lexicon.* Retrieved July 6, 2008, from http://bible1.crosswalk.com/Lexicons/Greek/grk.cgi?number=1384&version=kjv

Collins, Paul, Bunty, and David. *Back to the Gospel.* Newcastle, Australia: Fountaingate Christian Foundation, 1994.

Maxwell, L.E. *Born Crucified.* Chicago: Moody Press, 1945, 1973.

Strong, James. *New Strong's exhaustive concordance of the Bible.* Nashville, TN: Thomas Nelson Publishers, 1990.

Zodhiates, Spiros. *The Hebrew – Greek Key Study Bible King James Version The Old Testament The New Testament Zodhiates' original and complete system of Bible study.* Chattanooga, TN: AMG Publishers, 1984.

Endorsements

Chad has been a vital part of our staff here at Free Chapel. The powerful principles in this book have been proven time again as Chad has put them into practice with hundreds of new converts in our congregation who were seeking to discover God's destiny and calling for their lives. "Making disciples" is the passion of Chad's life, and in this book I pray his passion will ignite yours as never before.

Jentezen Franklin
Senior Pastor, Free Chapel
Author of NY Times Best Seller, Fasting

Life's lessons are not always easily learned, and many believers become discouraged in their journey with the Lord. Chad Craig's new book *Divine Design for Discipleship* will be a valuable tool to every believer no matter where they are in their walk. Having a strong foundation built upon the Word of God will provide a steadying influence during those times when we wonder if He has forgotten about us. Reading this book will refresh, encourage, and motivate you to fulfill your special destiny in the kingdom of God. I had the privilege of serving as Chad and Michelle's pastor, and watched them grow and develop in their walk with Christ. I am very proud to endorse his book.

Dr. Bob Rodgers
Senior Pastor
Evangel World Prayer Center
Louisville, KY

ACKNOWLEDGMENTS

I want to first acknowledge and thank all of the men and women of God whose writings the Lord has used to speak into my life. The number of books and authors that I have gleaned from over the years are too numerous to acknowledge individually. I am forever grateful for their hours of study that have led to numerous truths being imparted into my life. However, during the writing of this book I did not consult any other book than those referenced above. Any truths, or the presentation of these truths, that may be similar to any previous copyrighted works was done unknowingly and therefore is asked to be forgiven.

I want to specifically acknowledge and honor Paul, Bunty, and David Collins for their original presentation of the terms: Christ Died For Me, Christ Died As Me, Christ Lives In Me, and Christ Lives Through Me. These biblical terms have been adapted and used in this book.

I want to thank Karol Scarborough for all her help, with the editing of this book.

Lastly, I want to acknowledge the three leaders that I have served under: Neil Bush, Bob Rodgers, and Jentezen Franklin. May God continue to bless and increase each of you!

Dedication

I dedicate this book to my wonderful wife, Michelle, and our child.

Lord Jesus, I dedicate more than a book to you, I give you my life. Thank you for your patience with me, your faithfulness, and your overwhelming grace. Holy Spirit, I want to thank you for your continual comfort and for leading me into all truth. Father, God, thanks for being the perfect Father and always loving me. May you alone be gloried through this book!

Table of Contents

Section I.

Foundation Phase – Christ Died For You

Chapter 1

Ages, Stages, & Phases

The term "discipleship" refers to the overall process that God uses to lead you toward maturity in Christ. This book is divided into five sections with each section representing a phase of God's divine design for your discipleship. Each phase of spiritual development is presented in the order that God has divinely designed. A chart is presented that highlights key information that is connected to each phase of discipleship.

Ages and the Elementary Principles of Christ

The term "ages" refers to the three major periods of time you will live through before you enter into eternity. The truths concerning these three ages establish the broadest part of the mental framework for spiritual development. The first age is connected to the first two elementary principles of Christ. There are six elementary principles of Christ and they can be grouped in three pairs of two. These first two elementary principles of Christ are repentance and faith toward God.

"Therefore, leaving the discussion of the elementary principles of Christ, let us go on to perfection (maturity), not laying again the foundation of repentance from dead works and of faith toward God,

of the doctrine of baptisms, of laying on of hands, of resurrection of the dead, and of eternal judgment."
          Hebrews 6:1-2 (Parenthesis Mine. NKJV Marginal Reading)

The reason they are the first two elementary principles of Christ is because they are the commanded responses to the person of Christ, and they are the principles that brought you out of the first age of your life and brought you into a second age. The first age represents the period of your life when you lived in sin, under the influence of Satan and his kingdom. You now live in the second age, or period, before you enter eternity. You now live under the reign of Jesus Christ while in a world that still remains under the influence of sin and Satan.

"We know that we are of God, and the whole world lies under the sway of the wicked one."
          1 John 5:19

Satan's kingdom of fear and death is reigning in the lives of all unbelievers. At one time in their life, all believers were under the influence of Satan and sin. That age was a time in your life when you walked according to the lust of your flesh.

"And you He made alive, who were dead in trespasses and sins, in which you once walked according to the course (age) of this world, according to the prince of the power of the air, the spirit who now works in the sons of disobedience, among whom also we all once conducted ourselves in the lusts of our flesh, fulfilling the desires of the flesh and of the mind, and were by nature children of wrath, just as the others."
          Ephesians 2:1-3 (Parenthesis Mine. Marginal Reading in NKJV)

This was the situation you found yourself in before you repented and believed in Christ to save you from your condition. However, when you received Christ as your Lord and Savior, God then *"delivered you from the power of darkness and conveyed (transferred) you into the kingdom of the Son of His love, in whom you have redemp-*

tion through His blood, the forgiveness of sins" Colossians 1:13-14 *(Parenthesis Mine. Marginal Reading in NKJV).* You have passed from death to life, from the kingdom of Satan to the kingdom of Jesus Christ. (See John 5:24) You no longer live under the reign of the first age but have now entered the second age of your experience before eternity.

The second pair of elementary principles of Christ are called the doctrine of baptisms and the laying on of hands. These two elementary principles deal with the second age in your life experience. This second age is the current experience for all of the followers of Jesus Christ who are living on the earth. This age is characterized by the contrast of being saved and living your life under the reign of Jesus Christ, while being surrounded by unbelievers who are still living under Satan's kingdom. You are part of the body of Christ, which is the chosen vessel of God to administer the rule and reign of Christ upon the earth and its inhabitants. The amazing truth about this age is that you can experience the power, works, and reign of the Millennium to come as well as be an instrument in the hand of God to rescue people's lives from the reign of Satan. As a believer, your life is going to be lived in this contrast: longing for what shall be while waiting for what is to pass away. These two principle doctrines of baptisms and the laying on of hands deal with your current experience as you live in the kingdom of God. These two principles instruct you in regards to your behavior and purposes in the kingdom of God.

The last group of two consists of the elementary principles of resurrection of the dead and eternal judgment. These two elementary principles deal with the last age in your experience before entering into eternity. The third age is the coming period of the Millennial reign of Jesus Christ over the nations of the world. Jesus Christ will return and establish the physical manifestation of His kingdom and Lordship. This period is what is referred to as the Millennial Reign of Christ or the age of the Millennium. Millennium is the Latin word for a thousand. This age to come is a period of time that will last for a thousand years before you enter into eternity. Truths found within the principles of the resurrection of the dead and eternal judgment of believers pertain to this last period before eternity. (See Revelation

20:4-6) These two principles of Christ instruct you about preparing for the age to come. Your life now determines the rewards you will receive from Christ during the Millennium. Therefore, the three pairs of elementary principles correspond with the three major ages in the life of every believer. These three ages coincide with the three pairs of principles and can be summed up as pertaining to: how to exit Satan's kingdom and enter the kingdom of God, life once in the kingdom, and the end judgment of our faithfulness to the kingdom of God.

Age 1: Satan is the god over this age.
Sin and death reign over unbelievers.
It is passing away.

Age 2: This is the age you currently live in.
You are living as a member of the body of Christ.
You can experience the age to come while you wait in hope.
You are to be an instrument of Christ to rescue people from
the current age of Satan's rule that is passing away.

Age 3: Christ returns.
He sets up His physical kingdom.
He is Lord over all the earth for 1,000 years.
This is referred to as the Millennium.
Christ rewards His followers for their obedience during
Age 2.

Stages and the Primary Division of Truth

As a follower of Christ, you find yourself living in age two as a member of the body of Christ. During this age, as you look forward with telescope vision concerning the spiritual journey you are on, other major milestones become apparent. These major milestones are four stages on your journey toward maturity in Christ. The stages reflect the ordinary growth patterns of humans. These stages are clearly presented in the Word of God as: babe, child, young man, and father. These growth stages, though spoken of in the masculine, apply likewise to female believers. These four stages illustrate the journey God has planned in order for you to become mature in Christ.

*"And I, brethren, could not speak to you as to spiritual people but as to carnal, as to **babes** in Christ."*

1 Corinthians 3:1(Bold mine.)

*"I write to you, little **children**, because your sins are forgiven you for His name's sake. I write to you, **fathers**, because you have known Him who is from the beginning. I write to you, **young men**, because you have overcome the wicked one."*

1 John 2:12-13 (Bold mine.)

Understanding what natural growth stage a person is in is extremely important. Your needs, diet, abilities, and knowledge differ according to the natural growth stage you are in. A baby has different needs than a father. Not only do their needs differ but also their diet. A baby cannot eat any kind of food but must have the specific diet that is necessary for the baby's current stage of growth. A baby does not receive correction and discipline for crying. As adults we understand that they have not matured and become capable of expressing themselves in a different manner. We do not hold them accountable for their actions because of the stage of growth they are in. However, if a teenager still cries when hungry then either their growth pattern is abnormal or they need to be seriously held accountable for their actions.

This is the same for your spiritual growth. Recognizing what spiritual growth stage you are in is just as important. If you view and deal with yourself as a father in the faith when you are in the stage of being a child in the faith, or vice versa, great damage can occur, hindering your spiritual growth. You must identify what stage of spiritual growth you are in because, what God wants to do currently in your life is determined by what spiritual growth stage you are in. God does not deal with His children who are babes on the spiritual journey as if they were fathers in the faith. The needs, diet, abilities, and knowledge differ according to what stage you are in spiritually.

For instance, if a baby eats meat, serious damage can occur and it is the same spiritually. Many times believers try to get ahead of the spiritual stage they are in. This always becomes a hindrance to their spiritual growth. I have seen this happen in the lives of many. Whether they pursued meat teachings found in the Word of God, or being involved in full time ministry before they were spiritually ready, the result was not positive. When you do not receive what God has for you in your current growth stage you become the biggest enemy to your destiny of being conformed to the image of Christ and living out your calling for His kingdom. You must recognize what growth stage you are in, be willing to learn from God's blueprint what diet of the Word of God you should be digesting, and grow up in all things according to the stage of spiritual growth you are in.

The chart also illustrates the primary divisions of truth contained in the Word of God and how they are connected to each phase of spiritual development. The primary division(s) of truth next to each phase demonstrates the portion of Scripture that should be your spiritual diet for that phase. The teachings contained in the primary division(s) of truth, is what are relevant to what God is doing in your life during that phase. All Scripture is profitable and necessary. However, certain divisions of its truth should be your primary spiritual diet during a certain phase.

Stages:
Babe
Child
Young Man or Young Woman
Father or Mother

Primary Divisions of Truth:
Gospel of Jesus Christ – This pertains to the person, life, finished work of Jesus Christ, the salvation made available for your life, and how you are commanded to respond.

Elementary Teachings of Christ – This pertains to the basic or beginning teachings or principles of Christ.

Gospel of Grace – This pertains to what God has freely provided for you through the finished work of the cross.

Paul's Gospel – This pertains to the completed revelation of God's plan.

Word of Righteousness – This pertains to the doctrine of being in right standing with God.

Revelation of the Mystery – This pertains to God's secret plan kept secret before the world began but accomplished through the cross of Christ.

Gospel of the Kingdom – This pertains to God's plan to establish His rule and authority upon the earth.

Phases

The term phases refer to the type of spiritual development that God is working toward during each stage of growth. As the temple of God, you are being built during each stage of growth by the Holy Spirit to be the dwelling place of God in the Spirit. (See Ephesians 2:22) God is constructing your life according to the blueprint in His Word. During this construction process there are phases of development. There are five phases of development that can be discovered in the Word of God concerning God's blueprint for His dwelling place. These phases are: foundation, transformation, formation, impartation, and multiplication. Each phase emphasizes a different aspect of what God desires to do in your life. Like building a house, each phase connects and continues from the work of the previous phase. If a builder does not follow the natural order of phases for the development of a home, the structure will not be built according to the blueprint and will lead to serious structural problems. Any good builder knows not to start the flooring and studding of a home without the foundation being completed. God also knows how to develop you into His dwelling place. We must follow His blueprint and no other.

God is ultimately the great architect. He laid the foundation of the earth and stretched out the heavens as a frame. The psalmist declares, *"Of old You laid the foundation of the earth, and the heavens are the work of Your hands" (Psalm 102:25).* You, also, as the temple of God are the work of His hands. As a human being, you are a person who is made of three distinct components. These three components are spirit, soul, and body. *"Now may the God of peace Himself sanctify you completely; and may your whole spirit, soul, and body be preserved blameless at the coming of our Lord Jesus Christ" (1 Thessalonians 5:23).* Your whole person consists of spirit, soul, and body. As God works in your life toward completing His blueprint for His temple, He starts in the deepest part of you and works out. God has a foundation for your life that pertains to your spirit. Paul speaks about this saying, *"For no other foundation can anyone lay than that which is laid, which is Jesus Christ" (1 Corinthians 3:11).* Jesus Christ, the Word of God, is the foundation for your life. When you received Jesus Christ, He came to dwell in your spirit.

After the foundation, which relates to the spirit of man, is completed, God begins the transformation and formation phases. These two phases deal primarily with the soul of man. The soul consists of your mind, will, and emotions. The soul affects your character and behavior. Then the last two phases, impartation and multiplication, deal primarily with the body of man. These phases deal with your activity and purpose within the kingdom of God.

God has a blueprint for His dwelling place. It is of great importance that you learn the phases of development God has planned for you and the order in which you are to experience them. As humans, we are tempted to follow our own pattern instead of God's, but we must humbly submit to His divine design.

"Trust in the Lord with all your heart, and lean not on your own understanding; in all your ways acknowledge Him, and He shall direct your path."

Proverbs 3:5-6

On this journey of spiritual growth and development, let God's blueprint, as revealed in His Word, direct your path. If you do, your path will be made straight. If you choose your own path, you will create great hindrances in reaching the goal of maturity in Christ. Lean on the understanding that God provides because He is the great architect. Acknowledge and trust in His divine design for discipleship because you are "God's building" (1 Corinthians 3:9).

Phases:
> Foundation
> Transformation
> Formation
> Impartation
> Multiplication

The Primary Methods ("M")

For the phases of discipleship, there are primary methods that helps facilitate your spiritual development. Each method aids and assists your spiritual development for the phase that it is correlated with. These methods are tools that God desires to use to accomplish what He has divinely designed. Each of these methods is important and has a place in your life; however, each method has a special importance to the phase it is connected with. The four primary methods all begin with the letter "M." Therefore, I refer to these methods as the four "M's" or the primary "M." Each method is explained during the section on the phase for which it is the primary factor that facilitates spiritual development.

Methods:
> Ministry of the Word
> My Role
> Modeling Community
> Mentoring

Three Ages Elementary Teachings of Christ Represent	Spiritual Growth Stages	Phases for Discipleship	Primary Division of Truth	Primary "M" Facilitates Growth for Phase
Age 1 Transferring Kingdoms *Repentance from Dead Works and Faith toward God*	Babes	I. Foundation 1 Cor.3:11 (Spirit)	Gospel of Jesus Christ, Elementary Teachings of Christ Overview	Ministry of the Word
	Little Children		Gospel of Grace, Paul's Gospel, Word Of Righteousness	
Age 2 Life in God's Kingdom *Doctrine of Baptisms and Laying on of Hands*	Little Children	II.Transformation Rom. 12:2 (Soul)	Revelation of the Mystery	My Role
	Children			
	Children	III.Formation Gal.4:19 (Soul)	Revelation of the Mystery	Modeling Community
	Young Men			
	Young Men	IV.Impartation Matt.10:7-8 (Body)	Gospel of the Kingdom	Mentoring
Age 3 Life in the Millennium *Rewards for Resurrection and Judgment*	Father	V.Multiplication John17:6-8,20 (Entire Person)	Whole Counsel of Scripture	All the M's

Phase
Introduction

Foundation phase is connected to the first pair of the elementary teachings of Christ that consists of repentance from dead works and faith toward God. This first pair of elementary teachings represent the first age of your life experience before receiving Christ. These two elementary teachings are the responses a person are to have to the gospel and person of Christ in order to enter the kingdom of God through the new birth. The next pair of elementary teachings also applies to the latter part of the phase. The second pair of elementary teachings consists of the doctrine of baptism and the laying on of hands. These two doctrines speak to the age and period of time that you are now living in within the kingdom of God. It is because a new believer has become a part of the body of Christ and been command to be water baptized that also makes this pair connected to this phase of spiritual development.

During this phase a believer should progress in the spiritual development stages from being a babe in Christ to a little child. Foundation phase deals primarily with the spirit of man and what happens when you receive Christ. As a believer feeds on the right division of truth they will continue to grow. The primary divisions of truth that are relevant for this period of spiritual development are the gospel of Jesus Christ, the elementary teachings of Christ, and Paul's gospel. Within the gospel Paul received from the Lord are found the fulfilled teachings of the gospel of grace and the word of righteousness and are relevant for this phase. The primary method that facilitates growth for foundation phase is the ministry of the word through both its preaching and teaching. See the chart on the previous page!

Chapter 2

Christ Crucified

"And I, brethren, when I came to you, did not come with excellence of speech or of wisdom declaring to you the testimony of God. For I determined not to know anything among you except Jesus Christ and Him crucified. I was with you in weakness, in fear, and in much trembling. And my speech and my preaching were not with persuasive words of human wisdom, but in demonstration of the Spirit and of power, that you faith should not be in the wisdom of men but in the power of God."

1 Corinthians 2:1-5

Jesus Christ and Him crucified is the core of what you needed to hear and understand in order to come into a relationship with God. Through the finished work of Christ, the forgiveness of your sins and peace with God is offered to you. Jesus has become an open door for you to come into a right relationship with God the Father. Jesus' death provides you with the option of no longer living in sin, rebellion, or apart from God's will for your life. Jesus died to give you a new life. A life lived in right standing with God and for His glory. To live for God's glory means you live no longer for yourself but for His will. Jesus died so you can be changed, and to remove any excuses of why you can't change. God, through Jesus Christ, offers to change you. He offers to save you from your sin. He offers to save you from an eternity of being separated from God. Christ crucified is God's testimony that you can be saved. Christ crucified is God's testimony that you can be forgiven. Jesus died for you. He took the punishment you deserved. He shed His blood so you could be cleansed from your sin. He took your place. He took your sins. He took your guilt. Through this message God is saying, "Jesus is the Christ, the way, the truth, and the life!"

When the gospel is preached it is declaring the testimony of God concerning His Son Jesus Christ. The message of the gospel is to be presented in simplicity in order for your faith to be in the power of God and not in the wisdom of men. God chose and was pleased *"through the foolishness of the message preached to save those who believe"* (1 Corinthians 1:21). Christ crucified is both the power of God and the wisdom of God. (See 1 Corinthians 1:24) Through the hearing of the gospel you are confronted with the person of Jesus Christ. It is through this encounter with Jesus that God gives individuals the revelation that Jesus is the Christ, the Son of the living God. Becoming a follower of Christ is more than just believing in certain facts it is responding to an encounter and revelation of who Jesus Christ is. The very person and presence of Jesus Christ is present when the testimony of God is being proclaimed. Accepting that the preaching of the gospel is bringing you into an encounter with Christ will help you more accurately understand how God has commanded for you to respond.

The Rock Revealed

"When Jesus came into the region of Caesarea Philippi, He asked his disciples, saying, 'Who do men say that I, the Son of man, am?' So they said, 'Some say John the Baptist, some Elijah, and others Jeremiah or one of the prophets.' He said to them, 'But who do you say that I am?' Simon Peter answered and said, 'You are the Christ, the Son of the living God.' Jesus answered and said to him, 'Blessed are you, Simon Bar-Jonah, for flesh and blood has not revealed this to you, but My Father who is in heaven. And I also say to you that

you are Peter, and on this rock I will build My church, and the gates of Hades shall not prevail against it.'"

Matthew 16:13-18

The foundation for the New Testament church is the confession that Jesus is the Christ, the Son of the living God. It is upon this understanding that the church is founded or built. This also is the foundational truth that unifies the body of Christ. However, in order for a person to be able to confess this truth, God the Father must first reveal Christ to them. The revelation, or spiritual understanding, that Jesus is the Christ does not come from man but only from God the Father. Jesus told Simon-Peter that it was the Father in heaven who had revealed that truth to him. This is important for you to understand. Paul was making the same point when he said, *"that your faith should not be in the wisdom of men but in the power of God"* (1 Corinthians 2:5). Whether it was through a friend, a preacher, a dream, a vision, or any other means that you heard the gospel, the revelation that Jesus is the Christ comes only from God the Father. He may work through different means but ultimately, if you recognize that Jesus is the Christ, the Son of the living God, the Father Himself has revealed it to you. When this happens your understanding concerning Jesus Christ is not based on your opinion, your friends' opinion, a denomination's opinion, or any other opinion but upon a revelation you were given from God the Father.

"For no other foundation can anyone lay than that which is laid, which is Jesus Christ."

1 Corinthians 3:11

Jesus Christ is the foundation. Any other foundation is faulty and will not endure. The foundation phase is about that you having the Jesus Christ as the foundation to build your life on. The revelation that the Father gives concerning Jesus does not automatically save you from your sins and put you in a right relationship with God. When the Father reveals to you that Jesus is the Christ a question follows, "How will you respond to what you now know?" You must respond to the person of Jesus Christ. You can no longer deny that He is the way, the truth, the life. You can no longer live in ignorance of the truth. God has revealed the truth to you. Now, how you respond to the truth is your decision, not God's.

When you have received this revelation from God the Father, it is easy to accept the authority of the written Word of God. Why? The Bible is the book that contains the record of the life and teachings of Jesus. Jesus was the living word of God. (See John 1:1,14) The Bible is the written Word of God, and just as powerful, alive, and active as Jesus was when He walked on this earth. (See Hebrews 4:12 and 2 Timothy 3:14) Since God has revealed to you that Jesus is the truth, the Scriptures He taught from, and that contain His life and teachings, must also be true. The revelation the Father gives becomes an authoritative witness of truth concerning Jesus Christ and the Bible.

Another witness the Father has provided for you concerning Jesus Christ is the fact of His resurrection. The resurrection declares that Jesus is King, Lord, and Judge. In Romans 1:4 we read Jesus was, *"declared to be the Son of God with power according to the Spirit of holiness, by the resurrection from the dead."* The resurrection is therefore another testimony of God the Father's that Jesus is the Christ.

Jesus, who the Father has witnessed is the truth, taught from all the Old Testament Scriptures and also said, *"The Scripture cannot be broken"* (John 10:35). The Bible is the trustworthy and authoritative source of spiritual truth. It is in the Bible that you can find out how you are to respond to the truth that Jesus is the Christ, the Son of the living God.

"But why do you call Me 'Lord, Lord,' and not do the things which I say? Whoever comes to Me, and hears My sayings and does them, I will show you whom he is like: He is like a man building a house, who dug deep and laid the foundation on the rock. And when the flood arose, the stream beat vehemently against that house, and could not shake it, for it was founded on the rock. But he who heard and did nothing is like a man who built a house on the earth without a foundation, against which the stream beat vehemently; and immediately it fell. And the ruin of that house was great."

Luke 6:46-49

To build your life upon the foundation of Jesus Christ also means to build your life upon the written Word of God. Notice that Jesus said that only if your life is built upon the Word of God will you have an everlasting foundation. If you will build your life on the rock of God's Word you will have an unshakable foundation. Your life cannot be built upon an experience and you have a solid foundation. Your life cannot be built upon emotions and you have a solid foundation. Experiencing God's presence and weeping is not a solid foundation. However, when your life is built upon Jesus, and His words, you will be able to stand the trials and test of time.

"Repent, for the kingdom of heaven is at hand."

Matthew 4:17

Truly, these times of ignorance God overlooked, but now commands all men everywhere to repent, because He has appointed a day on which He will judge the world in righteousness by the Man whom He has ordained. He has given assurance of this to all by raising Him from the dead."

Acts 17:30-31

The first response Jesus said you are to have to what the Father has revealed to you concerning Him is to repent. The Apostle Paul also said that God has commanded all people to repent because He has appointed a day when Jesus will judge the world. Repenting is having a change of mind. You come to a place where you no longer want to live your life in rebellion against God. You are willing to turn from a life of selfishness and sin. True repentance is experiencing godly sorrow. (See 2 Corinthians 7:9-10) You have sorrow that your sin sent Jesus to be crucified. It was your actions that drove the nails into the Lord's body. It was your rebellion that put the crown of thorns upon His head. He was crucified for your sin.

Repentance is important because it is commanded. It is necessary for you to understand that you must be willing to forsake your life of sin in order to be a follower of Christ. Any gospel presentation that gives the idea that you can keep your life of self will and sin and receive eternal life is false. The Apostle Paul said, *"Nevertheless the solid foundation of God stands, having this seal: 'The Lord knows those who are His,' and, 'Let everyone who names the name of Christ depart from iniquity'"* (2 Timothy 2:19). A solid foundation that has God's seal of approval comes from true repentance. If you desire to be a follower of Christ, or called a Christian, then you must be willing to depart from your lifestyle of sin.

Christ crucified is the power of God to change you. True repentance is desiring to have God save you from your life of sin; not just save you from an eternity in hell. True repentance is seeing your sin in the light of God's holiness. True repentance causes you to view sin differently. Christ crucified is the picture of how sin must be punished by God. When you encounter Christ you must respond with repentance. You must be willing to turn from a life that was in rebellion to Jesus to a life that is in submission to Him.

"Testifying to Jews, and also to Greeks, repentance toward God and faith toward our Lord Jesus Christ."

Acts 20:21

The second response that is commanded by the Word of God is sincere faith. Faith is being assured and confident that what God has said and promises is true. Faith is being assured that Jesus is the Christ. Faith is having confidence that the claims of the gospel of Jesus Christ are true. Sincere faith leads you to receive and believe on Christ as your Lord and Savior.

"That whoever believes in Him should not perish but have eternal live. For God so loved the world that He gave His only begotten Son, that whoever believes in Him should not perish but have everlasting life. For God did not send the His Son into the world to condemn the world, but that the world through Him might be saved. He who believes in Him is not condemned; but he who does not believe is condemned already, because he has not believed in the name of the only begotten Son of God. And this is the condemnation, that the light has come into the world, and men loved darkness rather than light, because their deeds were evil."

John 3:15-19

Believing is more than faith. Faith is a noun but believing is a verb. Believing speaks of the commanded responses. It is more than mentally agreeing. When the Bible speaks of believing it entails repentance and faith. Believing is to receive the person of Christ as your Lord and Savior. Believing is to receive the Spirit of Christ to dwell on the inside of you. Believing leads to confessing Jesus as Lord with your mouth and through water baptism. This is more than just facts. This is the power of God to change your life. God does not condemn people; they condemn themselves by not believing. Notice in the above verses that loving darkness and participating in evil deeds is the definition of not believing. When you heard the gospel and encountered Christ you were at a crossroad. How would you respond to Him? We are talking about more than just responding to facts. We are talking about responding to the person of Jesus Christ. You are commanded by the Word of God to respond to Jesus by repentance and faith.

"But as many as received Him, to them He gave the right to become children of God, to those who believe in His name."

John 1:12

Notice to receive Him is what it means to believe in Him; and to believe in Him is to receive Him. You are not just receiving facts you are receiving Jesus Christ, the Son of the living God. You are receiving all that He is and all that He represents. You are receiving His Kingdom and authority over your life. You are receiving His Lordship for your life. You are surrendering your life and will to the King. You are receiving a Savior. You are receiving His forgiveness. You are receiving His peace. You are receiving His power to change you on the inside. You are choosing to identify yourself with Jesus Christ. This is what the Scripture means by obeying the gospel.

"But they have not all obeyed the gospel. For Isaiah says, 'Lord, who has believed our report?'"

Romans 10:16

To believe is to obey. Jesus said, *"This is the work of God, that you believe in Him whom He sent"* (John 6:29). The fruit of true repentance and sincere faith is confession. When Peter obeyed the revelation that the Father had given him, he outwardly confessed Jesus as the Christ. Confession is agreeing with God and His truth. Paul said, *"I believed and therefore I spoke"* (2 Corinthians 4:13). Biblical believing leads to biblical confession. To confess is to acknowledge what God has said about you, about Christ, and about coming into a relationship with Him. This is why often time's ministers or believers lead those responding to Christ in a prayer. Prayer is a way to call, talk, or confess to God.

"That if you confess with your mouth the Lord Jesus and believe in your heart that God has raised Him from the dead, you will be saved. For with the heart one believes unto righteousness, and with the mouth confession is made unto salvation. For the Scripture says, 'Whoever believes on Him will not be put to shame.' For there is no distinction between Jew and Greek, for the same Lord over all is rich to all who call upon Him. For 'whoever calls on the name of the Lord shall be saved.'"

Romans 10:9-13

I believe there are many who are reading this and have realized that you never have responded correctly to the revelation of Christ. Now is the time. Respond to Christ through repentance and faith, and also with the fruit of confession. Confess and call upon Him to save you. If that is you, this prayer might help you express your heart:

Father God, I thank you for revealing to me that Jesus is the Christ and the only way to a relationship with you. I acknowledge that I am a sinner. I have lived contrary to your will for my life. I need your forgiveness. I choose to turn from my life of selfishness and sin. I acknowledge that Jesus is Lord and that you Father have raised Him from the dead. I receive Christ into my life to be my Savior and Lord. Thank you, that Christ died for me and through Him I receive forgiveness of all my sins, and peace with you Father God. I am free from condemnation. I am saved from sin and hell. I am now your child God. I want you, Christ, to live in me and empower me to live in obedience to your will. In Jesus name: Let it be so!

Confessing also includes identifying yourself publicly with Jesus Christ and a community of His followers. You are to make this public confession through water baptism. This is carrying out believing in Christ to completion or to the full. (We will discuss this more in the next chapter.) The foundation phase is about being assured through the Word of God that you have received the right foundation. Taking time to check the foundation of your life is extremely important. With a wrong foundation you would be destined to build a house that would not endure what you will encounter throughout your life-time. You would be building a spiritual walk that would not have the foundation to support it.

Whether you have just received Jesus Christ as the foundation of your life or had already previously, you must now sit and learn what God accomplished in your life when you received Christ as your Savior and Lord. In order for you to live in obedience to God, you must first know your new identity in Christ and grow in spiritual understanding. Yes, you must sit in order to learn how you should walk. The primary method that facilitates your spiritual development during this foundation phase is receiving the ministry of the Word of God that includes both the preaching and teaching of the Word, but primarily the teaching.

Chapter 3

The Word of Righteousness

"For what does the Scripture say? 'Abraham believed God, and it was accounted (counted) to him for righteousness.'"
Romans 4:3 (Parenthesis Mine. NKJV Marginal Reading)

Abraham was righteous because he believed God. When Abraham believed God, it was counted to him for righteousness. To be righteous is to be in right standing with God. Righteousness is the ability to stand in a position acceptable before God. Righteousness allows you to be fully accepted, approved, and loved by God the Father so when you approach His throne you do so free from fear, condemnation, or guilt. When you believed in Christ, God brought you into a position of being righteous before Him. Believing in Christ has made you to be in right standing before God. You now have the right to a relationship with God. Previously your sin kept you from being able to have a relationship with God. But now in Christ Jesus *"you have been brought near by the blood of Christ"* (Ephesians 2:13).

What Jesus Christ accomplished made a way for all of mankind to come into a position of being in right standing with God and to be in right standing means that there is nothing separating you from God. No guilt! No condemnation! No sins! No rebellion! No demon! Nothing! When you repented and believed in Christ you received what Christ had made available for you. You received a position of being in right standing with God. The moment you received Christ, God declared you to be righteous. You have been brought into a position of being right with God. Any walls that may have separated you from God were removed when you received the benefits of Christ being crucified. (See Ephesians 2:14-15) Righteousness is also the right to eternal life. Death is the penalty for sin. (See Romans 3:23) However, since your sins have been forgiven you therefore have no penalty to pay. You are in right standing with God and have been given as a gift eternal life through Jesus Christ. Righteousness was offered by promise and by grace, and you received it through faith.

By Promise

"But now the righteousness of God apart from the law is revealed, being witnessed by the Law and the Prophets, even the righteousness of God, through faith in Jesus Christ, to all and on all who believe. For there is no difference; for all have sinned and fall short of the glory of God."

Romans 3:21-23

From the beginning of Scriptures God promised that He would provide a way for mankind to be brought into a right relationship with Him. The Law and the Prophets in the Old Testament witnessed this promise of God. The Old Testament looks forward to the day that God would provide a provision for mankind's sins to be forgiven. That day came when Jesus was crucified, died, and buried for your sins. The prophet Jeremiah prophesied concerning Christ saying, *"Now this is His name by which He will be called: The Lord our Righteousness"* (Jeremiah 23:6). You have the testimony of the Old Testament and New Testament Scriptures that right standing with God is provided through Jesus Christ and Him alone. Through God's promise you can have assurance that Jesus has made you righteous. This is one of the reasons righteousness was offered by promise. You can have confidence that you are righteous and a sure foundation to build your life upon.

"Thus God, determining to show more abundantly to the heirs of promise the immutability (unchangeableness) of His counsel, confirmed (guaranteed) it by an oath, that by two immutable things, in which it is impossible for God to lie, we might have strong consolation."
  Hebrews 6:17-18 (Parenthesizes Mine. NKJV Marginal Reading)

By Grace

"Therefore it is of faith that it might be according to grace, so that the promise might be sure (certain) to all the seed, not only to those who are of the law, but also to those who are of the faith of Abraham, who is the father of us all."
  Romans 4:16 (Parenthesis Mine. NKJV Marginal Reading)

God by grace provided righteousness for you so that you can be sure or certain of being in right standing with God. Grace is God's ability. Grace is God giving you something freely without you doing anything to earn it. Grace is free and grace is a gift! You do not pay for or earn a gift. You simply receive it. When you received Christ you received the gift of righteousness that God provided for you by grace. It was the grace of God that planned and provided the finished work of Christ. The finished work of Christ refers to what Jesus accomplished through His crucifixion, death, burial, resurrection, and ascension. Paul said in Ephesians 2:4, *"But God, who is rich in mercy, because of His great love with which He loved us, even when we were dead in trespasses, made us alive together with Christ (by grace you have been saved)."* While you were living in sin and rebellion God had already provided by His grace a way to come into right standing with Him. That way is Jesus.

It is not through following the Law of Moses that a person can become righteous before God. It is not by any works, good deeds, or religious service that you were brought into a position of being righteous before God. It is by God's promise and by His grace that it was available to you. If righteousness was based on your good works or performance you would not be able to be certain of your position before God. None of us are sinless and live in complete obedience to all of God's will. If your acceptance before God was based on your performance then you would never have a sure foundation to stand on. Ephesians 2:8-9 states, *"For by grace you have been saved through faith, and that not of yourselves; it is the gift of God, not of works."* Righteousness is by God's grace and not by your works. Righteousness was given to you as a gift through Jesus Christ. (See Romans 5:15-18) You received this gift when you received Christ.

"But of Him you are in Christ Jesus, who became for us wisdom from God – and righteousness."

1 Corinthians 1:30

Through Faith

"Where is boasting then? It is excluded. By what law? Of works? No, but by the law of faith. Therefore we conclude that a man is justified by faith apart from the deeds of the law."

Romans 3:27-28

"And the Scripture, foreseeing that God would justify the Gentiles by faith, preached the gospel to Abraham beforehand, saying, 'In you all the nations shall be blessed.'"

Galatians 3:8

"But the Scripture has confined all under sin, that the promise by faith in Jesus Christ might be given to those who believe."

Galatians 3:22

"For by grace you have been saved through faith, and that not of yourselves; it is the gift of God, not of works, lest anyone should boast."

Ephesians 2:8-9

God chose to bring you into a righteous position through the law of faith. He did this to ensure that no one would get the glory except Him. How can you boast about what was freely given to you? You did not earn your right standing with God. You good works did not save you from sin and hell. You did not transfer yourself out of the kingdom of darkness into the kingdom of Jesus Christ. God did all of this for you through Jesus Christ. Boasting or feeling that you are better than other people is excluded.

You have been declared righteous by God apart from your deeds and only because you have believed in Christ. You have received what God made available for you through the finished work of Christ. You have no reason to boast because your acceptance before God is not based on your works. God's approval and love for you is not based on your works or performance. He has once and for all accepted and received you as His child through your faith in Christ. You have been justified or declared no longer guilty because of your faith in Christ and not your works.

"Therefore, brethren, having boldness to enter the Holiest by the blood of Jesus, by a new and living way which He consecrated for us, through the veil, that is His flesh, and having a High Priest over the house of God, let us draw near with a true heart in full assurance of faith, having our hearts sprinkled from an evil conscience."
Hebrews 10:19-22

You can now come before God's holy presence boldly through the blood of Jesus. You can draw near to God with a heart of full assurance because of your faith in Christ. You no longer have to doubt if God accepts you. You no longer have to wonder if God loves you. You no longer have to question if God receives you just as you are. You can have a heart fully assured that you are righteous before God. You can be fully assured that you are in a position of being in right standing with God. No barriers, no walls, and no hindrances. You can approach God and He will receive you with open arms. Your father may have rejected you, a friend, or a family member, but God fully accepts you through your faith in the finished work of Christ. Be assured today that you are righteous before God. In fact, you are the righteousness of God. You are a person who is in a position acceptable before God. Christ finished it and His work is complete. There is nothing left for you to add to it. Go ahead and lift up your head to the Father and recognize He has received you just as you are through your faith in Christ.

"But of Him you are in Christ Jesus, who became for us wisdom from God- and righteousness."
1 Corinthians 1:30

Christ has become your righteousness. Christ is the only way you can be accepted and received by God. Christ is your right standing with God. The fact that Christ has become your righteousness means that God the Father receives and accepts you the exact same way that He accepted Jesus Christ when He ascended into heaven and sat down at the right hand of God. (See Hebrews 1:3) Since Jesus is your righteousness you can experience what He experiences in God's presence. You can experience complete acceptance, approval, peace, and love in the presence of God. You are received by God just as Jesus was received. That is a reason to shout!

Skilled in Righteousness

"For though by this time you ought to be teachers, you need someone to teach you again the first principles of the oracles (Scriptures) of God; and you have come to need milk and not solid food. For everyone who partakes only of milk is unskilled in the word of righteousness, for he is a babe."
Hebrews 5:12-13 (Parenthesis Mine. NKJV Marginal Reading)

This passage from Hebrews exposes an unfortunate situation that can still be found in the body of Christ today. What is this situation? Believers who have been saved long enough that they should no longer be babes in Christ. The passage is speaking to a group of believers who "by that time" should have been able to teach others the first principles of God's word. Unfortunately they were unable because they had not progressed in their spiritual development but were still in the spiritual growth stage of being a babe in Christ. These believers were unable to receive teachings and truth that are considered "solid food" teachings. They were still in need of milk which is the beginning truths for Christians.

Babes in Christ need spiritual milk. Peter said, *"As newborn babes, desire the pure milk of the word, that you may grow thereby"* (1 Peter 2:2). As a new believer you are in the spiritual growth stage of being a babe in Christ and are in need of "milk" teachings found in the Word of God. Your spiritual growth is dependant upon you receiving the right teachings for where you are spiritually. You must guard yourself from entertaining teachings that are beyond where you are spiritually. You need to receive teachings that are "pure milk." You need only the milk teachings in their purest form and not deeper truths mixed in. This will ensure that you grow up into what Christ has made available for you when you were saved.

Every believer who needs milk is still a babe in Christ. The passage in Hebrews informs us that in order for you to move on to the next spiritual growth stage you must be taught the first principles of Scripture and become skilled in the word of righteousness. Therefore, a babe in Christ is a believer who has not become skilled or experienced in the word of righteousness. You will remain a babe in Christ until you become skilled in the word of righteousness. During this season in your life you must diligently devote yourself to the subject of righteousness.

To be skilled in the word of righteousness is more than just hearing a teaching on righteousness. Yes, you must be taught righteousness but this Scripture is referring to you also becoming experienced, acquainted, and changed by the truth of righteousness. This is what Scripture says is necessary for where you are currently in your spiritual growth. Righteousness is relevant to the current situation you find yourself in. When you become skilled in the word of righteousness you will no longer be a babe in Christ.

Becoming skilled or experienced in the word of righteousness is living out daily the reality of the position God has brought you into when you received Christ. You now have a relationship with God. You now can come before Him and talk with Him. When you spend time talking with your new heavenly Father that is what it means to pray. God has given you the gift of righteousness through Christ. This gift gives you the ability at any time to speak with God. This gift gives you the ability to worship Him at any time. This gift gives you the ability to come before God, and for Him to receive you with open arms. Now that you are in right standing with God, He receives you just the way you are. You can talk to Him and He will receive and hear you.

You must understand that righteousness has nothing to do with your daily behavior or performance. Righteousness has to do with a position that God has brought you into when you received Christ. Let me emphasize again, righteousness has nothing do to with your performance or behavior. It has to do with a position given to you in Christ. You did nothing to attain this position of being in right standing with God. You just received the gift God offered you through Jesus Christ. It was God's grace that saved you and brought you into this position of being fully accepted and approved by Him. Now, through the gift of righteousness you can approach God and His presence at any time. You have been given, as a gift, the ability to have a relationship with God. You have been given the right to live forever. Your relationship with God will always be founded upon the gift of righteousness that He has given you. You will never be able to approach God and have Him hear you because of your good works. You will never be able to earn God's love, acceptance, and approval. You have already been given them as a gift when you received Christ. The only reason you will ever be able to have a relationship with God is because of the fact you received Christ.

You never will have the right to a relationship with God because of your behavior or good works that you perform on a daily basis. The only reason God accepts and approves of you is because you have received Christ. Do you see that your performance and behavior has nothing to do with those truths? At no time during your life are you righteous before God because of your own works or deeds. Being in a position of acceptance before God is never a matter of how much you prayed that day, or how many chapters you read in the Bible, or how many people you told about Jesus, or how many church services you attended that week. You are only righteous and able to approach God because of your trust in God's provision for you through the finished work of Christ. Thank God for the gift of righteousness provided through the finished work of Christ.

So the question remains, 'What then about my behavior?' First, your behavior is extremely important to God. Peter states, *"But as He who called you is holy, you also be holy in all your conduct, because it is written, 'Be holy, for I am holy'"* (1 Peter 1:15-16). However, the issue of your behavior is separate from the issue of your position before God. If not, it would mean every time you sin or fail in your conduct you would no longer have a relationship with God. Remember righteousness is the ability to stand in a position of acceptance and right standing with God free from fear or guilt. Let me ask, 'What got you into the position of being in right standing with God in the first place?' Was it your conduct? Was it your behavior? Was it your performance? Was it your good works? Was it attending church? Was it giving money to the poor? No!

You were brought into a position of being righteous by God *"not of works lest any man should boast"* (Ephesians 2:9). It was God's divine grace and saving work that brought you into that position. So, if your mistake, sin, or bad performance can take you out of that position of being righteous then you would need God to save you again every time you sinned. If every time you sinned you lost your position of being righteous then you will continually be losing your ability to have a relationship with God. Remember, to be righteous is the right to have a relationship with God. Therefore, you do not lose your position of being righteous when you fail to live according to God's will. This is why the way for you to have a relationship with God is based on the free gift of righteousness He gave to you when you received Christ and not based on your behavior or performance. God, through the finished work of Christ, has made a way for you to always have a relationship with Him.

You can have a sure foundation to build your life upon because of the gift of righteousness through Christ. You can have assurance that you are in right standing with God always through the free gift of righteousness. You can be assured that you always have God's acceptance, approval, and unconditional love because of the free gift of righteousness. That is good news. People might reject you because of your mistakes, performance, or because you don't live to up to their expectation, but not God. The matter was settled through the finished work of Christ.

Your behavior does not change the fact that you are in a position of being righteous before God but it does affect your fellowship or intimacy with the Holy Spirit and Lord. So your behavior is never connected to your position of being righteous before God, but it is always connected to your personal fellowship with Holy Spirit and Jesus Christ. Your behavior does not change your position of being righteous because that was a free gift given from God when you received Christ. Your behavior affects your ability to experience some of the benefits of being in a position of right standing before God.

"The work of righteousness will be peace, and the effect of righteousness, quietness and assurance forever."

Isaiah 32:17

The effects of being righteous before God are experiencing peace, quietness, confidence, and assurance forever. When you received Christ, guilt and condemnation was removed from your life and replaced with peace and confidence. You become aware of God's love and acceptance of you. You experience peace and joy like never before. Romans 14:17 states, *"The kingdom of God is not eating and drinking, but righteousness and peace and joy in the Holy Spirit."* When you came under God's authority or kingdom you were able to experience righteousness, peace, and joy. You were able to experience the benefits of being in right standing with God.

Notice that the effects of peace and joy come from the Holy Spirit. When you received Christ it was the Holy Spirit who caused you to experience the peace, joy, confidence, sense of forgiveness, and acceptance. The Holy Spirit takes the facts of what Jesus has accomplished for you and makes you experience or become aware of the benefits. This is important because you must understand that when you sin you grieve the Holy Spirit. (See Ephesians 4:30) And when you grieve the Holy Spirit you are resisting the very person of God who causes you to experience and become aware of the benefits of being in right standing with God. In fact, the Holy Spirit is one of the ways that God gives you witness that you are righteous. Jesus speaking concerning the coming of the Holy Spirit said:

"And when he has come, He will convict the world of sin, and of righteousness, and of judgment...of righteousness, because I go to My Father and you see Me no more."

John 16:8,10

So when you sin, you do not lose your position of being righteous, but you lose the ability to sense the benefits of the fact of you being righteous. When you sin, your behavior will keep you from being able to achieve the awareness of God's unconditional love, acceptance, and approval. You will lose the sense of peace, joy, and confidence. However, you must understand that when you sin you are still in a position before God where He loves you, accepts you, and approves of you. The fact is you still have peace with God through Christ. You will just be unable to experience those facts because you have grieved the Holy Spirit who enables you to be aware of those benefits of being righteous. Your behavior does not change the eternal facts of what Christ has accomplished for you. It just changes your ability to enjoy some of the benefits of those truths.

"If we confess our sins, He is faithful and just to forgive us our sins and to cleanse us from all unrighteousness."

1 John 1:9

When you find yourself in this type of situation there are three main options for you. The first option is to follow the Biblical solution above. What again is the gift of righteousness? The gift of righteousness is your ability through Christ to approach God and Him receive you. In the Old Testament if a person approached God and He did not accept them they would be struck dead. God is holy and awesome and yet He has made a way for you through Christ to be able to approach Him at anytime! This is why you must learn the importance of the gift of righteousness. Even when you failed, sinned, messed up, or blew it, you through the gift of righteousness have the ability to come before God and Him receive you with complete love, acceptance, and approval through the gift of righteousness. God's approval of you is not based on your behavior but on your personhood. Personhood means it is based on the fact that you are a person who has received Christ and become a child of God.

So when you sin you are to use the gift God gave you and run to Him, not from Him. Even though you messed up you still have the right to a relationship with Him through Christ. Even though you messed up you still have the ability to talk or pray to God through Christ. So use the gift of righteousness, come before God and do what the Scripture instructs you to do. You are to confess that what you did was sin or wrong. Confession is just agreeing with God. You are confessing or agreeing that the sin you just committed was wrong and not something that is proper for a child of God. Confession means you don't try to justify to God why you did it or try and blame what you did on another person. You take responsibility and confess, "Lord I was wrong and guilty of committing a sin.' When you are willing to do that God said, 'He is faithful.' He is faithful to forgive you of the sin you committed and to cleanse you from all unrighteousness.

The reference of being cleansed means that all that grieved the Holy Spirit will be removed and you will be able once again to experience those benefits of being righteous such as peace, joy, and confidence. Your fellowship and intimacy with the Holy Spirit and Jesus Christ will no longer be hindered. So when you sin, quickly take advantage of the gift of righteousness and come before God to confess your sin. Then continue on your day experiencing the benefits of being in right standing with God. Remember that through this entire situation you remained in a position of being righteous, but, due to the sin you committed, you lost your awareness of the benefits of your position.

The second option of how to respond when you sin is not what God intends for you. In fact, if you are not quick to come before God confessing your sin and using the gift of righteousness to approach God then tragedy will soon follow. The longer your fellowship with the Lord is hindered the more vulnerable you become to wrong desires and the attacks of Satan. The longer you go without being cleansed and having your confidence, sense of acceptance, and sense of approval restored, the harder it will be to believe God's word and eternal facts over your feelings. The fact is God does accept you and still loves you regardless of your mistake and sin. The fact is you still are righteous before God through Christ. The fact is you still are God's child and are able to pray and worship Him.

However, the longer you allow your fellowship with the Lord to be hindered the harder it becomes to believe in those truths over the emotions of fear, guilt, and condemnation that you feel. You no longer are aware or able to sense God's peace, joy, confidence, and acceptance, so you begin to doubt that what God's Word says concerning your position is even true. Then the devil comes and begins to take advantage of how you feel. Satan begins to tell you lies that God is mad at you, or that He doesn't accept you, or He has left you. The battle becomes greater and greater until you begin to sin more, be accused more, and listen to more lies. Your faith that you can approach God and have Him receive and accept you becomes weaker, and instead of running to God, you run from God, falling into a season of continual sin and defeat. In my experience of ministering to young believers, this has been the number one reason they said caused them to backslide or not grow spiritually.

The last major option of how to respond is to become religious. You become a hypocrite. You choose to try and play the part of a person who is intimately fellowshipping with the Holy Spirit and Jesus Christ. How does that happen? You try through your behavior, performance, or good works to achieve the benefits of being righteous that you lost when you committed the sin. You begin to live what is called a "works mentality." Having a works mentality means you try through your behavior to achieve the awareness or sense of being in right standing with God and experience joy, peace, and confidence. The problem is you can never achieve the awareness of being in right standing with God through your performance. You can never achieve the awareness of God's approval and acceptance of you through your good works or religious activities.

The people who end up in this category are usually disciplined people because of their personality or upbringing. Therefore, through their discipline they will pray longer than others, read more chapters in the Bible than others, attend more services, or do more religious activities than others but only to try and make them feel better about themselves. Through your self effort and performance you are

51

trying to silence the guilt and accusations of your conscience and the enemy. A works mentality will always lead to pride. Since you base God's love and acceptance of you upon your behavior, you begin to think you have achieved a right standing with God that other people were not disciplined enough to attain. Therefore you boast in your works because you think you have earned your relationship with God and His approval, love, and acceptance.

The reality is you are not experiencing a vibrant fellowship with God but are just focused on your performance. You are doing good deeds without God being involved. This is what is called "dead works." There is no life because you are resisting the Holy Spirit. The reality is God resist the proud. (See James 4:6) He resists such an attitude because it thinks you are better than other people. The gift of righteousness leaves no room for any one to boast because it was given freely to us through God's grace in Jesus Christ. (See Romans 4:2) Until you are willing to give up your pride, humble yourself and acknowledge God's grace you are living just a religious life with no true joy, peace, or power of the Holy Spirit.

My prayer for you is that you do not become religious or backslide but become skilled in the word of righteousness for every day life. Choose to be quick to confess your sin and keep your intimacy with the Holy Spirit active. You need to constantly feed on these truths. I encourage you to read the books of Paul: Romans, Galatians, Ephesians, Philippians, and Colossians. As you become experienced in the word of righteousness you will move out of being a babe in Christ to the next spiritual growth stage.

Water Baptism

"Then Jesus came from Galilee to John at the Jordan to be baptized by him. And John tried to prevent Him, saying, 'I need to be baptized by You, and are You coming to me?' But Jesus answered and said to him, 'Permit it to be so now, for thus it is fitting for us to fulfill all righteousness.' Then he allowed Him."

Matthew 3:13-15

Jesus was water baptized. He provided an example for us to follow. It is interesting that Jesus spoke of water baptism as "fulfilling all righteousness" for His life. The word translated "fulfill" also can be interpreted to mean "carrying out something to the end" (Strong's # 4137).

"And Jesus came and spoke to them, saying, "All authority has been given to Me in heaven and on earth. Go therefore and make disciples of all the nations, baptizing them in the name of the Father and of the Son and of the Holy Spirit, teaching them to observe all things that I have commanded you."

Matthew 28:18-20

Jesus has commanded all His followers to be water baptized. Peter also when he preached to people, *"Commanded them to be baptized in the name of the Lord"* (Acts 10:48). Since water baptism is commanded for those who receive Christ, it is related to the topic of carrying out righteousness to the end. When you obey the Lord and are water baptized you are carrying out to the end your obedience to the faith. Acts 6:7 speaks of many people who "were obedient to the faith." Water Baptism is publicly confessing that you have repented of your sins and received Christ as your Lord and Savior.

"Nevertheless even among the rulers many believed in Him, but because of the Pharisees they did not confess Him, lest they should be put out of the synagogue; for they loved the praise of men more than the praise of God."

John 12:42

Notice that there were people who believed in Jesus but were unwilling to confess Him publicly. They were not willing to carry out their believing to the full. You are commanded by the Scriptures to confess Christ both with your mouth and through water baptism. This is what it means to carry out your righteousness to the end or to the full. Peter spoke of water baptism being the answer of a good conscience toward God. (See 1 Peter 3:21) Water baptism is answering the demand or command of God. This answering, or obedience of yours, gives you a good conscience toward God. I have ministered to countless of people who have considered themselves to be rededicating their lives back to the Lord and had never been water baptized. Not obeying the command to be water baptized will always hinder a person's ability to live with an awareness of being in right standing with God. This leads people to back slide and not grow spiritually in the will of God for their life. When believing in Christ leads you to obey the command to be water baptized, you will experience a joyful and clear conscience. Obeying the Lord is very important.

If you have not been water baptized, you need to make plans to do so immediately. I believe you desire to be a person that carries out your believing fully to the end. This will enable you to experience all the benefits of the righteousness God offers through believing in Christ. Do not allow your believing to stop short of the responses God has commanded you to have to the person of Jesus Christ. It is time for you to go ahead and confess Him publicly through water baptism. Water baptism is a ceremony of identification by which you as a new believer become associated with Jesus Christ and His followers. Water baptism symbolizes your identification with the death, burial, and resurrection of Jesus Christ. You are identifying that Jesus' death was your death. It was death to your old life. Death to who you use to be. It was death to your old habits and sins. Everything that represented your life outside of having a relationship with God has been buried. And when Jesus was resurrected it was your resurrection. You have been made to be a new person, with a new life, and a new start.

"For there are three that bear witness: the Spirit, the water, and the blood; and these three agree as one."
1 John 5:7-8 (Early Greek Manuscripts)

Water baptism is one of the witnesses provided by God that testifies to your position of righteousness. The blood of Jesus cleans your heart and also provides a witness. Hebrews 10:22 states, *"Let us draw near with a true heart in full assurance of faith, having our hearts sprinkled from an evil conscience and our bodies washed with pure water."* This verse speaks of the full assurance of faith you can experience and it mentions the effects of the blood and water. Having your heart sprinkled is referring to the blood of Jesus and your body being washed with pure water refers to water baptism. (See Hebrews 10:19) You can become skilled and experienced in the word of righteousness. You can have a sure foundation to build your life upon. God has given you the ability to have certainty and confidence through Christ.

Fear Not

For anyone reading this that has a mistaken concern that the teaching of righteousness and confidence may produce a mentality that leads to sinfulness or lawless living, fear not. First, the Apostle Paul when he taught the word of righteousness and God's free gift of grace he caused people with mistaken concerns to make false accusations also. Paul said, *"And why not say, 'Let us do evil that good may come?' - as we are slanderously reported and as some affirm that we say. Their condemnation is just"* (Romans 3:8). Paul had people wrongly slander and accuse him along with the truth of what the Scriptures teach. However, Paul understood the power of what Christ had done for a new believer.

"What shall we say then? Shall we continue in sin that grace may abound? Certainly not! How shall we who died to sin live any longer in it?"

Romans 6:1-2

When a person understands the reality of what water baptism signifies they would never fear the power and pull of sin over the power of what God has accomplished on the inside of a new believer in Christ. As a babe in Christ, you not only have been brought into a position of right standing with God but a miracle or change has happened on the inside of you. Fear not and keep reading. The next chapter will unfold the power and miracle of the new birth when a person receives Christ. You do not have to fear or try and control people from sinning. God has taken care of that issue when he made them a new creation in Christ. When you truly understand what the Bible teaches concerning the issue of grace you will see how wrong such a fearful mentality is. Biblical teaching on God's grace does not lead to sin but actually to holiness.

"For the grace of God that brings salvation has appeared to all men, teaching us that, denying ungodliness and worldly lusts, we should live soberly, righteously, and godly in the present age, looking for the blessed hope and glorious appearing of our great God and Savior Jesus Christ, who gave Himself for us, that He might redeem us from every lawless deed and purify for Himself His own special people, zealous for good works. Speak these things, exhort, and rebuke with all authority. Let no one despise you."

Titus 2:11-15

Fear not, God knows more than man.

Chapter 4

The New Birth

"Whoever believes that Jesus is the Christ is born of God, and everyone who loves Him who begot also loves him who is begotten of Him."

1 John 5:1

You have learned that Christ died for you, providing you with a position of righteousness before God. Also when you repented and believed in Jesus Christ, God then miraculously changed you on the inside. Since your believing in the finished work of Christ allows God to consider you righteous, you then were made alive through what is called the new birth. Remember, to be righteous is the right to have eternal life. Eternal life is to have an eternal relationship with God. (See John 17:3) You were dead in trespasses and sins but through the new birth you were made alive together with Christ. (See Ephesians 2:5) It is through the resurrection of Jesus Christ, and your believing that God raised Him from the dead, that you have experienced the same power, resulting in your new birth. You have been born again. You have been born of God. This new birth took place in the deepest part of your being, in your spirit. When the Spirit of Christ entered your life you were made alive in your spirit. To be made alive means you came into a relationship or in contact with God. The Apostle Paul said, *"But he who is joined to the Lord is one spirit with Him"* (1 Corinthians 6:17). You have come into union with the Lord. Your spirit that was dead and in sin was made alive and recreated in Christ. You were made new. You were born again. You have been joined to the Lord.

"But as many as received Him, to them He gave the right to become children of God, to those who believe in His name: who were born, not of blood, nor of the will of the flesh, nor of the will of man, but of God."

John 1:12-13

You are now a child of God. God has created you new. You are created according to God's image. Observe you were born not by man or by flesh. Your earthly parents no longer dictate your identity. The issues or circumstances surrounding your natural birth no longer determine your identity or significance. You have been born by the will of God. God delighted for you to become His child.

"Having been born again, not of corruptible seed but incorruptible, through the word of God which lives and abides forever...But the word of the Lord endures forever. Now this is the word which by the gospel was preached to you."

1 Peter 1: 23, 25

God did such a miracle on the inside of you. You were born by the incorruptible Word of God. Remember Jesus Christ is the Word of God. (See John 1:14) Like we saw before, when you heard the gospel you were confronted by Jesus Christ Himself. When you received and believed in the gospel you received and believed in Christ. His life and power brought forth this new you, through the new birth.

"But when the kindness and the love of God our Savior toward man appeared, not by works of righteousness which we have done, but according to His mercy He saved us, through the washing of regeneration and renewing of the Holy Spirit."

Titus 3:5

It was not your behavior that brought about this miracle. It was God's kindness and love for you that provided for your spirit to be changed or saved from its previous condition. God, in His mercy, regenerated you on the inside. The grace of God, His ability, brought about this change in your nature. You are not the same on the inside. Don't look in the natural mirror for certainty that you have been born again but look in the mirror of God's Word. God is not a man that He should lie. (See Numbers 23:19) His Word is true. You are a child of God born by the will of God.

Through the provision of the resurrection of Jesus Christ and your believing, you have been born again and received and new nature. Your new birth was your entrance into the kingdom of God. You are now a citizen of heaven. You have been born from above. You live in the kingdom of God or under His authority. You now are "In Christ." To be "in Christ" is a phrase that illustrates the fact that you are a child of God and have received the nature of Christ. Peter said through God's promises we have become "partakers of the divine nature" (2 Peter 1:4). The fact that you are "in Christ" means that you are under the lordship of Jesus Christ and from His lineage. (See Hebrews 2:11-12) You are a part of the family of God. To be "in Christ" also means that your new identity is found in Jesus Christ.

"Therefore, if anyone is in Christ, he is a new creation; old things have passed away; behold, all things have become new."
2 Corinthians 5:17

You are now a new creation. The person you use to be no longer exists. The old things have passed away and all things have become new. Your old identity has passed away. Your old nature has passed away. The person you use to be has died. You have become a new person. Your born again spirit is the new creation. God has created you new. God miraculously did that for you when you were born again. Being a new creation is your new identity.

The old you that loved and enjoyed to sin no longer exists. Now that you have been born again you have the nature of God and a desire to live for God. It is now natural for you to live for God. It is natural for you to worship and spend time in God's presence. Do you know who are the most miserable people on the earth? Children of God who have backslid and are not enjoying intimacy and fellowship with God. Why? Because they are living a life contrary to who they truly are. As a child of God it is contrary to your nature to rebel against God and live in sin. Unbelievers live in sin because it is their nature to sin. However, you as a child of God have become a new creation that has been made to desire the will of God. I have never met a born again person that did not desire to live for God's will, because that is what God created the new creation to be. New creations desire to live for God and obey His will. The apostle John stated, *"That people who had been born again could not live a life of sin and rebellion because God's seed remains in them and because they have been born of God"* (My Paraphrase. 1 John 3:9).

As a new creation when you deliberately sin, immediately you will know it. Your heart will condemn you and you will lose the experience of having confidence toward God. (See 1 John 3:21) This is because you did something that was contrary to the person God created you to be. Due to the new birth and God's Spirit dwelling in you, God has put "His laws in your mind and on your heart" (Hebrews 8:10). Ezekiel 36:27 states, *"I will put My spirit within you and cause you to walk in My statues, and you will keep My judgments and do them."* When you truly repented and desired to be saved from your sin, God took it serious. God took it so seriously that, through the provisions of Christ, He made you a new creation that was made to live in obedience to His will, and He put His Spirit within you for empowerment. Listen, you will instantly know when you deliberately grieve the Holy Spirit. (See Ephesians 4:30) Do you recognize this great miracle that God has done on the inside of you?

As a person who lives on the earth you are made up of three parts. You are a spirit who lives in a body and you have a soul that consists of your mind, will, and emotions. Your body is called an "earthly tent" (2 Corinthians 5:1). (We will learn more about your soul in the chapters to come.) One day you will leave your body. Therefore, your body is not your true identity. Your body is just a temporary house that you use to express yourself through while living here on earth. Your body did not become a new creation. The real you, your spirit, was born again and made a new creation. So what is the new you made to be like?

"And that you put on the new man which was created according to God, in true righteousness and holiness."

Ephesians 4:24

The new you was created according to the image of God. As a new creation you have been made righteous and holy. You must understand that you are not just in a position of being righteous; but have been made righteous through the new birth. You have been created by God to have a relationship with Him. You have been created to live forever. You have been created to live in God's holy presence. You have been created righteous as a new creation. You have been created holy. You are a child of God and have been created according to His image and the characteristics of being righteous and holy. Now do you see why you can fear not? God has changed you into a new person. A miracle has taken place in your spirit. You have been created righteous and holy in the image of God. God through the new birth has made it possible for you "to be an imitator of God" (Ephesians 5:1).

"But according to His promise we are looking for a new heavens and a new earth, in which righteousness dwells."

2 Peter 3:13

There is coming a day in the future when God will create new the heavens and the earth. However, you have already been created and fitted to live in them. Take in the fact that only righteousness will dwell in the new heavens and new earth and that you have already been created righteous through the new birth. God has already prepared you to live in the new heavens and earth. Only righteousness dwells there and you have been made righteous. As a citizen of heaven, the current earth you live in is not your eternal home. In fact, the Apostle Peter says you are a "sojourner and pilgrim" passing through the current but temporary earth (1 Peter 2:11). Even though you do not live yet in the new heavens and new earth you have been created and called by God to reflect the customs, laws, attitudes, and habits of the kingdom of God.

"For whom He foreknew, He also predestined to be conformed to the image of His Son, that He might be the firstborn among many brethren."

Romans 8:29

As a new creation in Christ, God has predestined you to be conformed into the same image of His Son, Jesus Christ. This means that God has pre-determined or planned for you to become like Christ. God through the new birth performed such a miracle on the inside of you that He has made it possible for every area of your life to reflect Christ likeness. God used the image of Jesus Christ as a model for what He created you to be like. Jesus was the firstborn but you have been created to follow in His footsteps. God has made this possible, not you. When you grow in your knowledge of who Jesus is, you will be growing in understanding what God has created you to be. This testifies to the power of what the new birth has made possible for your life. Thank God for His wonderful grace! Go ahead and say, 'I am a new creation!' God is good! The new birth is just the beginning of what God has planned for you. You have just started a journey of having a relationship with God and walking with Christ. Be willing for God to continually show you what is next for you on this journey.

"For we are His workmanship, created in Christ Jesus for good works, which God prepared beforehand that we should walk in them."

Ephesians 2:10

As a new creation you are God's workmanship. God skillfully created you to be this person you have become in Christ. When God created you as a new creation you were also created to perform good works. These good works and serving in God's kingdom is not something you just do, but it is the result of who you are through the new birth. God did such a miracle in your life that it is going to affect what and how you do things. Good works will begin to flow from your identity. You do not have to do good works to earn a sense of identity. No! The reality is your identity, in Christ, will determine your good works. Your good works do not determine your identity, but your identity determines your good works. As a child of God you have been created for a purpose in the kingdom of God.

As you continue to grow in understanding and accept your new identity, you will began to discover your spiritual gifts and calling in the kingdom of God. Your call and purpose is intended by God to flow out of you living in line with who you are as a new creation in Christ. Therefore, it is absolutely necessary for you to first learn to live in accordance to who God has created you to be before you seek to know, understand, experience, and carry out your purposes and calling. The next chapter will help prepare you for the journey and process that God has planned for you to participate in as you move toward your calling and purposes. It is only as you follow the Lord that you will be able to navigate successfully into what God has prepared beforehand for you.

New Family

"Behold what manner of love the Father has bestowed on us, that we should be called children of God."

1 John 3:1

As a child of God you have become part of the family of God. You have not only been brought into a relationship with Jesus Christ and the Father but also with other believers. All of God's children make up His family. You are to develop healthy relationships with other believers or children of God. These relationships are to grow and to lead to genuine fellowship with other believers. As you continue to fellowship with members of the family of God you will begin to learn characteristics of God's family. As a child of God you have been brought into a relationship with the community of followers of Christ. In this community as you fellowship and observe other believers you will begin to pick up many characteristics of God's family. There are many things that are more caught than taught in your new life as a child of God. You will observe how your new family prays, sings, worships, gives, fasts, reads the Bible, and so on.

"Not forsaking the assembling of ourselves together, as is the manner of some, but exhorting one another, and so much the more as you see the Day approaching."

Hebrews 10:25

As you wait for the return of Christ you are to continue assembling and fellowshipping with other believers. When you come together with other believers to hear the Word of God and celebrate the Father's goodness, it is called the assembly or congregation of believers. Through these times of assembling together, you will be exhorted and encouraged as you continue to mature into the image of Christ. As a member of the family of God, when you assemble with other believers this is what the Bible refers to as the "church."

The word "church" refers to the gathering of believers, or people who have been called out from sin into a relationship with Jesus Christ. The term "church" refers both to all the universal believers in Christ and also to when believers in a local area gather together. The church is not a building. The church is the called out believers of Jesus Christ or the family of God. The church is also called the body of Christ. You are one member of the body of Christ. You are a member of the family of God. You are a member of the church. Therefore the family of God, the church, and the body of Christ are different ways to express the same truth.

Chapter 5

The Framework

"Therefore gird up the loins of your mind, be sober, and rest your hope fully upon the grace that is to be brought to you at the revelation of Jesus Christ."

1 Peter 1:13

When you responded to Christ through repentance and by believing in Him, you were *"delivered from the authority of darkness and transferred into the kingdom of Jesus Christ"* (Colossians 1:13 Paraphrase Mine.) When you asked Jesus to come into your life you made a choice to depart from a life of iniquity or sin. Christ saved you from the life you previously lived. You now have a new life under a new Lord. Therefore, it is extremely important for you to begin to grow in spiritual understanding of the new kingdom that you live in. There are principles and laws in the kingdom of Christ that are different from those you previously followed or obeyed while living in sin. When you were born again you became a babe in Christ or a babe spiritually speaking. God intends for you to continue to grow similar to the way you have developed physically. This is what we refer to as growing spiritually. When you become skilled in the word of righteousness you move from being a spiritual babe to a little child in the faith. These are the two stages of spiritual growth during the foundation phase.

Another term that describes the process of spiritual growth is discipleship. As a child of God you are a disciple of Jesus Christ. A disciple is a learner or follower of a teacher. You are now a follower or pupil of Jesus Christ. Like every good teacher, He knows the plans and purposes He has prepared to lead you in. (See Jeremiah 29:11) It is important for you to understand that Christ desires disciples who learn and obey all of His commands.

"Go therefore and make disciples of all the nations, baptizing them in the name of the Father, and of the Son and of the Holy Spirit, teaching them to observe all things that I have commanded you; and lo, I am with you always, even to the end of the age."

Matthew 28:19-20

As a disciple of Jesus Christ you have become part of a community of followers of Christ. Another way the Word of God expresses this truth is that you are part of the body of Christ. We read, *"For as the body is one and has many members, but all the members of that one body, being many, are one body, so also is Christ"* (1 Corinthians 12:12). When you were brought into a relationship with God you were also brought into a relationship with the people of God. You are now one member of the body of Christ. We are called the body of Christ because we are the instruments that God lives through on the earth. Just as you live through your body, God also lives through His body. The body of Christ is God's dwelling place. So as a member of the body of Christ you are God's dwelling place.

When you were born again and the Spirit of God came into your life you became the dwelling place of God. The dwelling place of God is His people. God does not dwell in man-made buildings. (See Acts 7:48) God dwells in His people. You have been born again and have become part of the family of God and a member of His house.

*"Now, therefore, you are no longer strangers and foreigners, but fellow citizens with the saints and members of the **household** of God...in whom the whole building, being fitted together, grows into*

*a holy **temple** in the Lord, in whom you also are being built together
for a **dwelling place** of God in the Spirit."*
Ephesians 2:19, 21-22 (Bolds Mine.)

God lives in His children; therefore, you with them have become
His house or the temple of God. Paul said, *"Do you not know that
you are the temple of God and that the Spirit of God dwells in you"* (1
Corinthians 3:16)? In the construction process for any building there
is a blueprint that is to be followed. If the blueprint is not followed
the building will not become what it was intended to be. The same
is true for God's people. God has a blueprint for the building of His
dwelling place or temple. In the Old Testament God gave Moses the
pattern for His tabernacle. (See Exodus 25:40) God gave David the
plans for the Temple of Solomon. (See 1 Chronicles 28:12, 19) In
the New Testament the life of Jesus modeled God's blueprint for His
current dwelling place, His people. (See Hebrews 1:1-3)

God has a blueprint for your life. God has a blueprint for your
spiritual development. The rest of this book is intended to lead you
in this spiritual development according to the blueprint of God. It is
during this season of your life that God has laid the foundation and
you are learning what He has accomplished for you.

*"For no other foundation can anyone lay than that which is laid,
which is Jesus Christ."*
1 Corinthians 3:11

When you received Christ you received the foundation for your
life to be built upon. The foundation phase of your spiritual development pertains to what God instantaneously accomplished in your
life when you received Christ. Therefore, the foundation phase is
related to what God has accomplished in the deepest part of your
being, in your spirit. As you learn what God has freely accomplished for you, the framework for your life is being established.
Therefore, the framework for your spiritual development is only set
in place as you receive spiritual understanding. Remember you are
God's dwelling place or temple, and spiritual understanding is the
framework according to God's blueprint. Without growing in your

67

understanding of what God has accomplished in your life you will be unable to be developed according to God's blueprint. Without this framework of spiritual understanding you will not have adequate support for what you are about to experience.

What you have already been taught concerning Christ crucified, the Rock revealed, the word of righteousness, and the new birth are necessary in order for you to have a sufficient framework to move forward in spiritual development. God performed it and you just learn about it. God laid the foundation through the new birth. As you understand what God has done, this mental framework is built upon the foundation. It is also very important for you to examine the blueprint in order for you to have a strong enough framework that will support what God has planned to do in your life as you follow Christ. This framework is having the right perception of God's will, ways, and purposes for your life. If you do not understand what God's blueprint for you life is, then it would be impossible for your life to be built according to God's plan. This framework of spiritual understanding will prepare you to follow the blueprint for your spiritual development. This will give you a clear mental picture or vision to follow during this journey. You must not overlook the importance of you first receiving this framework of spiritual understanding before you seek to fulfill the will of God for your life. Without it your life will not be built according to God's divine design.

A Mental Framework

A framework is a structure that supports something. A mental framework is a perspective on a subject that sets the boundaries for the truths it contains. As a believer this mental framework of God's plan for your spiritual growth is very important. This mental framework will become the support that guides you through every day life and its circumstances. This mental framework will give you a perspective on the seasons of life you go through and their relation to your spiritual growth. This is your perspective on life where by faith you understand that in all seasons of life God is working toward your spiritual growth.

"By faith we understand that the worlds (ages) were framed by the word of God, so that the things which are seen were not made of things which are visible."
Hebrews 11:3 (Parenthesis Mine. Marginal Reading in NKJV)

This verse says that by faith believers have a perspective concerning the ages. The word "worlds" in the Greek is *"aion"*, which refers to a period of time or ages (Strong's #165). This word refers to an age of time not to people or space (Zodhiates pg. 1660). In God's plan there are ages or periods of time that have been framed by the Word of God. These major moments in history have come to pass or will come to pass because of the Word of God, which has framed them. The word "framework" is the Greek word *"katartizo"* which means to put in order and arrange (Strong's # 2675). The invisible Word of God has framed the ages of time and what has transpired during them. The invisible Word of God has framed the visible circumstances of history. History has not just happened by chance. God through His Word has arranged and put in order the history of the world. That which is visible has been brought to pass by that which is invisible. The invisible God is Lord over history and the ages it contains. This is the same for your spiritual development.

God's Word frames the major ages of your existence as well as other stages and phases He has prepared for those who continue to follow Christ on this spiritual journey (we will learn more of this later). Also, the visible things you will experience throughout your lifetime will have been allowed to be brought to pass by the unseen hand of God. In all seasons of your life God will be working toward the goal of maturity in Christ. By faith you must understand that your spiritual growth journey has been framed by the Word of God. The circumstances you face will not just be happening by chance. God has put in order, arranged, and will allow events in your life that will be opportunities for you to grow spiritually. During these moments you will need by faith to have this mental framework so that regardless of the circumstances, pain, discouragement, or questions you face, you perceive God is moving you toward the goal of maturity in Christ.

"Telescope" Vision

"Where there is no revelation (prophetic vision), the people cast off restraint."
     Proverbs 29:18 (Parenthesis Mine. Marginal Reading in NKJV)

The blueprint for your spiritual development is a prophetic vision for your life. This prophetic vision will keep you from wandering aimlessly through your spiritual journey. In this Scripture the word "prophetic" carries the idea of divine communication that has been revealed and provides you with understanding for the future. If you lose sight of the fact that God has predestined you to be conformed to the image of Christ, you will become vulnerable to either the circumstances of your life or to your own desires. You must keep as your vision the intended goal of maturity in Christ that God has created you to reach. The Apostle Paul spoke about vision through the idea of running a race in such a way that you may attain the prize.

Do you not know that those who run in a race all run, but one receives the prize? Run in such a way that you may obtain it. And everyone who competes for the prize is temperate (exercises self-control) in all things. Now they do it to obtain a perishable crown, but we for an imperishable crown. Therefore I run thus: not with uncertainty.
1 Corinthians 9:24-26 Parenthesis Mine. Marginal Reading in NKJV)

When people run in a race they have an end goal in mind. They are not running with uncertainty, but they are moving forward with purpose and vision. Runners have to run in such a way that they may obtain the goal. They exercise self-control in all things because their heart and mind are set upon reaching the goal and obtaining the prize. It is the same for spiritual growth; for you to grow up in all things, into the image of Christ, you will need to learn how to exercise self-control in all things. As you pursue the end goal of maturity in Christ you will need to follow God's blueprint, His timing, and His ways, not your own. Exercise self-control by not giving in to the tendency to lose sight of the goal.

You need what is called "telescope vision." A telescope has a lens that when you look through it provides you with the ability to view an object brighter, clearer, and nearer. This is referred to as the telescopes: Light Gathering Power, Resolving Power, and Magnifying Power according to the (Astronomical League, 2008). A telescope will not change the reality of things around you. However, it will provide you with the ability to see the reality of things brighter, more comprehensively, and nearer. So a telescope does not change your reality but your perception of reality and what is around you. When you look through a telescope, things become easier to see. You are able to comprehend the details of an object in a way that the natural eye could not. Also objects in the far distance are seemingly brought nearer to where you stand. "Telescope vision" will allow you to view your present circumstances with a supernatural eye. In the midst of a life storm you will be able to see things through a spiritual lens that provides: divine light, better comprehension, (that God is working through the storm for your good) and a view of the end goal, of being conformed to the image of Christ brought nearer.

The root words for telescope are two Greek words that are used in the Bible: *"telos"* and *"skopos."*

Paul uses a form of the first of the two Greek words in Colossians 1:29 where he says, *"Him we preach, warning every man and teaching every man in all wisdom, that we may present every man perfect in Christ Jesus."* The word translated "perfect" in English is the Greek word "teleios" which is the adjective form of "telos" (Strong's #5046). This word means: fully grown, mature, or that which is brought to its completion. Paul tells us that his desire was to present every believer mature in Christ. He had captured the heart of God to see believers mature and reach their potential in Christ.

In another place he speaks concerning himself, *"I press toward the goal for the prize of the upward call of God in Christ Jesus"* (Philippians 3:14). The word "goal" is translated from the last of the two Greek words, which makes up our English word "telescope", which is *skopos (Strong's Greek Lexicon #4649)*. It carries the idea of fixing ones attention on a goal.

When you put those words together the meaning could be: Fixing ones attention on the goal of reaching maturity in Christ. This is the prophetic vision that must capture your perception. You need to be as determined as Paul was to press toward the goal of being conformed to the image of Christ. "Telescope" vision will provide you with a perspective on spiritual growth that you can view your life circumstances through. Keeping your attention on the goal of becoming mature in Christ will not change the circumstances and trials that you will face. However, it will provide you with a lens through which you can view the reality of your circumstances with the end goal in mind. If you lose the "telescope" vision during a hard time in the future you will be unable to perceive correctly how God is working during that season to move you forward in your spiritual growth. "Telescope" vision will provide you with the motivation, strength, and encouragement you need during difficult times.

Telescope Overview

"Set up signposts, make landmarks; set your heart toward the highway."

Jeremiah 31:21

If you were hiking across the country to a desired location, a telescope or pair of binoculars would be a great tool in helping you reach your destination. If you stood on a large hill looking toward the destination, your natural eye's vision would be limited. However, if you looked through the lens of the telescope you were carrying you would become aware of landmarks that you would pass on the path toward your destination. Your vision through the telescope would be able to see the path to your destination a lot brighter, clearer, and the landmarks you would pass a lot nearer. This is what "telescope vision" will enable you to do on your journey of spiritual growth. As you fix your attention on the goal of reaching maturity in Christ your understanding will become brighter, clearer, as well as the end result appearing a lot nearer. With "telescope vision" you are able to see landmarks that you will pass on your journey toward maturity in Christ. These landmarks are illustrated in the Word of God as ages, stages, and phases. God wants you to receive "telescope vision" in order that you may perceive an overview of those landmarks He has planned to lead you through on this journey to grow spiritually and reach the goal of maturity in Christ.

Chapter 6

Preparation for Transformation

"Lest, after he has laid the foundation, and is not able to finish, all who see it begin to mock him, saying, 'This man began to build and was not able to finish.'"

Luke 14:29-30

It is extremely important for you to be prepared for the next phase of spiritual development. Before you are ready to experience transformation there are certain truths you must understand about it. As stated before, foundation phase deals primarily with your spirit and receiving a mental framework through spiritually understanding what God has already accomplished in your life when you received Christ. Transformation phases deals with your soul.

What God has accomplished through the finished work of Christ provides salvation for your entire being: spirit, soul, and body. However, when Christ came into your life it was only your spirit that was instantaneously changed or saved through the new birth. Your spirit has been saved or delivered from sin and its results. God did not instantly change your body when you received Christ. You can look in the mirror and verify the truth of that statement. Your body will be changed or experience the salvation God has provided for it in the future. When Christ returns, all believers will receive a glorified body similar to the one Jesus possessed after His resurrection.

As a result, you will be delivered from your current body in the future. However, you can experience God's power now for divine strength, healing, and restoration in your body. (See Romans 8:11)

Your soul also was not instantly changed when you received Christ. This is why you can still recall memories of events from before you became a child of God. Along with those memories you are still able to experience painful emotions from the time before you were born again. Your mind and your emotions need to be renewed and healed. This is what it means for your soul to be saved. Your soul is being saved as you are able to experience the salvation that God has made available for you through the finished work of Jesus Christ. There are mentalities, thought patterns, or strongholds in your mind from years of thinking contrary to God's will and truth. Also, there are still places in your will that you have previously given to sin that must become submitted to your new Lord, Jesus Christ. This process of experiencing the salvation that God has provided through Christ for your soul is called sanctification. During this process your soul is being saved, renewed, or delivered from sin and its results. Therefore, your spirit has been saved, your body will be saved, and your soul is being saved.

As a child of God, you are only prepared to experience transformation when you have a solid foundation and framework for spiritual development. God's salvation for your life started in the deepest part of your being and works outward. After a secure foundation and thorough framework has been laid in your life, it is time to begin to experience the salvation of the soul. Jesus gives us an example of this in His dealings with the Apostle Peter. We have already looked at the story when Peter made the confession that Jesus was the Christ the Son of the living God in Matthew 16:16. In that story Jesus informs us that His church would be built upon the confession of such a revelation. Let us now read what happens after those events.

*"Then He commanded His disciples that they should tell no one that He was Jesus the Christ. **From that time** Jesus **began** to show to His disciples that he must go to Jerusalem, and suffer many things from the elders and chief priests and scribes, and be killed, and be raised the third day. Then Peter took Him aside and began to rebuke*

Him, saying, 'Far be it from You, Lord; this shall not happen to You!' But He turned and said to Peter, 'Get behind Me, Satan! You are an offense to me, for you are not mindful of the things of God, but the things of men.' Then Jesus said to His disciples, 'If anyone desires to come after Me, let him deny himself, and take up his cross, and follow Me. For whoever desires to save his life will lose it, but whoever loses his life for My sake will find it. For what profit is it to a man if he gains the whole world, and loses his own soul? Or what will a man give in exchange for his soul? For the Son of Man will come in the glory of His Father with His angels, and then He will reward each according to his works.'"

Matthew 16:20-27 (Bold Mine.)

It is not by chance that after the disciples had received the foundation of Jesus' identity that He begins to deal with teachings concerning the soul. Only after the disciples were sure that Jesus was the Christ, the Son of the living God, and that He alone had the words of eternal life, did Jesus begin to teach them certain truths. (See John 6:67-69). The same is true for your life. There are things in your soul that are not mindful of the things of God. You have wrong habits, wrong thought patterns, wrong emotions, and wrong attitudes that effects how you live each day.

Notice the initial reaction of Peter to what Jesus began to teach them in the story. Peter took Jesus aside and begins to rebuke Him. There are mentalities, bondages, and places that have been given over to sin and Satan in your soul that are contrary to the ways and truths of God. The Scriptures confirm this in another place stating, *"For My thoughts are not your thoughts, nor are your ways My ways,' says the Lord. 'For as the heavens are higher than the earth, so are my ways higher than your ways, and my thoughts than your thoughts.'"* (Isaiah 55:8-9).

The truth of this Scripture is evident with how Jesus responded to Peter. Jesus turned to Peter and rebuked the devil. Why? Because the unchanged mentalities, beliefs, or perceptions that were in Peter's mind were an offense to the ways, will, and truths of God. They hindered Peter from understanding or living out God's will for His daily life. They resisted the voice and teachings of Jesus.

They sought to control Jesus. They sought to dictate what was right or wrong. If you do not engage in the process of sanctification, the salvation of your soul, it will allow the enemy to be able to work through these unchanged areas. The result will be that you will have areas in your life that are an offense to the ways of God and you will respond to Jesus wrongfully like Peter did in this story.

Peter had the foundation laid in his life but was still in need of experiencing the transformation of his soul. Through your previous life of sin and rebellion, before you were born again, you opened up your soul to demonic influences. Sin or wrong mentalities in your soul allows demonic influences to come and work in your life. Peter went from being the first person to confess that Jesus is the Christ to being rebuked for allowing Satan's influence to work in his life. Whatever is not from God is from the devil. Any thoughts or ways that are not in line with the things of God are sided with the devil and become areas in your life that resist the Lordship of Christ in your daily life. Issues and struggles can continue to exist and operate in your life if you do not allow them to be confronted and dealt with. When this occurred in Peter's life, Jesus spoke of the need for believers to take up their cross and follow after Him. The cross speaks of death. The cross speaks of you denying yourself or surrendering the areas of your soul to the Lordship of Christ in your daily life. You must learn to die to anything that is in your soul that is contrary to the ways of God.

"And do not be conformed to this world, but be transformed by the renewing of your mind, that you may prove what is that good and acceptable and perfect will of God."

Romans 12:2

This is what transformation phase is about. The renewing of your mind will allow you do be able to prove what the will of God is for you life. Peter's unrenewed mind caused him to rebuke or resist Jesus. Peter's unrenewed mind affected the way he reacted. It is the same in your life. To experience this renewing is to experience a renovation. As the temple of God anything that exists in your life that is not according to the blueprint of God must be transformed or renovated. Renovation means to go in and tear out the old and replace it with something new. God must deal with the old habits, old thought patterns, old attitudes, old emotions, old desires in order for you life to be built and lived according to the plan of God. This process is also referred to as being delivered. One of the reasons for this is because the definition of the word "saved" carries the idea of being delivered (Strong's # 4982).

"Therefore lay aside all filthiness and overflow of wickedness, and receive with meekness the implanted word, which is able to save (deliver) your souls."

James 1:21 (Parenthesis Mine.)

You must lay aside anything that is in your soul from your previous life of sin. All those areas of your soul that were given to sin or demonic influences must be renovated or renewed. (See also 1 Peter 3:15 and Ephesians 3:17) You must learn to lay aside the wrong thoughts. Lay aside the wrong desires. Lay aside the wrong attitudes. Lay aside the wrong emotions. Lay aside the hurts. Lay aside what people have done to you. Lay aside anything that is contrary to God's will for your life.

One of the characteristics that must be in your life in order for you to be prepared for transformation is an attitude of meekness. Humility or remaining in a position of being humble before the Lord is extremely necessary for you continue to be move forward in spiritual development. The Scripture exhorts you to receive the Word of God with meekness. It will result in you experiencing the salvation Christ has purchased for your soul. If you do not humbly receive the Word of God, you will never experience the complete freedom that Jesus died to give you. Since you have recently been born again you are like a newborn child. You have a lot to learn. You have a lot of room for spiritual development.

A result of being humble is that you understand your physical age, education, or occupation has nothing to do with where you are in your spiritual development. You might be fifty years old but you are at the same spiritual stage as a twelve year old who just got born again. This is the way of the kingdom of God. (See Mark 10:15)

When you came to the cross and received Jesus you became as a newborn baby regardless of your outward characteristics. The cross creates the same starting point for all new believers. You need the same spiritual food and teachings that all new believers need and therefore you are at a place of humility.

Another extremely important characteristic for your preparation for transformation is being secure in the love of God. This ultimately flows out of the cross of Christ and the word of righteousness. You must be secure in God's love and acceptance of you in order to allow God to renovate your soul. If you are not secure in God's love you will not be able to perceive correctly what God is doing when He confronts the areas in your soul. Jesus rebuked Peter. If you are not secure that God accepts you as a person then you will take such a rebuke in the wrong way. You are accepted by God through Christ. However, you have behaviors, thought patterns, attitudes, and emotions that are not acceptable for you to continue having in God's kingdom. You are accepted but you can still have unacceptable behavior.

Remember your identity is not found in your behavior but in who you have been created to be through the new birth. To be secure in God's love is to be secure in your identity in Christ. Only with this security will you have the right perception to allow God to deal with your wrong behaviors, thoughts, attitudes, and so on. The rebuke that Peter received from Jesus was not against who Peter was as a person but to the things in Peter that were an offense to God and that allowed Satan to work through him. It will be the same in your life and there is a huge difference in the two. You need to continue to re-read the chapters within the foundation phase if you are not clear on this issue.

The last characteristic I want to cover is your need to stay disciplined and feed on the right division of Scripture. The New Testament Epistles or letters are written to deal with exactly what you are going through and therefore contain the relevant truths for where you are in your spiritual development. Your spiritual development determines your ability to understand the truths found throughout the Word of God. Your heart determines your response to what you hear or read. Therefore, if you spend time on teachings and truths that are for the spiritually mature you will in result misunderstand or misapply them to your life. You need to continue to digest the teachings that concern the truths that you have learned in these chapters within the foundation phase as you continue to move forward in experiencing transformation. Stay within the Scriptures that were written after the finished work of Christ and to born again believers like you. These Scriptures will speak relevantly to the phase of transformation you are entering into. When you spend time reading or mediating on the Word of God, do so from New Testament letters.

Elementary Principles for your Spiritual Development

As you move forward in spiritual development you must continue to understand the place the elementary principles of Christ have throughout your journey of being spiritually developed. All Scripture is connected to and concerning the person of Jesus Christ. (See Colossians 2:3) Therefore, the elementary principles of Christ are to help you throughout your relationship with Jesus Christ and with His Word as you continue toward maturity in Christ. These six principles help guide and instruct you throughout your spiritual development. They become tools that help you navigate toward your goal of maturity in Christ. The six elementary principles of Christ listed in Hebrews 6:1-2 are: repentance from dead works, faith toward God, doctrine of baptisms, laying on of hands, resurrection of the dead, and eternal judgment.

Repentance
The principle of repentance has a place throughout your entire walk with Christ, not just when you first turned from your previous life of sin and rebellion. As God begins to deal with areas in your soul that needs to be transformed it will require you to live a lifestyle of repentance. To repent is to have a change of mind. As God reveals areas in your soul that are not pleasing to Him you will need to change your mind to see those areas in light of God's holiness and presence. You will need to turn from those areas and turn to God and His ways, His truth, and His thoughts. Repentance includes turning from wrong beliefs. Repentance includes turning from previous acts

or behaviors that are not proper for a child of God as God chooses to deal with them. Repentance means you receive a hatred of sin and that which displeases God.

Without experiencing true repentance you will not experience true deliverance from an issue you struggle with. If God delivered you from a struggle without you experiencing true repentance then you would never be able to acknowledge completely the grace of God that made your freedom possible. However, when you have seen your sin or struggles in the same manner that God sees them and are set free from them, you will truly be grateful and humbled by God's overwhelming goodness. This is why true repentance leads to certain types of fruits in your life. (See 2 Corinthians 7:10) It produces diligence and zeal. When you experience God's grace that comes from true repentance, it becomes the empowerment for you to be diligent and zealous for God. When you repent, times of refreshing will come from the Lord's presence as areas in your soul that were previously given over to sin are surrendered to the Lordship of Christ. (See Acts 3:19) Continue to give the principle of repentance a place in your life as you walk with the Lord.

Faith

The second elementary principle of Christ is faith toward God. Faith is extremely important for you during your walk with Christ. In fact, Scripture says, *"Without faith it is impossible to please Him, for he who comes to God must believe that He is, and that He is a rewarder of those who diligently seek Him"* (Hebrews 11:6). You must operate in the principle of faith in order to please God. Your relationship with God is not based on your works or performance but on faith. Faith motivates you to come before God and spend time with Him. You are to walk not by sight but by faith (2 Corinthians 5:7). Faith is like a door that allows God to have continual access into your life. It is through faith that you receive what God has made possible for you. (See Matthew 17:20)

Faith is a principle or law for you to enter into God's promises for your life. (See Romans 3:27) The principle of faith removes the right for you to boast about anything God does for you. God responds not to your good works but to your faith. Faith comes as you spend time with God through prayer, reading the Bible, fasting, worship, and other ways of drawing near to God. (See Romans 4:17, 10:17) Faith is having confidence and trust that what God has said is true. Faith is to be based on the Word of God and not on the things that are seen in your life. You will be challenged throughout your walk with Christ on whether you believe God's Word despite your experience. This is why the Bible says that we are to *"fight the good fight of faith"* (1 Timothy 6:12).

Identification

The third elementary principle of Christ is the doctrine of baptisms. The principle of baptism is the principle of identification. As you move forward in your spiritual development you must learn to continue to identify yourself with Jesus Christ and what He has accomplished for you. When you were water baptized you identified yourself with Jesus' death, burial, and resurrection. As you learn to continually identify yourself with the eternal facts of the finished work of Christ you will put off the deeds of the old man and put on the new man. You will learn more about this in the upcoming transformation phase section.

Laying on of hands

The fourth elementary principle of Christ is the laying on of hands. The laying on of hands was the primary method that Jesus used to impart the ministry and anointing of the Holy Spirit upon a person. The laying on of hands is also a way that Jesus still imparts the anointing of the Holy Spirit into your life through other believers. When a mature believer or minister lays his or her hands upon you, the anointing of the Holy Spirit can be released to minister to your needs. The laying on of hands is a primary way for the anointing and ministry of the Holy Spirit to be administered into your life.

"It shall come to pass in that day that his burden will be taken away from your shoulder, and his yoke from your neck, and the yoke will be destroyed because of the anointing oil."

Isaiah 10:27

"And He was handed the book of the prophet Isaiah. And when He had opened the book, He found the place where it was written: 'The Spirit of the Lord is upon Me, because He has anointed Me to preach the gospel to the poor; He has sent Me to heal the brokenhearted, to proclaim liberty to the captives and recovery of sight to the blind, to set at liberty those who are oppressed; to proclaim the acceptable year of the Lord."

Luke 4:17-19

The anointing of the Holy Spirit, when transferred upon your life through the laying on of hands, can accomplish any of the above purposes. The laying on of hands through an anointed believer is one of the primary ways that you will experience the transformation that God has designed for you. When you receive by faith the anointing of the Holy Spirit through the laying on of hands you can receive:

Emotional healing – "heal the brokenhearted"

Freedom from bondages – "liberty to the captives"

Revelation knowledge/ Spiritual Understanding – "recovery of the sight to the blind

Physical healing – "recovery of sight to the blind, set at liberty those who are oppressed"

The practice of the laying on of hands is an elementary principle of the church for how the anointing and power of God can be transferred into your life. You need to by faith continually receive from the ministry of the Holy Spirit through the laying on of hands. When you do it will be a way that you experience being set free from hurts, negative attitudes, wrong beliefs, demonic influences, or any area of your soul that needs to experience transformation. The anointing can break every yoke that would try and hinder you from experiencing what Jesus has made possible through His finished work. The laying on of hands is extremely vital in helping you receive the anointing of the Holy Spirit for your souls needs during the transformation phase.

Eternal Perspective

The last two elementary principles of Christ are the resurrection from the dead and eternal judgment. These two principles are to establish an eternal perspective for you as you live your life. You must continually live with an understanding that your current existence on earth is temporary and that there is coming a day that you will have to give an account for your life. These two principles help you live for eternity and not the temporary desires of your flesh or body. When you live with an eternal perspective it will help you to overcome temptation easier. As a follower of Christ you have passed from death to life. (See John 5:24) However, there still remains an eternal judgment for believers called the judgment seat of Christ.

"Therefore we make it our aim, whether present or absent, to be well pleasing to Him. For we must all appear before the judgment seat of Christ, that each one may receive the things done in the body, according to what he has done, whether good or bad."
2 Corinthians 5:10

As a born again believer you will give an account to Christ on whether you reached the goal of your journey with Him. You will give an account for your spiritual development which also includes whether you fulfilled your purposes in the kingdom of God. This eternal perspective becomes a healthy motivation for you to engage in sanctification and the transformation of your soul. Your soul ultimately dictates your behavior and how you live. And since you are going to give an account for the deeds you do in the body, you should understand the importance of the transformation phase of your spiritual development. Notice, you give an account for the deeds that you do in the body. Remember, you are a spirit and your body is to be an instrument for you to live out the will of God. Whether you are able to use your body for good is determined by how much transformation of your soul you experience. Thus, the transformation of your soul prepares you for the coming resurrection of the dead and eternal judgment of God. An eternal perspective leads you to present your body and soul as a living sacrifice unto the Lord. (See Romans 12:1-2)

Section II.

Transformation Phase – Christ Died As You

Phase
Introduction

Transformation phase is also connected to the second pair of elementary teachings of Christ. This is because it is during transformation phase that the deeper truths and application of the doctrine of baptisms, specifically water baptism, is relevant. The application of these truths greatly affects a believer's life in the kingdom. The doctrine of laying on of hands speaks to believers learning to receive the anointing of the Holy Spirit through mature believers for the transformation of their soul. A believer should progress in the spiritual development stages from being a little child to that of a child during this phase. Transformation phase deals primarily with the soul of man. The relevant division of truth is the revelation of the mystery contained in Paul's gospel. The primary method that facilitates spiritual growth for transformation phase is what is called the "My Role" factor. This means that each individual believer is the main facilitator that determines how much spiritual growth takes place during this phase. Observe the chart on the next page!

Three Ages Elementary Teachings of Christ Represent	Spiritual Growth Stages	Phases for Discipleship	Primary Division of Truth	Primary "M" Facilitates Growth for Phase
Age 1 Transferring Kingdoms *Repentance from Dead Works and Faith toward God*	Babes	I. Foundation 1 Cor.3:11 (Spirit)	Gospel of Jesus Christ, Elementary Teachings of Christ Overview	Ministry of the Word
	Little Children		Gospel of Grace, Paul's Gospel, Word Of Righteousness	
Age 2 Life in God's Kingdom *Doctrine of Baptisms and Laying on of Hands*	Little Children	II.Transformation Rom. 12:2 (Soul)	Revelation of the Mystery	My Role
	Children			
	Children	III.Formation Gal.4:19 (Soul)	Revelation of the Mystery	Modeling Community
	Young Men			
	Young Men	IV.Impartation Matt.10:7-8 (Body)	Gospel of the Kingdom	Mentoring
Age 3 Life in the Millennium *Rewards for Resurrection and Judgment*	Father	V.Multiplication John17:6-8,20 (Entire Person)	Whole Counsel of Scripture	All the M's

Chapter 7

The Spirit of Revelation

*"That the God of our Lord Jesus Christ, the Father of glory, may give to you the **spirit of** wisdom and **revelation** in the knowledge of Him, the eyes of your understanding being enlightened; that you may know what is the hope of His calling, what are the riches of the glory of His inheritance in the saints, and what is the exceeding greatness of His power toward us who believe, according to the working of His mighty power which He worked in Christ when he raised Him from the dead and seated Him at His right hand in the heavenly places, far above all principality and power and might and dominion, and every name that is named, not only in this age but also in that which is to come."*

Ephesians 1:17-21 (Bold Mine.)

God the Father desires to give you the spirit of wisdom and the spirit of revelation. The spirit of revelation is an aspect of the ministry of the Holy Spirit. This ministry of the Holy Spirit is related only to the New Covenant and what Jesus accomplished through His finished work. God accomplished His eternal purpose through the finished work of Jesus Christ (Ephesians 3:11). What God desired and planned from before the foundation of the world was made possible through Jesus' crucifixion, death, burial, resurrection, and ascension. Therefore, the cross and the resurrection are to become our focal point, and yet, you in your own ability are limited to see, perceive, and understand the importance of what Jesus did for you through His finished work. Jesus hung on the cross around two thousand years ago before you were even born and nevertheless it has power, relevance, and provisions for your life. Through the spirit of revelation, what God accomplished for you through the finished work of Christ will be made real and alive in your life. God desires for you to know the power which He worked in Christ.

"And to make all see what is the fellowship of the mystery, which from the beginning of the ages has been hidden in God who created all things through Jesus Christ."

Ephesians 3:9

It is the ministry of the spirit of revelation to reveal the mystery surrounding the cross and resurrection of Jesus Christ. All of the provisions that God has made possible for mankind through the finished work of Jesus Christ remained a mystery until the spirit of revelation revealed it to the Apostle Paul. Paul said, *"If indeed you have heard of the dispensation of the grace of God which was given to me for you, how that by revelation He made known to me the mystery"* (Ephesians 3:2-3). The spirit of revelation made known the mystery surrounding the finished work of Christ to Paul and desires to also make it known to you. Observe that God desires for all to be made to see the truths surrounding the mystery of the cross and resurrection of Jesus Christ. It was a mystery because God did not reveal completely what He was going to accomplish through the finished work of Christ beforehand. (See Deuteronomy 29:29) It was only made known by the spirit of revelation after the eternal purpose had been accomplished in Christ. God wants for you know the truths concerning what He has done for you through Christ.

"Now to Him who is able to establish you according to my gospel and the preaching of Jesus Christ, according to the revelation of the mystery kept secret since the world began."

Romans 16:25

After the foundation and framework has been performed in your life, you need to be established as the temple of God. To be established is to be spiritually developed where you have put off deeds of the old man and have put on the deeds of the new man you have been created to be in Christ. Notice that the division of the Scriptures that God has provided for you to be established is what Paul called "his gospel." Paul referred to the truths that God had revealed to him as his gospel. His gospel includes the teachings of the revelation of the mystery that were kept secret since the world began and the word of righteousness. You have already been presented the teachings surrounding the word of righteousness, and the preaching of Jesus Christ refers to the core of the gospel.

*"Moreover, brethren, I declare to you the gospel, which I preached to you, which also your received and in which **you stand**, by which also you are saved, if you hold fast the word which I preached to you-unless you believed in vain. For I **delivered to you first of all** that which I also received: that Christ died for our sins according to the Scriptures, and that He was buried, and that He rose again the third day according to the Scriptures, and that He was seen by Peter, then by the twelve."*

1 Corinthians 15:1-4 (Bold Mine.)

To stand implies that those truths are foundational. Paul said that he first preached and delivered to the believers in the city of Corinth the gospel that emphasized the death, burial, and resurrection of Christ. The preaching of Jesus Christ refers to the truths that are to be first preached or delivered to a person. When a person receives and responds correctly to those first truths the foundation is laid in their life. The preaching of Jesus Christ refers to the foundational truths concerning Christ that you stand upon. It is upon this foundation, that you first received concerning Christ, that you are to be spiritually developed and established in your walk with Christ. The spirit of revelation will make known and alive to you the truths contained in the revelation of the mystery.

This is why it is important for you to spend time in the letters of Paul. Paul said concerning his ministry, *"I became a minister according to the stewardship from God which was given to me for you, to fulfill the word of God, the mystery which has been hidden from ages and from generations, but now has been revealed to His saints"* (Colossians 1:25-26). The truths God revealed to Paul completed the Word of God. These truths completed the Word of God because they were not revealed or contained in the Old Testament Scriptures. As you learn and apply the truths contained in the revelation of the mystery by the spirit of revelation, you will become established in your walk with Christ.

It was through responding to the revelation that Jesus is the Christ that the foundation was laid in your life, and it is through understanding and applying the revelation of the mystery that you will be established in the faith. You begin through revelation and will be established in the faith through revelation. This is why it is so important for you to spend time learning these truths found in the Word of God. As you continue to be spiritually developed you must guard against striving. Your spiritual development will not be *"by might nor by power, but by My Spirit, says the Lord of hosts"* (Zechariah 4:6).

God accomplished His eternal purpose through the finished work of Christ. This also means He has accomplished and made possible His purpose for your life. The key is He has accomplished it and made it possible. Remember, you have been *"created in Christ Jesus for good works, which God prepared beforehand that you should walk in them"* (Ephesians 2:10). You must learn to rest in the finished work of Christ and allow God to lead and develop you. This is what it means to abide in the rest of God.

"For he who has entered His rest has himself also ceased from his works as God did from His."

Hebrews 4:10

Through Christ you have entered the rest of God. However, you must guard yourself from not abiding in the benefits of the rest you have through the finished work of Christ. Notice that when you abide in the rest of God you cease from working. This does not mean you do nothing but it does mean that striving and a works mentality will not bring spiritual development. When you abide in the rest of God you are allowing God to do in you and through your life what He has already accomplished for you through the finished work of Christ. It seems like a paradox but it is not. You are just choosing to remain in position where you humbly receive what God has freely done for you in Christ. Just as you received Christ, you also are to learn to walk in Him and be established in the faith. (See Colossians 2:6-7) You receive God's grace through faith!

"Now we have received, not the spirit of the world, but the Spirit who is from God, that we might know the things that have been freely given to us by God."

1 Corinthians 2:12

As the Spirit of God causes you to know the things that you have been freely given by God, you are able to experience those truths through faith. Through the spirit of revelation you can learn everything that you have been freely given through the finished work of Christ. God's work in Christ has accomplished all you will ever need to live for God. Let us now look at how you determine how much of God's provisions you experience.

The "My Role" Factor

"Work out your own salvation with fear and trembling; for it is God who works in you both to will and to do for His good pleasure."

Philippians 2:12-13

During the transformation phase, the most prominent factor that facilitates your spiritual development is you. This is what is referred to as the "my role" factor. You are the major factor during this phase that determines if you will experience what God has freely given you through Christ. Understand that as you abide, resting in the finished work of Christ, God will work on the inside of you. God will create desires on the inside of you and He will provide you with the ability to perform them. God will influence both your will and your performance or daily behavior. However, notice that you are commanded to do something. Out of reverence to God, you must remain willing to live out or perform what God wants to do in your life. This is the essence of what it means to work out your own salvation. It is remaining in a position where you allow what God is doing on the inside of you to affect how you live each day.

This Scripture speaks to the role that you have in order for you to experience transformation. You are to keep the fear of the Lord in your heart. You are to humbly and respectfully give God the place He deserves in your life. God will change your mind, your will, and emotions if you will humbly let Him. There are three primary ways that you allow what God is doing on the inside of you to be "worked out."

"Therefore do not be unwise, but understand what the will of the Lord is."

Ephesians 5:17

You must grow in spiritual understanding. In order for you to have acceptable behavior in the kingdom of God you must learn what God's will is for you. (See Ephesians 5:10) This is what it means to grow in spiritual understanding. It is impossible to "walk worthy of the Lord" without increasing in spiritual understanding (Colossians 1:9-10). In Hosea 4:6 it states, *"My people are destroyed for lack of knowledge."* If you do not choose to grow in spiritual understanding you will hinder what God wants to do in your life. The result of such a choice will lead to tragedy or destruction in your life. Your life must be built upon the Word of God in order to withstand the trials and storms of life. It is important that you accept the spiritual understanding that is being given to you when the spirit of revelation reveals truth to you.

If you do not learn what God has freely given to you through Christ how will you be able to experience those provisions? It is impossible to live according to God's blueprint without growing in spiritual understanding. You must spend time reading the Word of God. This is part of the role you play in your spiritual development. God cannot read His Word for you. Your pastors or leaders cannot make that choice for you. This is the power of the "my role" factor.

Your work is to spend time in God's Word. As you do this it will allow God to continue to work *"both to will and to do"* in your life (Philippians 2:13). The psalmist declared, *"The entrance of Your words gives light; it gives understanding to the simple"* (Psalm 119:130). The Word of God is spiritual food and therefore extremely vital for your spiritual development.

"Therefore, as the Holy Spirit says: 'Today, if you will hear His voice, do not harden your hearts as in the rebellion."
Hebrews 3:7-8

The Lord will speak to you as you spend time reading the Word of God. When you read the Word of God you are spending time with the Lord. You must understand that when God is dealing with you about something, that is what it means for God to speak to you. God may cause a Scripture, word, or phrase to stand out to you as you read the Bible. Don't expect God to speak audibly to you like when you are talking to a friend. However, God knows how to get your attention. He may choose to get your attention through a preacher, through a conversation, or through circumstances. Jesus said you would know when He is communicating something to you. (See John 10:27) Hearing God speak is not listening to a voice that speaks in your ear. The Bible says, *"The spirit of a man is the lamp of the Lord, searching all the inner depths of his heart"* (Proverbs 20:27). Your born again spirit is the lamp of the Lord. This means that God communicates with you spirit. When this occurs you will be able, through your spirit, to become aware that God is communicating with you. This is a function of your born again spirit and is called intuition.

God can communicate with you in many ways, but you must obey what God communicates to you. To not obey what God's is dealing with you about is to harden your heart to God's work in your life. You hold this key for your spiritual development. You must obey what God speaks to you for God to have continual access to work *"to will and to do"* in your life (Philippians 2:13). If you rebel or disobey the voice of God, it will absolutely keep you from developing spiritually. God has already made provision through

Christ for you to be changed. God, by His grace and power, will do it for you if you will obey what He asks you to do. This is the role or work you must do in order for you to experience transformation in your soul and continue to grow spiritually. Nobody else can obey for you. Let the word of the Lord "run swiftly" in your life (2 Thessalonians 3:1).

"And do not grieve the Holy Spirit of God...Do not quench the Spirit."

Ephesians 4:30 and 1 Thessalonians 5:19

You must stay yielded to the Holy Spirit. To grieve or quench the Holy Spirit is to resist what God is doing in your life. God desires to continually work to will and to do in your life, but you can resist Him. Your work is to stay yielded to the working of the Holy Spirit in you life. The Holy Spirit works to enforce the Lordship of Christ to every area of your life. As you stay yielded to the Spirit of God, He will heal your emotions, set your mind free, and form your will to God's. God works in your life through the Holy Spirit. Therefore, to resist the Holy Spirit is to resist God the Father and the Son Jesus Christ.

You resist the Holy Spirit when you are not willing to surrender areas of your soul that need to experience transformation. When you remain yielded to the Holy Spirit He can deal with any area in your soul that He desires to restore. When you remain yielded you are living out the experience of the Lordship of Christ in your life. God will not make you yield to His Spirit. Your pastors, teachers, and leaders cannot make you stay yielded to the Spirit of God. This is a part of the role and work you play in your transformation and spiritual development. This is what it means to work out your salvation. You have a role that no one else can ever perform for you. I pray you will allow God *"to work in you what is well pleasing in His sight, through Jesus Christ"* (Hebrews 13:21).

Diligence

"Not lagging in diligence, fervent in spirit, serving the Lord."

Romans 12:11

Engaging privately in spiritual disciplines is a biblical way for you to diligently grow in spiritual understanding, obedience, and yieldedness. The most common private spiritual disciplines include: reading the Bible, praying, singing to God, fasting, meditating on God, and confessing the Word of God. This is how you can be diligent in fulfilling your role or work of allowing God to work in your life. Spiritual disciplines are ways that you continually open the door of your heart to the work of God in your life. When you diligently give yourself to spiritual disciplines you remain in a position where God can work unhindered in your life. Spiritual disciplines are how you abide and rest in the finished work of Christ.

"Let us therefore be diligent to enter that rest, lest anyone fall according to the same example of disobedience."
Hebrews 4:11

You will be able to continually experience the rest of God when you are diligent to participate in these spiritual disciplines. Many people have a wrong perception that effects how they feel concerning spiritual disciplines. Spiritual disciplines are not boring when you understand that they are ways that you draw near to God and spend time with Him. (See James 4:8) You are not performing spiritual disciplines to earn God's love, approval, or acceptance. Remember you already have those because you are the righteousness of God in Christ Jesus. (See 2 Corinthians 5:21) You do not perform spiritual disciplines out of a works mentality but from a heart that desires to spend time with God. You are providing opportunities for the Holy Spirit to work in your life to change you more and more into the image of Christ. When you participate in private spiritual disciplines you are positioning yourself to receive and experience what God has freely provided for you through the finished work of Christ. You will add to your faith more and more of the character of Christ. (See 2 Peter 1:5)

As you participate in private spiritual disciplines you should believe that God is working in your life. God is the only one who can change you. With an attitude of dependence and hunger you should partake in the spiritual disciplines. You are inviting God to change you more into the image of Christ every time you spend time with Him through the disciplines. If you want to experience what God has made possible for you through Christ then you need to spend intimate time with the Lord.

You are not to be casual in your fellowship with God. You are to diligently spend time with Him. Spiritual disciplines will help you set aside time each day to be alone with God. Without these times of intimacy with the Lord you will hinder what God wants to do on the inside of you. Seek God first each day. Remain in a position where you invite God to change any area in your soul. Be diligent daily to take part in private spiritual disciplines. Diligence keeps you fervent in spirit. Diligence helps you to faithfully serve and obey the Lord.

"Keep your heart with all diligence, for out of it spring the issues of life."

Proverbs 4:23

Prayer

I want to pray for you:

Father, I ask in the name of Jesus Christ that you would impart the spirit of revelation into this person's life. Father, I ask that the finished work of Christ would be made known to them. Give them a revelation of the cross of Christ and the power of His resurrection. May their spiritual understanding be enlightened to what you have freely given them in Christ. May you strengthen them in their spirit as they engage in the transformation of their soul. May your peace and love fill their heart. May the mystery of what you accomplished through Christ become extremely clear to them that they are able to live the life you made possible for them. May the spirit of wisdom help them apply what is revealed to them. Be blessed. Be encouraged. Receive what the Lord has for you in Jesus Name. So be it!

Chapter 8

Christ Died As You

"I have been crucified with Christ; it is no longer I who live."
Galatians 2:20a

W ho you use to be has died. When Christ died you died with Him. In fact, Christ died as you. He took your place. When He hung on the cross the old you was being crucified. The old you no longer lives. Jesus did not just die for you but He died as you. He died and buried your old identity through His finished work. All that you were before was taken care of by God when Christ died as you. The spirit of revelation will make these truths come alive to you. This changes the way you should see yourself. This is the answer for you to have a healthy self-image and self-esteem.

The power of the cross is God's answer for every need of yours. God, through the death of Christ, arranged for you also to die with Him. Your old self or old man died with Christ. God has provided for you to be completely free of everything that you were before. You have been provided freedom from your entire past. What Christ has accomplished provides more than just your sins being forgiven and you coming into a right relationship with God but remaining unchanged. Christ crucified is also your freedom from all wrong attitudes, thoughts, habits, sins, and bondages. When Christ died as you He also took to the cross all the areas of your soul or self that need to be transformed. The cross is the power of God for your soul to be transformed.

Did you have an anger problem? Christ buried it! Did you struggle with sexual sins? Christ buried it! Did you have a problem with lying? Christ buried it! This is the power of the finished work of Christ. Self effort will not change your soul and behavior. Trying harder will not change your soul and behavior. In fact, such an attitude would be pride and would hinder the power of the cross to transform your soul. (See 1 Corinthians 1:23) God's grace through the finished work of Christ has made it possible for you to be free and free indeed. Free from all that you were or did before you were born again and this includes the areas of your soul that God did not instantaneously change but now desires to progressively transform.

"Knowing this, that our old man was crucified with Him, that the body of sin might be done away with (rendered inoperative), that we should no longer be slaves of sin."

Romans 6:6

The old you was crucified and buried with Christ. Notice that the verse emphasizes the need for you to "know" this. It is impossible to live the life that Jesus Christ has made possible for you without knowing, by the spirit of revelation, the truths that your old man has been crucified. What was done to Christ was done to the old you. You are not the person that you use to be, therefore the desires of your body do not have to control you. You do not have to obey or be a slave to sin. You have become a completely new person in Christ. You are a new creation.

The old man is one of the ways the Bible refers to who you were before you were born again. The old man refers to your old self. It is in your soul that you are self conscious. This old self or your soul was crucified with Christ. When your old self was alive you were considered to be in Adam. The Bible speaks of all those who have not been born again as people that are in Adam and the terms "old man" or being "in Adam" are synonymous. Paul said, *"For as in Adam all die"* (1 Corinthians 15:22). To be in Adam means that you are a descendant of the first man named Adam and that you inherit his life and characteristics. When you were in Adam you bore his fallen and sinful image. To be in Adam is to be a sinner and also includes all the results of sin. You can look in the world today and see the image of Adam being displayed in the lives of all unbelievers.

Your old man or self was crucified with Christ. Your old man died. When the Bible speaks concerning your old man or self it refers to three things. The first thing that makes up your old man is what you received from previous generations. This is what the Bible refers to as generational curses. God said that He *"visits the iniquity or sin of the fathers upon the children to the third and fourth generations"* (Exodus 20:5). Sinful habits, attitudes, and desires were passed down as curses to you from your family line.

The second thing that makes up your old man is what has been done to you. This consists of what you have received from the experiences of life. Maybe you have received rejection from an earthly father who abandoned you. Maybe you received self-worth issues because you were raped. What you have received refers to hurts, memories, and emotions. These issues affect your soul. They cause the way you feel, how you think, perceive things, and react in certain situations.

The last item that the old man refers to is what you have done. Your personal decisions, actions, and life before you were born again affects your soul and also makes up your old man. Wrong choices you made allowed strongholds to be formed in your soul. The life you previously sowed has reaped consequences in your life. These wrong habits, evil thinking, and every rebellious thing that was apart of your life also made up your old self. These three things make up what the Bible speaks of as your old man or being in Adam. (I must give credit to the book Back to the Gospel concerning this issue. God used this book to conform what He was teaching me concerning this issue and I am forever grateful.)

When Christ died as you this is what died. Your old self died. Who you were when you were in Adam has died. The power of the cross has made it possible for you to experience complete freedom from all three of those areas. The cross has provided for you to be free from every generational curse. The cross has provided for you to be healed and restored from what people have previously done to you. The cross has provided for you to be free from what you have brought upon yourself.

Your old man's family history does not have to dictate your experience, your life, or your future. You are no longer a person that is from the lineage of Adam or your earthy parents. You have been born from above. You have been born of God. You are a child of God now and a part of His family. You are now from the lineage of Jesus Christ. You are no longer in Adam but are in Christ. Your old man may have come from poverty but you are now a new creation. Poverty no longer has power over your life. You are a new creation in Christ and have the resources of heaven. Your old man may have come from a family of obesity but who you were was crucified and buried. You are a new creation in Christ and come from the lineage of Jesus Christ. You are a new person, a new man, a new self.

"Christ has redeemed us from the curse of the law, having become a curse for us (for it is written, 'Cursed is everyone who hangs on a tree')."

Galatians 3:13

What people have done to you does not have to dictate your experience, your life, or you future. You do not have to be a product of other peoples mistakes. The past does not have influence over you. It was crucified. Those hurts were crucified. The abuses were crucified. The evil things said to you were crucified. The rejections were crucified. Jesus took them upon Himself. He bore your shame so you can be free. He bore your rejection so you can experience acceptance. He bore your hurts and pains so you can experience wholeness. He bore your wounds so you can be healed. Jesus died as you. His bloody body is your freedom. His pierced head is your peace. His pierced feet are your freedom. What you were died when Jesus died. What was done to you died when Jesus died. The curses you inherited died when Jesus died.

"Knowing this, that our old man was crucified with Him, that the body of sin might be done away with (rendered inoperative), that we should no longer be slaves of sin."

Romans 6:6

Your old man was crucified – past tense. You do not need to be crucified. It has already happened. Your old man has been crucified with Christ. What you were in Adam has been crucified in Christ. What God did to Jesus in His mind He was doing for you! You are not waiting to get the victory, God has already given you the victory in Christ. It has already been provided for you. Praise God.

"For the love of Christ compels us, because we judge thus: that if One died for all, then all died."

2 Corinthians 5:14

When Jesus died your old man died. What you were has died-past tense. You have a new identity. You are a new man. You are a new self. You are a new creation. Those hurts have died. Those curses have died. Your sins have died. Your wrong attitudes have died. Your old self died with Christ.

"How shall we who died to sin live any longer in it? Or do you not know that as many of us as were baptized into Christ Jesus were baptized into His death?

Romans 6:2-3

You do not have to live in defeat. You do not have to continue to behave the way you did before you were born again. The old you died. Those old habits died. His death was your death. He made a way for all things to become new. Thank God for His grace.

"Therefore we were buried with Him through baptism into death."

Romans 6:4

Your old man was crucified and then died. When people die they need to be buried. Your old self was buried with Christ. When Christ was buried you were buried. The curses, the sins, wrong attitudes, and bad habits not only have died in Christ but have been buried never to rise again. Water baptism was the ceremony in which you buried the body the old you lived through. Your body has now been raised in order for the new you to live through it. Your body no longer is to be used for sin because the old you died. You have become a new man and therefore use your body to live for God.

The entire person you were before has been crucified, died, and buried. There is nothing from your previous age of living in sin that God has not already dealt with through the finished work of Jesus Christ. These are the facts of what God has accomplished and made possible for you through the cross. God cannot lie. It is true, Christ died as you. Your old identity has died and been buried. You have to accept that the old you is gone. All that you were in Adam is gone. Thank God for the finished work of the cross. You can exchange the effects of your past upon your soul for the freedom Christ has purchased for you. God will give you a revelation of this truth like He did to the nation of Israel. God wants you to see that your old man is dead.

*"So the Lord saved Israel that day out of the hand of the Egyptians, and Israel **saw** the Egyptians **dead on the seashore**. Thus Israel **saw** the great work which the Lord had done in Egypt; so the people feared the Lord, and believed the Lord and His servant Moses."*
Exodus 14:30-31 (Bold Mine.)

Free Indeed

"Therefore if the Son makes you free, you shall be free indeed."
John 8:36

The Son has made you free through His finished work. The eternal truth is that you are truly free in Christ. You are free from having to live according to the image of Adam or fallen man. The cross has not only provided you with freedom from your entire old man or who you were in Adam but also provides you with freedom over any influence. The cross is the power of God for your entire life. The Bible speaks of the influence of the flesh, the world, the devil, and the Law. Let us now briefly look at each of them.

Flesh

"And those who are Christ's have crucified the flesh with its passions and desires."

Galatians 5:24

You are now in Christ. Your identity is found only in Him. In Christ the power and influence of the flesh has been dealt with. The power of the cross is greater than the influence of the flesh. The Bible speaks of the flesh in a couple of ways. The term "flesh" refers to the physical body you live in. Pinch yourself, that is flesh. (See 2 John 1:7) Your physical flesh also includes your nationality or from whom you have descended. (See Romans 1:3) This use of the term flesh refers to human beings. The flesh also refers to the appetites or desires of your body. Natural sexual desires, the desire to eat, desire for rest, the desire for safety or comfort, and so on. Except, now that sin has affected our bodies, it desires to meet those needs excessively or outside of God's will. These are called the sinful passions. (See Romans 7:5)

However, the flesh also refers to any activity that is done without God's involvement. When persons live depending on their own ability, strength, wisdom, knowledge, and so on, it is what the Bible defines as living in the flesh. So the flesh also refers to the sphere of activity outside of God's assistance or will. This is why every unbeliever lives in the flesh. They are not in a right relationship with God where His Spirit can empower and help them in their daily life. They live outside of God's help and ability. Believers can also choose to walk in the flesh and not depend upon the provisions God has made for them. (See Galatians 5:25) We will learn more about this later.

World

"But God forbid that I should boast except in the cross of our Lord Jesus Christ, by whom the world has been crucified to me, and I to the world."
Galatians 6:14

"For all that is in the world—the lust of the flesh, the lust of the eyes, and the pride of life—is not of the Father but is of the world."
1 John 2:16

The power of the cross has broken the power, influence, and pull of the world in your life. The cross of Christ is God's provision for all your needs. Your victory is in the cross. The cross is the only reason and foundation for you to boast. The cross is God's grace for all of your life. When you were crucified with Christ you died to the world and its influence. Notice that the world is defined as the lust of the flesh, the lust of the eyes, and the pride of life. It is the flesh of man that has led to the world in which you live. Those areas of the flesh motivate the world. When you died in Christ you died to all that the world consists of. You do not have to follow the pattern or ways of the world all around you. You have died to the methods, styles, and practices of the world's lust. You have died to trying to meet the culture's standard. You have been born from above and now live according to the culture of the kingdom of God. You have been crucified to the world. You have died to the peer pressure of the world.

Devil

"For he who has died has been freed from sin...For the death that He died, He died to sin once for all... For sin shall not have dominion over you...And having been set free from sin.
Romans 6:7, 10, 14, 18

"Therefore submit to God. Resist the devil and he will flee from you."
James 4:7

Jesus died to the power of sin once and for all. When your old self died with Christ you also died to the power of sin. Before you were born again you were a slave to sin and its control. Sin and the influence of Satan dictated your life. However, when your old man died, the person sin and Satan reigned over died also. Therefore, when you were born again, the power of sin and Satan no longer had any legal right to be your master. You do not have to submit and be controlled by the power and influence of sin any longer. The cross of Christ has provided you with freedom from the slavery and torment of sin and Satan. You can resist the devil as you stay submitted to God and he will flee from you. God's Word said he will flee from you when you resist him and that means he does not have authority over your life.

Law

"Therefore, my brethren, you also have become dead to the law through the body of Christ, that you may be married to another- to Him who was raised from the dead... But now we have been delivered from the law having died to what we were held by, so that we should serve in the newness of the Spirit and not in the oldness of the letter."

Romans 7:4, 6

Through the death of Christ you have also died to the law. The law refers to the Law of Moses. However, the law also refers to any system of rule-keeping. You have died from having to follow a list of commandments. As a born again child of God you serve in the newness of the Spirit and not by following a list of rules. You have been delivered from the weight and burden of trying to keep a bunch of rules. You do not have to live under a system of religious rule keeping. A relationship with Christ is the exact opposite of religion. Religion is to believe and adhere to a set of beliefs. This means a person's religion can be based on a letter or on a list of commands. You can try and believe and follow those commands on that list without having any relationship with a person. However, you have been brought into a relationship with Christ. Your relationship with

Christ is not based on trying to follow a list of commands just as any healthy relationship does not consist of that. Out of your time spent with the Lord you are to follow His leading. You have died to religious law-keeping and have come into a living relationship with God.

God gave the Law of Moses to show mankind their sin. Romans 3:20 states, *"For by the law is the knowledge of sin."* The law reveals to mankind their inability to obey it completely and therefore their need for a Savior. This is the main purpose why God gave the Law. The law was to lead people to Christ. Galatians 3:24 reads, *"Therefore the law was our tutor to bring us to Christ."* The word tutor refers to a hired slave who was responsible for the training and discipline of the children. Any time the child did something wrong the tutor would guide them by a spanking. This is what the law accomplishes in a person's life. The law condemns a person when they fail to completely keep it. (See James 2:10) The law was to drive or lead a person to find righteousness in Jesus Christ. Paul said, *"For Christ is the end of the law for righteousness to everyone who believes"* (Romans 10:4). You have died to the law and have come into a living relationship with Christ. You no longer have to try and follow a list of rules but are to obey what Christ speaks to you. Your obedience is to flow out of your relationship with Christ. Jesus offers freedom from a religion of burdens. In Christ you have died to the law.

"Come to Me, all you who labor and are heavy laden, and I will give you rest. Take My yoke upon you and learn from Me, for I am gentle and lowly in heart, and you will find rest for your souls. For My yoke is easy and My burden is light."

Matthew 11:28-30

Chapter 9

Put Off the Old Ways

"That you put off, concerning your former conduct, the old man which grows corrupt according to the deceitful lusts."

Ephesians 4:22

"Do not lie to one another, since you have put off the old man with his deeds."

Colossians 3:9

It is a fact that Christ died as you. It is a fact that the power of the cross has provided for your complete freedom. And it is a fact that you must choose to deliberately put off the deeds or conduct of your old man. You must put off the characteristics of your old identity. You are no longer that person therefore you should no longer live or act the same. The old you died so you are able to put off the ways of your old self. Transformation phase pertains to the process of your soul being restored in order for your conduct or behavior to be transformed. Your old man, old self, or old identity has died with Christ. Now you must purposefully put off the former conduct of who you were before the new birth. The finished work of Christ has made it possible, and now you must actively work out the salvation that has been provided for you. This is the process of sanctification. Sanctification is setting apart every area of your soul for God and

His purposes. You have been set apart in Christ so now you are to work out that sanctification in your soul. (See 1 Corinthians 1:30) Though this process will continue until the day you meet Christ, the most significant transformation is to take place now.

It is not the old man that you are exhorted to put off because he has already been crucified, died, and buried once and for all in Christ. You are told to put off the conduct or deeds of the person you use to be. To put off the deeds of the old man means you no longer display them. You put them off like you take off a coat or pair of jeans. The deeds of the old man are to no longer be visible to the people around you.

However, in order for you to put off the deeds of the old man there are some areas in your soul that will need to receive deliverance, healing, and transformation. This will allow you to put off any of the consequences in your soul that were the result from what took place in the previous age before you were born again. When Christ died as you He also bore your wrong thinking, your emotional hurts, and wrong desires in your will. He died completely representing everything that you were in Adam or that was in your life.

God, through the finished work of Christ, took care of the root of the problem. In your spirit you have been born again and created according to the image and likeness of God. Now that you have experienced such a great salvation you are more than able to no longer live the same way. A dead person does not smoke. A dead person does not lie. A dead person does not commit sexual immorality. A dead person is not prideful. A dead person does not overeat. A dead person is dead and your old man has died once and for all.

Why are you still acting as if the old you is alive? Your soul determines your conduct. Your mind, will, and emotions affect your behavior. You have to inform your soul that you are a new person in Christ. Your soul is like a computer that has stored everything that has occurred to you since you were a baby. Therefore, like a computer your soul has been programmed to function certain ways. These ways of thinking, feeling, and desires must be overridden with new information. This is how you put off the deeds or conduct of your old man. Your old man is dead and now you are putting off his ways.

The salvation of your soul and the putting off the deeds of the old man refer to the same process. The word "salvation" in Scripture represents many truths such as deliverance, making whole, to heal, restore, and to be persevered (Strong's # 4982). For that reason, in order for you to no longer behave like your old self, your mind, will, and emotions must experience transformation. If not, when you go to act according to who you are in Christ, your soul will not agree and will become a barrier. Only as your soul begins to be renewed will your conduct line up with who you already have been created to be through the new birth. This process is spoken of often throughout the book of Psalms. Below are a couple of verses that refer to the salvation of the soul.

"The Lord redeems the soul of His servants, and none of those who trust in Him shall be condemned."

Psalm 34:22

Draw near to my soul, and redeem it; deliver me because of my enemies."

Psalm 69:18

"The law of the Lord is perfect, converting (restoring) the soul."
Psalm 19:7 (Parenthesis Mine. NKJV Marginal Reading)

"Deliver my soul, O Lord, from lying lips and from a deceitful tongue."

Psalm 120:2

"How long shall I take counsel in my soul, having sorrow in my heart daily? How long will my enemy be exalted over me?

Psalm 13:2

The initial transformation of the soul will take longer for some believers than others. Your background determines how much restoration you need. The amount of hurts, emotional traumas, and bondages, sin, and so on in your past determines how much restoration of the soul you need to experience. Believers who have not previously experienced abuse or major emotional traumas will not need to address such issues during their spiritual development. You might have to. You know the amount of darkness that existed in your past. Understand that God must restore all of it in order for you to experience the freedom He has purchased for you through Christ. Do not get in a hurry and try to move into other phases of spiritual development before you have allowed God to work what is well pleasing in His sight. Most believers who make a serious mistake and fall into sin are those who do not allow God adequate time to restore all the major hurts and areas in their soul. David said of the Lord, *"He restores my soul"* (Psalm 23:3a). He will restore yours also if you will allow Him.

Willing to Change

"Then Jesus entered and passed through Jericho. Now behold, there was a man named Zacchaeus who was a chief tax collector, and he was rich. And he sought to see who Jesus was, but could not because of the crowd, for he was of short stature. So he ran ahead and climbed up into a sycamore tree to see Him, for He was going to pass that way. And when Jesus came to the place, He looked up and saw him, and said to him, Zacchaeus, make haste and come down, for today I must stay at your house.' So he made haste and came down, and received Him joyfully. But when they saw it, they all complained, saying, 'He has gone to be a guest with a man who is a sinner.' Then Zacchaeus stood and said to the Lord, 'Look, Lord, I give half of my goods to the poor; and if I have taken anything from anyone by false accusation, I restore fourfold.'"

Luke 19:1-8

There are things in your soul that keep you from being able to see who Jesus truly is. Zacchaeus also had this problem. The Scripture informs us that he was a short man and that it kept him from being able to see Jesus. There are wrong mentalities, hurts, and areas of sin in your soul that keep you from being able to see Jesus' character, thoughts, ways, or behaviors. These areas must be dealt with in order for you to be conformed into the image of Christ. Without being able to see and know Jesus clearly you will be unable to live according to God's blueprint for your life. It is only as you see Jesus that you see who God has created you to be through the new birth.

There are many things that have happened in your life that have affected your soul. Some of these have been done to you. Notice that the Scripture says that when Zacchaeus sought to see Jesus that the crowd was in the way. If you choose you can continue to blame circumstances or people for the areas in your life that need to be transformed or you can do what Zacchaeus did. Zacchaeus did not allow circumstances or people around him to keep Him from receiving what Jesus had for him. The reality was he needed to be changed. He was of short stature. There were areas in his life that did not measure up to God's standard. The same is true in your life. You have behaviors that do not meet God's standard for His children. You have been accepted but those wrong mentalities and behaviors are not acceptable because they are contrary to the person you have become through the new birth. Zacchaeus made a choice to be willing to change. He made a choice to allow nothing to become an excuse and keep him from the freedom he could receive from Jesus. You must do the same!

Zaccheaus ran to the provision of God to meet his need and his desire to see Jesus. He ran to a tree. God has provided a tree for you; the cross that Jesus hung upon. The cross has made it possible for you to be conformed into the image of Christ. Like Zaccheaus you must climb into what God has made possible for you. Zaccheaus had to become humble in order to climb the tree. He most likely had to roll up his long robe and climb up the trunk of the tree. You also will have to humbly receive the provisions of the cross of Christ. You must cast off pride, religion, or the opinions of man to experience the power of the cross. To encounter Jesus you must run to the cross. That is the place that Jesus passes by in order that God's children can experience the transformation of their soul. Jesus came into the house of Zaccheaus in the story and Jesus will come into the areas of your soul that need to be healed, changed, and transformed. When this happens you also will experience more and more the joy of your salvation given to you in Christ.

People all around you may complain. Religious people hate true transformation because they are unwilling to humble themselves and receive it. It did not stop Zaccheaus, so don't let it stop you. Instantly areas in Zaccheaus' life that needed to be changed were changed when He encountered Christ. God has provided a way for you to have continuous encounters with Christ to receive the transformation of your soul. Each time you do, areas of your soul will be restored and you will be able to live according to the person God has created you to be. Are you willing to experience the transformation that God has made available for you through Christ? Will you humble yourself and allow the power of the cross to renew your mind, heal your wounded emotions, and establish the Lordship of Christ in your will. The cross is God's only provision for the areas in your soul that need to be changed. You cannot do it yourself. You are not able to see Jesus and be transformed through your own strength or ability. Let go of pride and receive God's grace!

Fact, Faith, Experience

"If you are willing and obedient, you shall eat the good of the land."

Isaiah 1:19

What Isaiah spoke to the nation of Israel is what God is saying to you. If you are willing to experience transformation and are obedient, you will partake of what God has made available for you. The way for you to be obedient during the transformation phase is the same way that you were obedient to the gospel of Jesus Christ and that is through the law of faith. As a person who has been justified or become righteous you are to "live by faith" (Romans 1:17). You must understand that the finished work of Christ applies to your every need in life. As you apply the power and provisions of the cross more and more in your life you will grow into the image of Christ. The power of the gospel is revealed or experienced in your life "from faith to faith" (Romans 1:16-17). You experience more and more transformation of your soul as you obediently respond in faith to what God is teaching and applying to your life. This is why you are to live by faith. You continue to progress in spiritual development as you grow from one place of faith to another place of faith.

You will only be able to put off the deeds of the old man as you learn the facts of God's Word and place faith in them. The Word of God is to be your anchor for every issue that you are struggling with. The Word of God provides you with a sure foundation. Your emotions will change. Your mind will not always perceive a situation correctly. Your will and desires will not always be pure or consistent. However, the Word of God is unchangeable and everlasting. The eternal facts from God's Word of who you are in Christ provide you with the ability to live in constant faith. If your faith is dependant on how you feel you will be unstable. If your faith is dependant on your own understanding you will be unstable. If your faith is dependant on the desires you experience then you will be unstable. Your mind, will, and emotions fluctuate all the time. Nevertheless, the Word of God never changes. It is only as you fix your focus and attention on the Word of God will you have a stable foundation to live out God's will each day. This is why the Scripture exhorts you to *"look unto Jesus the author and finisher of your faith"* (Hebrews 12:2).

If the Word of God is not what you use to determine truth or reality then you will be unable to consistently put off the deeds of the old man. Why? Because one day you might not feel like your old man is dead. When this happens, what are you going to believe to be the truth; your feelings or the eternal facts in God's Word? Your own feelings or what the Word of God says concerning your old mind? What you believe to be true when you are faced with a similar situation will determine what you will experience that moment or for that day. In order for you to experience what God has accomplished for you through Christ, you must *"fight the good fight of faith"* (1 Timothy 6:12). Your battle is whether you will believe in what God says in His Word or will you believe what people say, what your emotions say, what your own understanding says, and so on. It is only by faith in the finished work of Christ that a life of victory and consistency is possible for you.

"As you therefore have received Christ Jesus the Lord, so walk in Him."

Colossians 2:6

The way that you received Christ is the same way you are to walk with Christ each day, and this is by faith. Your soul is never to be the basis for what you determine is true. The Word of God is your only sure foundation for truth. Your mind might tell you, "You are not free; you have not become a new person." However, the Word of God says, *"If the Son makes you free, you shall be free indeed"* (John 8:36). What are you going to base your belief on: your mind's thoughts or the Word of God? This battle of faith will always determine how you walk. What you believe determines whether you will put off the deeds of the old man or continue to live the same way even though the old you has died. It is only as you place faith in God's eternal facts that you will be able to experience what you have been freely given in Christ. How you feel or think is temporary but what God says is an eternal fact. When you believe the eternal facts over your temporary situation then eventually your experience will line up with what God's says.

"For the death that He died, he died to sin once for all; but the life that He lives, he lives to God. Likewise you also reckon (consider) yourselves to be dead indeed to sin, but alive to God in Christ Jesus our Lord. Therefore do not let sin reign in your mortal body, that you should obey it in its lusts."

Romans 6:10-12 (Parenthesis Mine. NKJV Marginal Reading)

Your old man died when Christ died. However, you only experienced the benefits of what God accomplished for you when you believed. When you believed and received Christ you were born again. As you believe in more of the provisions and power of the cross you will also enter into experiencing those truths. God has blessed you with every spiritual blessing in Christ but you will only experience them through placing faith in the facts of God's Word. In order for you to experience the truth that you have died to sin and are free from it, you must consider it to be true. The Scripture instructs you to "reckon" or "consider" what God says to be true. As you consider what God says to be true then you will be able to not let the lusts of your body lead you into sin. If you do not consider yourself to be dead to sin then it will become impossible for you not to obey the lusts of your body in the moment of temptation. However, if when the lusts of your body try to influence you to sin, you by faith consider yourself dead to its influence because the Bible says you have died to it, then you will not sin.

You have died to sin and therefore you should not let it rule how you use your body. Nevertheless, the determining factor will be whether or not you believe God's Word and consider yourself to be a new creation and dead to sin. To be dead to sin means you no longer have to obey it. To be dead to sin means it is no longer your master. What you consider to be true in the moment of temptation will determine what you do or experience. This is the fight of faith. Learn God's eternal facts. Believe God's eternal facts. Consider it true and reckon your old self to be dead, and then experience the facts of God's Word.

When you are tempted by the lusts in the world you must consider yourself dead to its influence through the power of the cross. When you are tempted by the lusts of your body you must consider yourself dead to its influence through the power of the cross. When you are tempted by the devil you must consider yourself dead to his influence through the power of the cross. When you are tempted to make your relationship with God dependant on following a list of rules you must consider yourself dead to the law through the power of the cross. When you place faith in God's eternal truth the Holy Spirit will release the power of the cross into your personal situation, experience, and life. This is how you experience the freedom that you have in Christ. This is how you experience the power of the gospel in your daily life. This is how you experience God's continual grace and empowerment for what you are going through. Faith in the provisions of the cross will release the power of God to meet your every need.

Identification

"How shall we who died to sin live any longer in it? Or do you not know that as many of us as were baptized into Christ Jesus were baptized into His death? Therefore we were buried with Him through baptism into death, that just as Christ was raised from the dead by the glory of the Father, even so we also should walk in the newness of life."

Romans 6:2-4

In every trial, in every temptation, and in every moment you are to identify with the finished work of Jesus Christ. You are to identity with His death. When you identify what happened to Jesus as happening to you then you are reckoning yourself to be dead. You might not feel dead. Your flesh might not feel crucified. Nevertheless, the way to walk in newness of life is to identify with Christ. Identifying or considering your old self crucified, dead, and buried with Christ is living by faith and that is the path of victory. Every circumstance, temptation, or struggle is an opportunity to exercise faith. If you choose to identify with the work of Christ you will by faith overcome anything you face. This is how you experience and live out the victory that Christ had accomplished for you. The Apostle John wrote, *"And this is the victory that has overcome the world- your faith"* (1 John 5:4). Paul said that sin is a result of not exercising faith (Romans 14:23b).

In the book <u>Born Crucified</u> L.E. Maxwell tells this story of identification.

"During the Civil War a man by the name of George Wyatt was drawn by lot to go to the front. He had a wife and six children. A young man named Richard Pratt offered to go in his stead. He was accepted and joined the ranks, bearing the name and number of George Wyatt. Before long Pratt was killed in action. The authorities later sought again to draft George Wyatt into service. He protested, entering the plea that he had died in the person of Pratt. He insisted that the authorities consult their own records as to the fact of his having died in identification with Pratt, his substitute. Wyatt was

thereby exempted as beyond the claims of law and further service. He had died in the person of this representative" (pg 13).

Jesus was your substitute. Jesus died your death. Your old man died in Christ. As you identify with these truths found in God's Word you will experience the power of God over temptation, sin, your flesh, the world, and the devil. When you feel angry and are about to sin, identify that your flesh and old man has been crucified, died, and buried with Christ. This is the life of faith that leads to you experiencing the freedom you have in Christ. When you are tempted to lust, identify that you have died with Christ. Consider those desires as crucified and buried in Christ. This is why faith pleases God. (See Hebrews 11:6) Faith is the way to experience the victory and abundant life you have been freely given in Christ. As you consider and identify that Christ died as you, you will be able to exchange any bondage or hurt in your soul and experience true freedom.

As you become secure from God's Word in your new identity in Christ it becomes easier to resist sin and temptation. If you know and consider yourself to be a new creation that has been made holy, in the moment of temptation you will not sin. Why? Because for you to commit the sin would be acting contrary to who you truly are as a new creation. The greatest weapon against sin is for you to know who you are in Christ and consider it so in the moment of temptation. You considering the eternal facts of God's Word to be true over any other data you receive will lead you to experience God's provision. You are to put off the deeds of your old man by faith in God's eternal facts. Only faith is what will allow you to live according to the person you already have become through the new birth.

Applying the Power of the Cross Deeper

Your spiritual development will only progress through faith. It is by faith from start to finish that you will be conformed into the image of Christ. You must resist the temptation to try and change areas of your soul and behavior through self effort or good works. The cross has forever made self effort and trying harder void. (See Galatians 3:1-5) If you rely on anything other than the finished work of the cross you will be resisting the power of God for your life. (See

1 Corinthians 1:17) Christ is not just your righteousness but He is also your holiness for conduct. True holiness comes only through the cross of Christ and God's grace that it provides. Christ alone has made a way for your soul to be transformed as well as your behavior. This ensures that from beginning to the end of your spiritual development you have no reason to boast, become prideful, or take credit for your transformation.

"I will not drive them out from before you in one year, lest the land become desolate and the beasts of the field become too numerous for you. Little by little I will drive them out from before you, until you have increased, and you inherit the land."

Exodus 23:29-30

God told the nation of Israel that He would not drive out all their enemies in one year. Over time little by little He would drive out their enemies and they would increasingly experience the inheritance or provision that God had promised them. From this we can illustrate the process of the salvation of your soul or transformation. God chose not to instantaneously transform your soul when you received Christ. He chose for you to enter into the inheritance that Christ purchased for you little by little. You are to go from glory to glory or be changed little by little. (See 2 Corinthians 3:18) One of the most important reasons that God chose this process is so you would continually have fresh encounters with the power of the cross and grow in your appreciation of what Christ did for you through the cross.

"Yet it pleased the Lord to bruise Him; He has put Him to grief. When You make His soul an offering for sin."

Isaiah 53:10a

The only reason you are ever able to put off a behavior of your old man is because of the great passion of your Lord Jesus Christ. It is only because of the extreme suffering Christ went through for you that your soul can be transformed. It is only because of the crown of thorns that was beat into Jesus' head that your mind can be set free. It is only because of the stripes upon His back that you can be healed. It is only because of His crucifixion that your will can be delivered and conformed to the will of God.

"Surely he has born our griefs and carried our sorrows; yet we esteemed Him stricken, smitten by God, and afflicted. But he was wounded for our transgressions, he was bruised for our iniquities; the chastisement for our peace was upon Him, and by His stripes we are healed."

Isaiah 53:4-5

The only way you can experience transformation for your soul is to continually visit the cross of Christ for each area you need to be restored. As you see the cross in a fresh light for your current need or situation you will be overwhelmed again by the mercy, love, and grace of God demonstrated through the cross of Christ. Each encounter with the power and provision of the cross renews your love, passion, and gratefulness towards the Lord. This process of transformation that God has chosen keeps us broken and humble before the Lord. Each time you experience transformation in an area of your soul, your walk with Christ is refreshed and you enter into more of the freedom God promised you.

You are to apply the power of the cross for your soul little by little. As you partake in experiencing transformation you are entering more deeply into the provisions of the cross for your life. The cross of Christ has application and relevance for every aspect of your life and experience. The cross of Christ has the power to deal with every deed of your old man. Growing in your intimacy with the Lord is learning to apply more deeply the power of the cross into your life. Never forsake the cross in your life.

*"For the message of **the cross** is foolishness to those who are perishing, but to us who are being saved it **is the power of God**."*

1 Corinthians 1:18 (Bold Mine.)

Your ability to believe and consider God's Word to be true in your life is highly dependant on whether you allow God to confront the areas in your mind, will, and emotions that resist His truth. There will be times during transformation phase that you will acknowledge that what God says is true, and yet you will still be unable to experience the reality of it in your daily life. When this happens it is a signal that there is an area of your soul that needs to be transformed. These areas in your soul will seek to hinder your faith and ability to consider things dead in Christ. These areas are resisting the Lordship and power of Christ. Therefore, you must seek God and allow Him to remove any barriers in your soul that hinder you from experiencing the life of victory God has made available for you through Christ. You must allow the power of the cross to be applied deeply into your soul.

Renewing of Your Mind

*"That you put off, concerning your former conduct, the old man which grows corrupt according to the deceitful lusts, **and be renewed in the spirit of your mind.**"*

Ephesians 4:22-23 (Bold Mine.)

For you to put off the conduct of your old man you must be renewed in your mind. The reason that unrenewed areas in your mind can hinder your ability to reckon yourself dead to sin is because they give place to demonic spirits. This is why the Scripture says you are to be renewed in the spirit of your mind. Your mind is to become subject to the Word of God and the Holy Spirit. You have patterns of thinking or strongholds for which you must repent. You have perceptions and attitudes that you must no longer allow to operate in your mind.

"For the weapons of our warfare are not carnal but mighty in God for pulling down strongholds, casting down arguments and every high thing that exalts itself against the knowledge of God, bringing every thought into captivity to the obedience of Christ."

2 Corinthians 10:5

Your wrong thoughts led to arguments being established in your mind that now resist the knowledge of God. These arguments keep you from being able to recognize and accept who God truly is. When you doubt the character of God it leads you to be unable to trust Him. From this you can see how your ability to reckon yourself dead to sin can be affected. When you are unable to trust God's character you are unable to believe in His promises. As these types of arguments continue they lead to strongholds in the mind. Strongholds act like blinders that keep you from seeing anything other than the pattern of thinking. Strongholds seek to dictate your path of thinking. They seek to control your mind and what you meditate and focus on. These must be confronted with the weapons that God provides us and not through your own ability or self effort.

These weapons are the Word of God and the Spirit of God. Paul said, *"Take up the sword of the Spirit, which is the word of God"* (Ephesians 6:17). As you draw near to God through the private spiritual disciplines you are to allow the Word of God and the Spirit of God to confront, renew, deliver, and set you free from areas in your mind. As God reveals to you these wrong areas be willing to repent of them and receive God's truth that will set you free. Remember it is not just the truth that sets you free but it is the truth that you know and receive. (See John 8:32) Also, there will be times through the laying on of hands that the anointing will be transferred upon you to set you free from strongholds in your mind.

"And do not be conformed to this world, but be transformed by the renewing of your mind, that you may prove what is the good and acceptable and perfect will of God."

Romans 12:2

The word "transformed" comes from the Greek word *"metamorphoo"* which is used to describe the process of a caterpillar changing into a butterfly. As your mind is renewed, your character and life will be changed into the image of Christ. You are only able to experience the potential you have as a new creation as your mind is renewed. Then you will put off the characteristics of the old you. You will begin to display the new you in your daily walk.

"Now after six days Jesus took Peter, James, and John his brother, led them up on a high mountain by themselves; and He was trans-figured before them. His face shone like the sun, and His clothes became as white as the light."

Matthew 17:1-2

The word "transfigured" comes from the same Greek word *"metamorphoo."* Notice Jesus was transfigured or morphed right before the eyes of Peter, James, and John. Who Jesus was became apparent to those around Him when He was transfigured. His glory was revealed. Jesus did not take on something He was not. No, who He always was just became clear.

It is the same in your life. People around you at this time may be unable to perceive who you truly have become through the new birth. Maybe even you have been unable to see yourself for who you truly are as a new creation in Christ. However, as your mind is renewed, who you truly are will be revealed or manifested. Your life and character will morph right before your eyes and the eyes of the people around you. Your life will begin to reflect the child of God you already are.

Your behavior will only be transformed as your mind is renewed. When your mind is renewed it will help guard you from conforming to the standard of the culture or world around you. It will become apparent that you are different from the people of this world. Without the renewing of your mind, you will be unable to discern the will of God for your life. You are to make the choice to be transformed by the renewing of your mind.

As you become aware of areas in your mind that need to be renewed you should make them a matter of prayer. Talk to God about them and find out what His Word says concerning the issue. Learn to guard what your mind thinks about. Do not allow your mind to dwell upon things from your life before you were born again. Discipline your imagination to only think upon what God would want you to think about. God will confront the issues in your mind but you must allow it to be renewed.

"For those who live according to the flesh set their minds on the things of the flesh."

Romans 8:5a

What you allow your mind to dwell upon determines how you will live. If you think about the things of the flesh you will obey the desires of the flesh. If you continue to think you are the same person who struggled with lying, pornography, smoking, drinking, or cussing then you will continue to act accordingly. You must take those old thoughts about you to the cross and get a clear picture of who you are in Christ. Negative pictures and memories of your past can be cleansed from your mind as it is renewed.

Emotional Healing

"He has sent Me to heal the brokenhearted."

Luke 4:18

'To comfort all who mourn, to console those who mourn in Zion, to give them beauty for ashes, the oil of joy for mourning, the garment of praise for the spirit of heaviness."

Isaiah 61:2-3

You do not have to hold onto negative emotions such as fear, shame, distrust, mourning, and so on. The cross has provided for your emotional healing. Your thoughts and emotions are highly related. If you think or mediate on old experiences it can affect your joy or peace. However, hurts and wrong emotions in your soul can also affect the way you think about yourself or others. Paul said, *"Be kind to one another, tenderhearted"* (Ephesians 4:32). In order for you to be kind to one another and tenderhearted, your heart will have to be healed. God wants to heal every emotional trauma you have ever experienced. God wants you to be free. Jesus took your shame so you do not have to carry it. He can turn the ashes of your past into a present beauty through Christ. He can turn your mourning into joy.

In order for you to experience the fruit of the Holy Spirit, wrong emotions must be removed and healed. You must be willing to face hurtful emotions from the past as God chooses to deal with them. It is definitely not easy at times. However, it is not worth holding on to those hurts and not experience the freedom that Christ died to give you. Choose not to compromise with your past. Do not settle for less than what Christ purchased for you. Do not allow the familiarity of your past hurts to become a hindrance to a new place of freedom and wholeness in Christ.

"But now you yourselves are to put off all these: anger, wrath, malice, blasphemy, filthy language out of your mouth."

Colossians 3:8

You can put off the things of the past. You can put off anger, wrath, and the hurts from the past. As you put them off, you will no longer be carrying them around with you. Therefore, you will experience the freedom that you have in Christ. You can exchange the results in your soul from your previous life for a new life in Christ. I promise it is worth allowing God to confront and heal your wounded emotions.

Christ as Lord in Your Will

"But sanctify the Lord God in your hearts, and always be ready to give a defense to everyone who asks you a reason for the hope that is in you, with meekness and fear; having a good conscience, that when they defame you as evildoers, those who revile your good conduct in Christ will be ashamed. For it is better, if it is the will of God, to suffer for doing good than for doing evil."

1 Peter 3:15-17

The word "sanctify" means to set apart. You must set apart your will for the will of God. As you allow Christ to be Lord in your will, your life will be set apart to obey God. It is only as Christ is directing your will that you will be able to have good conduct. Every area of your will that you previously yielded to sin must now become surrendered to the Lordship of Christ. Your choices in life must become submitted to the will of God. This is what it means to take up your cross daily and follow the Lord.

"When He had called the people to Himself, with His disciples also, He said to them, 'Whoever desires to come after Me, let him deny himself, and take up his cross, and follow Me."

Mark 8:34

The cross is to be applied to your will. This means that you no longer live for your own desires but for the will of God. As you do this, you are taking up your cross or allowing the power of the cross to be applied to your will. You must learn to live under the Lordship of Christ. As a child of God you are to follow Christ and what He commands you to do. He is your Lord. He is your King. Every day you are to learn to live for God's desire for you and not your own.

"That Christ may dwell in your hearts through faith."

Ephesians 3:17

As you consider yourself dead to sin, through faith you are to allow Christ to dwell in your heart. Where Christ dwells He is to be Lord. He is to direct the affairs of your life. He is to direct how you use your time. He is to direct how you use your body. Through faith in the finished work of Christ you can experience Christ being Lord in every area of your life. True freedom for living is only found where Christ is Lord. You will be unable to experience the freedom God has for you if you continue to control your will and life. You must surrender your will and desires to those that Christ has for you to know true freedom.

"Now the Lord is the Spirit; and where the Spirit of the Lord is, there is liberty."

2 Corinthians 3:17

God knows what is best for you. However, your thoughts and emotions greatly affect your ability to surrender and trust Christ as Lord for every area of your life. This is why experiencing transformation is so important. The restoration of your life will allow you to conduct yourself in a manner that reflects who you are in Christ.

Conclusion

I purposively have not provided potential examples of events that may have occurred in your life that need to experience transformation. The reason for this is that it is extremely important that you do not try and dig up things from your past on your own. The Holy Spirit will dictate what areas of your soul need to be addressed, and when to address them in order to experience transformation. You must keep your eyes on Christ and continue to draw near to God. As you do that, God will reveal to you what He desires to heal, restore, or set free in your soul. Maybe as you read this chapter the Holy Spirit already began to bring up areas that you need to allow the provision of the cross to transform. If that is you, then obey what the Lord is doing in your life. I cannot over emphasize the importance of allowing the Holy Spirit to dictate the process of transformation in you or anyone else. Your responsibility is to position yourself before God and provide Him with continual opportunities to restore your soul. Then simply trust and obey the Lord and all will be changed.

When you have been diligent to draw near to God and spend time with Him through worship, prayer, and reading the Word of God, and you still have been unable to obtain a measure of faith to experience victory over an area in your life, you probably are dealing with bondage in your soul. Such bondages in your mind, will, and emotions hinder your ability to reckon those areas of your old man crucified, dead, and buried in Christ. Situations such as this will at times require a season of prayer and fasting or a mature believer releasing the anointing of God through the laying on of hands to break the yoke. There are times when this is absolutely necessary. Jesus said concerning bondage and faith, *"However, this kind does not go out except by prayer and fasting"* (Matthew 17:21).

However, you must not think that this is always necessary in order for every area of your soul to experience transformation. Putting off the deeds or characteristics of your old man happens as you by faith consider them dead in Christ. Normally you will be able to reach the measure of faith you need to experience transformation as you encounter God's manifested presence through times of intimacy with Him. Be sensitive to God for He may lead you into a season of prayer and fasting or having a mature believer release the power of God upon you through the laying on of hands.

Chapter 10

Potential Hindrances

"Therefore we also, since we are surrounded by so great a cloud of witnesses, let us lay aside every weight, and the sin which so easily ensnares us, and let us run with endurance the race that is set before us."

Hebrews 12:1

There are weights and snares all around you that provide potential hindrances to your transformation. On this journey of being conformed into the image of Christ you need to successfully navigate through or around anything that seeks to be a hindrance to the transformation of your soul. In this chapter, I want to discuss some of the primary hindrances that have kept believers from progressing in their spiritual development. Stay sensitive to God and ask His help to guard you from these hindrances.

Circumstances & Trials

"Let no one say when he is tempted, 'I am tempted by God'; for God cannot be tempted by evil, nor does He Himself tempt anyone. But each one is tempted when he is drawn away by his own desires and enticed. Then when desire has conceived, it gives birth to sin."

James 1:13-15a

There will be numerous circumstances and opportunities to sin that you will come across each day. These circumstances are not sent from God. God does not create circumstances or opportunities to tempt you. There is a difference between being tempted and being tested or tried. The Scripture states that God never will tempt you through events or your surroundings. God never tempts anyone. If you are being tempted it is sent from the enemy and not from God. However, if you are drawn away by the temptation and sin, it is not the devil's fault, it's your own. The enemy can create circumstances and opportunities around you that provide you with a temptation. The enemy can use an unbeliever, an immature believer, or the lust of the world around you to try and tempt you to sin. However, the devil cannot make you sin. He can try and entice you by providing ways for you to sin but the choice is yours.

If you walk in the flesh, and do not apply the provision of the cross for your desires, you will sin. The devil uses circumstances and opportunities that seek to appeal to your own fleshly desires and appetites. If you are not reckoning yourself to be dead to sin and taking up your cross daily then you are making yourself vulnerable to the temptations of that day. When the devil appeals to your uncrucified desires and you yield to the temptation sin will occur. When you sin it is because your desire was joined with the enticement of the enemy and conception occurred. When the enemy is unable to hinder your transformation through using circumstances to cause you to sin then he tries to pervert your response to trials.

"In this you greatly rejoice, though now for a little while, if need be, you have been grieved by various trials, that the genuineness of your faith, being much more precious than gold that perishes, though it is tested by fire, may be found to praise, honor, and glory at the revelation of Jesus Christ, whom having not seen you love. Though now you do not see Him, yet believing, you rejoice with joy inexpressible and full of glory, receiving the end of your faith the salvation of your souls."
1 Peter 1:6-9

Trials are to provide opportunities for you to greatly rejoice. Why would you rejoice when you are experiencing a difficult trial in your life? Because it is to strengthen, purify, and produce genuine faith in your life. Trials are to become stepping stones to greater faith and trust in God. The end of your faith is the salvation of your soul. You can experience the power and life of the kingdom of God now by faith.

The enemy loves to try and use trials to discourage you, defeat you, and make you bitter or angry toward God. Trials are not bad when you see them with telescope vision. Trials become tools in the hand of God that strengthen your faith and mold your character into the image of Christ. Paul said that we are not only to rejoice in God's grace that made us righteous *"but we also glory in tribulations, knowing that tribulation produces perseverance; and perseverance, character (approved character); and character, hope"* (Romans 5:3-5/ Parenthesis Mine. NKJV Marginal Reading). You are to rejoice in tribulations and trials because of how God can use them to conform you into the image of Christ. God desires to use all trials for your good. Trials are to lead you to have approved character. Remember you are approved because of the gift of righteousness and the new birth but you need to begin to have approved or acceptable behavior in the kingdom of God. How you respond to trials, and the attitude that you possess during them, determines if your transformation will be hindered.

When you respond wrongly to trials in your life you hinder potential transformation. Also, when you do not navigate successfully through a trial, you will have to take the same test again. God allows trials to come into your life to reveal areas in your soul that need to be restored. When you do not allow the trial to produce the approved character or acceptable behavior in your life then God will see to it that you face a similar trial that addresses the same issue. Trust me, you can resist transformation but you cannot hide from God leading you into trials that address over and over the same issue that you are ignoring and not surrendering to God. You can leave churches but you will still run into the same trial. You can move cities but still run into the same trial. You can leave jobs and still run into the same trail. You must learn to be broken by recognizing that God has allowed this trial to come into your life for your own spiritual development. To run from the trial is to resist the transformation of your soul.

"But he who received the seed on stony places, this is he who hears the word and immediately receives it with joy; yet he has not root in himself, but endures only for a while. For when tribulation or persecution arises because of the word, immediately he stumbles."
Matthew 13:20-21

Unforgiveness

"Forgiving one another, even as God in Christ forgave you."
Ephesians 4:32

You are commanded to forgive. God in Christ forgave you of all your sin therefore you are to extend the same type of forgiveness to the people around you. The forgiveness that God provided for you in Christ is to be the example that you follow throughout your spiritual journey. You did not do anything to deserve the forgiveness that God extended to you and yet He still forgave you in Christ. As a child of God you are to follow in the footsteps of your Father and walk in forgiveness towards the people around you.

There will be people in your life that hurt you. Maybe you have already been hurt by people throughout your life. You cannot control what others do to you, but you can determine how you respond to the hurts. Every time a person has done something to hurt you, you face a crossroad. Will you choose to become bitter and hold on to unforgiveness or will you forgive them like God in Christ did towards you? Your response determines your spiritual development.

"For if you forgive men their trespasses, your heavenly Father will also forgive you. But if you do not forgive men their trespasses, neither will your Father forgive your trespasses."
Matthew 6:14-15

Jesus said that if you do not forgive others you would not be able to experience the Father's forgiveness. What this means is when you choose not to release a person of their debts against you, God will not release you. If you hold on to unforgiveness then your bondages will continue to hold on to you. If you choose to hold on to unforgiveness then the restoration of your soul will come to a complete stop. Holding unforgiveness in your heart will always tie up the flow of God's power in your life. God will not continue to heal and restore your soul when you are choosing to hold on to unforgiveness towards others.

You must never forget the forgiveness that God extended to you even after the great sins that you committed against Him. When you remember what God has forgiven you of, you will be able to forgive others for what they have committed against you. Even if the most horrible thing was done to you, God still commands you to forgive them because He freely forgave you through Christ. Jesus told a story about a servant who was forgiven by a king an enormous amount of money. However, when this servant found another person who owed him a small amount of money compared to the debt that the king forgave him of, he took the person by the throat and demanded that he pay immediately. When the person did not pay him, he threw the man into prison. Jesus finished the story saying:

"So when his fellow servants saw what had been done, they were very grieved, and came and told their master all that had been done. Then his master, after he had called him, said to him, 'You wicked servant! I forgave you all that debt because you begged me. Should you not also have had compassion on your fellow servant, just as I had pity on you?' And his master was angry, and delivered him to the torturers until he should pay all that was due to him. So My heavenly Father also will do you if each of you, from his heart, does not forgive his brother his trespasses."

Matthew 18:31-35

When you hold unforgivenss against a person it will always hurt you more than them. Jesus said that if you hold on to unforgiveness that you would be delivered over to torturers. Unforgiveness opens the door for your life to be tormented. You will not only be unable to progress in your spiritual development but your life will be tormented. Holding on to unforgiveness will destroy your walk and intimacy with the Lord. Not walking in forgiveness is one of the biggest hindrances to putting off the deeds of the old man and experiencing the transformation of the soul.

In order for you to receive emotional healing and deliverance from sins that have kept you bound, you must forgive anyone who has wronged you. For you to receive emotional healing from a hurt that someone has caused in your life, you must forgive them. If you choose to hold unforgiveness towards them then you will hinder God from healing your soul. God understands that what was done to you was absolutely wrong. He is not asking you to deny the fact that they wronged and hurt you, but He is asking you to forgive them. You forgiving them is more for your benefit than for theirs. They probably have gone on living their life. However, if you don't forgive, your spiritual development will not progress onward. God asks you to forgive so that your life is not hindered from reaching His purpose. Also when you choose to forgive you are manifesting a characteristic of Christ in your life.

You also must not hold unforgiveness against a person if you perceive that they have wronged you. Many people fall captive to torment because they become bitter at God. They perceive that God has wronged them. The reality is that God is just in all His ways. God has never wronged anyone. He always does what is right. (See Revelation 15:3 and Psalm 145:17) God never needs to be forgiven because He never has done anything wrong. God has never wronged you. However, if you perceive that God has wronged you then you might be holding unforgiveness against Him even though He has not sinned against you. In order for you to move on in your spiritual development you must release holding any unforgiveness in your heart towards God.

"And whenever you stand praying, if you have anything against anyone, forgive him, that your Father in heaven may also forgive you your trespasses. But if you do not forgive, neither will your Father in heaven forgive your trespasses."

Mark 11:25-26

Lastly, some believers need to forgive themselves. You are commanded to forgive anyone; including yourself. Self hatred must be released in order for you to receive the power of God to transform your soul. If God has forgiven you through Christ then you also need to forgive yourself. There are many people who demand sinlessness of themselves even when God Himself was aware that when He created you, you would make mistakes. If you are constantly beating yourself up over things that you have done in your life you need to let it go. Forgive yourself.

As you fix your eyes on God's goodness and provisions through Christ, your faith will be strengthened and you will acknowledge that God is bigger than your failure or mistakes. It is not too late to change. Your past does not have to dictate your future. God will restore and heal you as you choose to let go of any unforgivness towards yourself. The cross of Christ is able to cross it out. We have all sinned and made bad decisions but God's love through Christ has still been provided. Forgive yourself and receive the power of the cross to transform and restore you.

"Looking carefully lest anyone fall short of the grace of God; lest any root of bitterness springing up cause trouble, and by this many become defiled."

Hebrews 12:15

God's grace is available to transform you into the image of Christ. However, you will fall short of what God has made possible for you if a root of bitterness remains in your heart. Bitterness or unforgiveness will cause your life trouble and will lead to you being defiled. Harboring these negative attitudes will lead you into sin and your life will become defiled with all kinds of wrong behaviors and sins. If you have any unforgiveness towards a person who has wronged you, or you have become bitter toward God for a perceived wrong, you must release it. The cross of Christ has the power to turn your bitterness into sweetness. God had Moses throw a tree into bitter waters and it became sweet. (See Exodus 15:23-25) The tree of Calvary can release you from any bitterness or unforgiveness that you have been carrying. Choose to let go of it and God will be able to let you go from anything that has kept you bound. Do not fall short of what the grace of God desires to accomplish for your spiritual development.

Cares of this Life

"Now godliness with contentment is great gain. For we brought nothing into this world, and it is certain we can carry nothing out. And having food and clothing, with these we shall be content. But those who desire to be rich fall into temptation and a snare, and into many foolish and harmful lusts which drown men in destruction and perdition. For the love of money is a root of all kinds of evil, for which some have strayed from the faith in their greediness, and pierced themselves through with many sorrows."

1 Timothy 6:6-10

There are many responsibilities you have to fulfill each day. One of those responsibilities is making money and managing it wisely. However, if you take on more responsibilities than God has asked you to carry it will hinder your spiritual development. When you are over burdened you risk losing the contentment that comes from God. Instead of being thankful for what God has provided for your life you can become ungrateful, unsatisfied, and feel as if you are unfulfilled. This can be a dangerous place. If you allow the cares of this life to overwhelm you then you will become susceptible to harmful lusts. The Scripture speaks of how the desire to become rich leads to a snare. This snare will keep you from experiencing the transformation of the soul that you need.

The cares of this life and the love of money can absolutely bring sorrow and destruction into your spiritual development. All kinds of evil result from such attitudes. If you lose the contentment found in God you will stray from the faith or God's blueprint for your spiritual development. You will become more concerned over people's opinion of you than your spiritual development. You will care more about making money than the transformation of your soul. You will care more about the latest fashion to the destruction of your spiritual development. You will care more about the car that you drive than the building of God's temple. You must not fall into this snare.

"Now he who received seed among the thorns is he who hears the word, and the cares of this world and the deceitfulness of riches choke the word, and he becomes unfruitful."

Matthew 13:22

The cares of this world and the deceitfulness of riches can choke the power of the Word of God in your life. They can keep you from experiencing transformation. If you let them, they can keep you from being fruitful for the kingdom of God. You must not have wrong priorities in your life. Keep living with telescope vision and keep your eyes on the goal of being transformed into the image of Christ. Do not spend more time thinking about shopping malls than God's will for your life. Do not allow your heart to pursue selfish gain to the neglect of your spiritual development.

The Lord said to the prophet Ezekiel concerning religious people, *"So they come to you as people do, they sit before you as My people, and they hear your words, but they do not do them; for with their mouth they show much love, but their hearts pursue their own gain"* (Ezekiel 33:31). Allow the Word of God to transform your soul. Do not be distracted from God's blueprint for your spiritual development. Pursue God for the transformation of your soul. Do not pursue your own gain and be snared by the cares of this life and the deceitfulness of riches.

Willful Sin

"Moreover, brethren, I do not want you to be unaware that all our fathers were under the cloud, all passed through the sea, all were baptized into Moses in the cloud and in the sea, all ate the same spiritual food, and all drank the same spiritual drink. For they drank of that spiritual Rock that followed them, and that Rock was Christ. But with most of them God was not well pleased, for their bodies were scattered in the wilderness. Now these things became

our examples, to the intent that we should not lust after evil things
as they also lusted."

1 Corinthians 10:1-6

God was not well pleased with the most of the nation of Israel because they never navigated through the wilderness. God had said that He would lead them to the promise land. The Promised Land would be where they would experience the fullness of God's purpose for their life. On the way to the promise land however, God lead them by way of the wilderness. In the wilderness many lusted after evil things and they never managed to reach the promise land that God desired for them to inherit. Their bodies fell dead and were scattered throughout the wilderness. That story is given to you as an example and to teach you not to allow your spiritual development to be hindered. You do not want to fall dead in the wilderness and never reach the goal of being transformed into the image of Christ.

God has a place of promise for you. It is a place of experiencing all the provisions that He has made available for you through the finished work of Christ. You have been baptized into Christ. You eat spiritual food from the Word of God. You drink in the presence of Christ. And yet you can allow yourself not to experience the transformation of the soul and enter God's purpose for you in the kingdom. You must learn from their example and not fall into willful sin. Willful sin will absolutely hinder your transformation into the image of Christ. The Scripture lists four sins that some of the people committed because of their lust.

*"And do not become **idolaters** as were some of them. As it is written,*
'The people sat down to eat and drink, and rose up to play."
1 Corinthians 10:7 (Bold Mine.)

You must guard yourself from idolatry. The sin of idolatry is allowing anything in your life to come before God. Idolatry is allowing something to take the place that God deserves to have in your life. The peoples' idolatry caused them to lose telescope vision and cast off their purpose. Instead they sat down to eat, drink, and play. God does not want you to stop and sit where you are in your spiritual development. You have not reached the end goal. You must continue to yield to God and be built according to His blueprint. Do not replace Christ being sanctified as Lord in your will with an idol. Do not seek personal pleasure over your personal spiritual development. Paul warned in the last days that people would be *"lovers of pleasure rather than lovers of God"* (2 Timothy 3:4). Ask God to protect you from idolatry. Idolatry is an enemy to your spiritual development and personal promise land.

*"Nor let us commit **sexual immorality**, as some of them did, and in one day twenty-three thousand fell."*
1 Corinthians 10:8 (Bold Mine.)

Sexual immorality is the second sin that categorized those who fell dead in the wilderness. Sexual immorality is any sexual activity outside of the boundaries and standards given in God's Word. Sexual immorality also includes lusting in your heart and having perverted imaginations in your mind. Sexual sins are extremely serious and damaging to your spiritual development. Sexual sins create a connection between you and the person with whom they were committed. These become strongholds in your soul that affect your life. Sexual sins join you with things outside of God's will. Paul said, *"Or do you not know that he who is joined to a harlot is one body with her? For 'the two,' He says, 'shall become one flesh'"* (1 Corinthians 6:16). Sexual sin is sinning against your own body. (See 1 Corinthians 6:18) Do not allow your life to become entangled in sexual sins so that you never reach God's goal for you.

*"Nor let us **tempt (test)** Christ, as some of them also tempted, and were destroyed by serpents."*
1 Corinthians 10:9 (Bold Mine. Parenthesis NKJV Marginal Reading)

You tempt or test the Lord when you speak against Him. If you try and make God prove Himself to you, that is testing Him. The people in the nation of Israel tested God by accusing God of having brought them into the wilderness to die because there was no water and food. (See Numbers 21:4-7) God had already demonstrated His power and works to them. God has already made it clear to the nation that He was on their side. If you speak or act in a way to test God's love, presence, or faithfulness to you this is wrong.

Such an attitude will keep you from experiencing what God has for you. You test God when you refuse to believe what He has spoken to you and then ask Him to prove Himself by doing some great miracle. You test God when you try to deliberately provoke Him by your actions into performing the miraculous. Satan did this when he tried to get Jesus to jump off the top of the temple so the angels of God would have to rescue Him. (See Matthew 4:5-7) This type of attitude will invite serpents or demon spirits to come and destroy your life.

*"Nor **complain**, as some of them also complained, and were destroyed by the destroyer."*

1 Corinthians 10:10 (Bold Mine.)

The last sin that categorized those that fell dead in the wilderness was complaining. When you complain you open your life up to the work of the destroyer or Satan. Complaining is a sin. When you choose to complain you are choosing to be a companion of the devil. Negativity attracts the devil to you. If you always go around complaining and feeling sorry for yourself, you will be allowing more destruction to take place in your life. Proverbs 18:7 states, *"A fool's mouth is his destruction, and his lips are the snare of his soul."* Complaining is a snare that will hinder the transformation of your soul and keep you from reaching your promise land. Also, if you are always complaining, no one except the destroyer is going to want and be around you.

Get your mouth under the influence of God. The Bible commands us to *"give thanks always for all things to God the Father in the name of our Lord Jesus Christ"* (Ephesians 5:20). Learn to give thanks always to God through Jesus Christ. Put off the deeds of the old man by using your tongue for edification and not destruction.

God's Discipline

"For consider Him who endured such hostility from sinners against Himself, lest you become weary and discouraged in your souls... And you have forgotten the exhortation which speaks to you as to sons:

'My son, do not despise the chastening (discipline) of the Lord, nor be discouraged when you are rebuked by Him; for whom the Lord loves He chastens, and scourges every son whom He receives.'...

Furthermore, we have had human fathers who corrected us, and we paid them respect. Shall we not much more readily be in subjection to the Father of spirits and live? For they indeed for a few days chastened us as seemed best to them, but He for our profit, that we may be partakers of His holiness. Now no chastening (discipline) seems to be joyful for the present, but painful; nevertheless, afterward it yields the peaceable fruit of righteousness to those who have been trained by it."

Hebrews 12:3, 5-6, 9-11
(Parenthesizes Mine. NKJV Marginal Reading)

The discipline of God is a manifestation of His love for you. The Scriptures state that God disciplines all of His children that we may partake of His holiness. Now that you are righteous your fellowship with God will lead to bearing fruit for Him. This fruit is what is called the fruit of righteousness. The fruit of righteousness is the fruit that is the by-product of having fellowship with God. God desires for you to bear fruit. God has called you to bear fruit.

As you engage in spending time with God, areas of your soul that need to be transformed will be addressed by Him. When you refuse to allow God to restore, heal, and set free these areas in your soul, it will lead to you being disciplined. If you continue in willful sin, God will discipline you. It is painful when we experience discipline but it is for our own good. The discipline of God is to help direct and guide you back to following His blueprint for you life. You must have a mindset that views discipline correctly, as a manifestation of God's love for you. If you do not experience transformation your life will not be built according to God's blueprint and you will be unable to fulfill the purposes of God for you life.

Your relationship with your earthly father will greatly affect how you view and take the discipline of your heavenly Father. This is an area of your soul that may need to be restored depending on your past with your earthly father. We all subconsciously transfer our experience with our earthly father onto our relationship with our heavenly Father. Any wrong thoughts, hurt emotions, and areas of your will that were affected due to your relationship with your earthly father will need to be transformed in order for you to experience the type of intimacy God the Father desires to have with you. Learn to accept the discipline of God the Father in your life. Remember, unlike your earthly father, *"your Father in heaven is perfect"* (Matthew 5:48).

Scattered in the Wilderness

"But with most of them God was not well pleased, for their bodies were scattered in the wilderness."

1 Corinthians 10:5

If you do not allow God to transform your soul you will die in a spiritual wilderness and will never reach the goal of being conformed into the image of Christ. Holding on to weights and sins will cause you to be snared or captive to a life in the wilderness, outside of God's promise land for you. In order for your behavior and life to become well pleasing to the Lord, you must walk in your potential in Christ. Remember, God is pleased with you as a person but we are talking about your behavior and life becoming well pleasing to Him. To fall short of experiencing what God's grace has made possible for you is to die in the wilderness. God has incredible things in store for you. However, you will never be able to experience and enter into the vision and dream that God has given you without your soul being transformed.

During this transformation phase of your spiritual development there will be seasons that your fellowship with God seems dry. This is what we refer to as the wilderness season. During this time God will seem distant. You will not be able to sense or experience the revealed or manifested presence of God in your life. You will feel like God has left you or is hiding from you. However, this is how God prepares you for His purposes and creates opportunities for your faith to be developed in order for your soul to be transformed.

"And you shall remember that the Lord you God led you all the way these forty years in the wilderness, to humble you and test you, to know what was in your heart, whether you would keep His commandments or not. So He humbled you, allowed you to hunger, and fed you with manna which you did not know nor did you fathers know, that He might make you know that man shall not live by bread alone, but man lives by every word that proceeds from the mouth of the Lord. Your garments did not wear out on you, nor did your foot swell these forty years. You should know in your heart that as a man chastens his son, so the Lord your God chastens you. Therefore you shall keep the commandments of the Lord your God, to walk in His ways and to fear Him. For the Lord your God is bringing you into a good land, a land of brooks of water, of fountains and springs, that flow out of valleys and hills; a land of wheat and barley, of vines and fig trees and pomegranates, a land of olive oil and honey; a land in which you will eat bread without scarcity, in which you will lack nothing; a land whose stones are iron and out of whose hills you can dig copper."

Deuteronomy 8:1-9

God will lead you into the wilderness seasons. These seasons are to humble and test you. During these dry and difficult times your heart will be revealed. Issues and areas of your soul that need to be transformed will be made known to you. By faith you must trust that God is with you and is working to transform you into the image of Christ. This is a necessary process in order for you to be prepared for what God wants to do next in your life. If you do not allow God to change you and resist potential hindrances then you will not be prepared for the promise land God has planned for you. God brought the nation of Israel out of Egypt to bring them into the Promised Land. However, God chose to lead them through the wilderness to get to the promise.

This was their time of preparation. This was their time to learn acceptable behavior. This was their time to grow in their faith and intimacy with God. This was their time to be humbled and put off the deeds of the old man or the ways of Egypt. This was their time to learn to trust in the provisions of God and not in their own strength. This was a season to learn the fear of the Lord. This was a season of transformation. This was a time for their soul to be weaned from the ways of Egypt.

"Surely I have calmed and quieted my soul, like a weaned child with his mother; like a weaned child is my soul within me."

Psalm 131:2

Your soul must be weaned from your old ways. Your soul has to be weaned from the characteristics of the old man. It is during the wilderness season that this takes place. In the barrenness of a wilderness or desert there are no outward signs that your soul can depend upon. There is no food or provisions that your soul can depend upon. There are no resources or shelter that your soul can depend upon. This is to enable your soul to be weaned from depending on anything other than the Lord.

"And Moses was learned in all the wisdom of the Egyptians, and was mighty in words and deeds."

Acts 7:22

"By faith he (Moses) forsook Egypt, not fearing the wrath of the king; for he endured as seeing Him who is invisible."

Hebrews 11:27 (Parenthesis Mine.)

Moses forsook the ways of Egypt. He forsook the wisdom, words, and deeds that he had learned from the Egyptians. You also are to forsake the ways of the old man and the world around you. You are no longer to display the characteristics of the old man. This process happened to Moses as he spent time in the wilderness.

"Now Moses was tending the flock of Jethro his father-in-law, the priest of Midian. And he led the flock to the back of the desert, and came to Horeb, the mountain of God."

Exodus 3:1

Moses spent forty years in the wilderness or desert tending sheep. (See Acts 7:30) It was during this time that he unlearned the ways of Egypt. The end result was that he became the most humble man on the earth. (See Numbers 12:3) The wilderness season is a period that humbles you. It humbled Moses. It was to humble the nation of Israel. You become humble as your soul is weaned from the ways and characteristics of the old you. In the wilderness you learn to only depend on and trust in the Lord for all the areas and needs of your life. In the wilderness you are put in a place where you realize that true help can only come from the Lord. In the barrenness of the wilderness you learn that you are to live by faith! This is true humility; when you depend on and place faith in the Lord in all circumstances. This faith then enables you to put off the "ways of Egypt" or your old man. The wilderness season is to develop your faith and trust in God.

During this time, do not turn from obeying God and remaining yielded to the Holy Spirit. Do not die in the wilderness. It is in the wilderness that you are to prepare a highway for the Lord in order for Him to do what He planned for your life. Isaiah proclaimed, *"Make straight in the desert a highway for our God"* (Isaiah 40:3). When every crooked place in your soul is made straight, every exalted place of pride is brought low, and every rough place is made smooth then God will be able to accomplish mighty things through you and bring you into your promise land. (See Isaiah 40:4-5)

"The highway of the upright is to depart from evil; he who keeps his way preserves his soul."

Proverbs 16:17

The only way out of the wilderness is to depart from evil. As you put off the deeds and characteristics of your old man you are building a highway out of the wilderness. The prophet Isaiah spoke about a highway of holiness in the wilderness (Isaiah 35:8). As you experience transformation of your soul you will be able move forward into what God has planned for you. Without it you will die in the wilderness. To die in the wilderness means your life and behavior never become well pleasing to God. To die in the wilderness means you fall short of your purpose of being conformed into the image of Christ.

Fear of the Lord

"Because they do not change, therefore they do not fear God."
Psalm 55:19

If you resist God and allow hindrances in your life to the transformation of your soul you have lost the fear of God. If you become unwilling to change, you do not fear God. God has commanded you to put off the deeds of your old man. To refuse and be unwilling is to depart from giving God the reverence and respect that He deserves. Proverbs 8:13 says, *"The fear of the Lord is to hate evil; pride and arrogance and the evil way and the perverse mouth I hate."* You must never forget that Christ died so that you would no longer live for yourself. (See 2 Corinthians 5:15) You live for God's purpose. You live for God's pleasure and glory. If you become unwilling to change then you will be living for your own pleasure and purpose instead of the good works that God has planned beforehand for you to walk in. (See Ephesians 2:10)

"Therefore we make it our aim, whether present or absent, to be well pleasing to Him. For we must all appear before the judgment seat of Christ, that each one may receive the things done in the body, according to what he has done, whether good or bad."
2 Corinthians 5:9-10

You have passed from death to life when you were born again. And yet there remains a day when you will stand before the judgment seat of Christ and give account for how you followed God's blueprint for your life. This is not a judgment concerning heaven or hell. It is a judgment or evaluation of your life and whether it was built according to God's blueprint. Your aim throughout your life should be to live well pleasing to the Lord. It should be your goal to be transformed into the image of Christ and fulfill His purpose for you in His kingdom. Any areas that you are unwilling to be changed will cause you to suffer loss of rewards at the judgment seat of Christ. (See 1 Corinthians 3:15) The great news is that when you allow your life to be built according to God's blueprint you will receive rewards at the judgment seat of Christ. Your willingness to allow God to change you and transform you into the image of Christ determines the amounts of rewards you will receive in the Millennium reign of Christ.

Another way the Scripture expresses the rewards you may receive in the kingdom is by you being a partaker of Christ's glory. We are to follow in the footsteps of Jesus. When He first came to earth He took up His cross and suffered. When He returns He will take up His throne and reveal His glory. The measure to which you now allow the cross to transform your soul will determine the amount of glory or rewards you will experience when Christ returns. This is why some Scriptures speak of the salvation of the soul as to the glories that you will experience in the kingdom of Christ.

"For no other foundation can anyone lay than that which is laid, which is Jesus Christ. Now if anyone builds on this foundation with gold, silver, precious stones, wood, hay, straw, each one's work will become clear; for the Day will declare it, because it will be revealed by fire; and the fire will test each one's work, of what sort it is. If anyone's work which he has built on it endures, he will receive a reward. If anyone's work is burned, he will suffer loss; but he himself will be saved, yet so as through fire. Do you not know that you are the temple of God and that the Spirit of God dwells in you?"

1 Corinthians 3:11-16

What you allow God to do in your life after He has laid the foundation determines your future rewards in the kingdom of Christ. If the deeds of the old man remain in your life you will suffer loss. Continuing to operate in the deeds of the old man is building your life with wood, hay, and stubble. It will not stand the test of God's holy fire. It is serious to lose the fear of God and not allow God to conform you into the image of Christ. You are God's temple. You are to reflect His character, His ways, and His purposes. You are called to conduct yourself in holiness. (See 1 Peter 1:14-16)

"And who can stand when He appears? For He is like a refiner's fire and like launderers' soap. He will sit as a refiner and a purifier of silver; he will purify the sons of Levi, and purge them as gold and silver, that they may offer to the Lord an offering in righteousness."
Malachi 3:2-3

As God manifests His presence in your life He desires to refine and purify your soul. The presence of God is holy fire. The writer of Hebrews stated, *"For our God is a consuming fire"* (Hebrews 12:29). You can go ahead and allow the fire of God to purify your soul now of the wood, hay, and stubble or you can put it off until the judgment seat of Christ. However, if you will allow God to purify your soul now then you will receive rewards in the future. So the choice is yours and you make the choice now. Do you want to suffer loss in that day or do you want to receive rewards? Continue to embrace the transformation of your soul. Without it you will never be able to have acceptable behavior for the kingdom and walk worthy of the Lord. Choose to walk in the fear of the Lord and allow your life to be built according to the blueprint of God.

Section III.

Formation Phase – Christ Formed in You

Phase
Introduction

Formation phase is very similar to transformation phase. However, during this phase the emphasis is on the positive traits of Christ being formed in the life of a believer. It is the truths connected to the resurrection side of Christ's finished work that is relevant. The age that the elementary teachings of Christ represent remains the same in this phase as it was for transformation phase. The primary division of truth that is relevant during formation phase also remains the same and is the revelation of the mystery.

A believer should progress in the spiritual growth stages from being a child to a young man or young woman in the faith. Formation phase also deals primarily with the soul of a believer. The primary method that facilitates spiritual growth for this phase is a modeling community. A believer should be connected to a group of believers that models the ways of Christ and His kingdom. See the chart on the next page!

Three Ages Elementary Teachings of Christ Represent	Spiritual Growth Stages	Phases for Discipleship	Primary Division of Truth	Primary "M" Facilitates Growth for Phase
Age 1 Transferring Kingdoms *Repentance from Dead Works and Faith toward God*	Babes	I. Foundation 1 Cor.3:11 (Spirit)	Gospel of Jesus Christ, Elementary Teachings of Christ Overview	Ministry of the Word
	Little Children		Gospel of Grace, Paul's Gospel, Word Of Righteousness	
	Little Children	II.Transformation Rom. 12:2 (Soul)	Revelation of the Mystery	My Role
Age 2 Life in God's Kingdom *Doctrine of Baptisms and Laying on of Hands*	Children			
	Children	III.Formation Gal.4:19 (Soul)	Revelation of the Mystery	Modeling Community
	Young Men			
	Young Men	IV.Impartation Matt.10:7-8 (Body)	Gospel of the Kingdom	Mentoring
Age 3 Life in the Millennium *Rewards for Resurrection and Judgment*	Father	V.Multiplication John17:6-8,20 (Entire Person)	Whole Counsel of Scripture	All the M's

Chapter 11

Christ Lives in You

"I have been crucified with Christ; it is no longer I who live, but **Christ lives in me***."*

Galatians 2:20 (Bold Mine.)

C hrist died for you. Christ died as you. Christ lives in you. When you received Christ He came into your spirit. The moment that your spirit made contact with Christ you were made alive or born again. Paul said, *"But he who is joined to the Lord is one spirit with Him"* (1 Corinthians 6:17). Christ lives in you to provide you with all that you need to overcome anything that life will throw at you. You are not just in Christ but Christ is also in you. Transformation phase dealt with putting off the characteristics of the old man while formation phase deals with putting on the characteristics of the new man you have become in Christ.

"To them God willed to make known what are the riches of the glory of this mystery among the Gentiles: which is **Christ in you***, the hope of glory."*

Colossians 1:27 (Bold Mine.)

You are in union with Christ. This union brings into your life all the provisions of heaven. Through your union with Christ you have a continual connection to anything you need for life and godliness. You can have hope, because Christ is in you. You need strength, Christ is in you. You need encouragement, Christ is in you. You are facing depression, Christ is in you. You need joy, Christ is in you. You need humility, Christ is in you. This is why Paul could say, *"I can do all things through Christ who strengthens me"* (Philippians 4:13).

The mystery surrounding the crucifixion, death, burial, resurrection, and ascension of Jesus Christ was for the purpose of God making it possible for Christ to dwell in you. Christ dying for you and as you was so He could live in you. God did not just want to forgive you of your sins and then leave you dependant on your own ability to serve God. God did not want to restore your soul only to fall captive to bondage again. God made a way for the greatness of the power of Christ to live in you. Christ can keep you from sin. Christ can keep you from bondages. Christ is to be your life source.

Christ is on the inside of you. He can empower you to obey God on every occasion. You can do all of God's will for your life through Christ. He is your strength. He is your ability. He is your power. Paul said, *"You are complete in Christ who is the head of all principality and power"* (Colossians 2:10.) The reason that Paul could boast in the power of Christ within Him is because it was revealed to him. The same must happen in your life. God wants to reveal to you the greatness of Christ living in you.

*"But when it pleased God, who separated me from my mother's womb and called me through His grace, **to reveal His Son in me**, that I might preach Him among the Gentiles, I did not immediately confer with flesh and blood, nor did I go up to Jerusalem to those who were apostles before me; but I went to Arabia, and returned again to Damascus."*

Galatians 1:15-17

Before Paul could ever fulfill his purpose and preach Christ he had to have a revelation of Christ in him. Flesh and blood did not reveal this to Paul. This is like what Jesus said to Peter when he confessed that He was the Christ. The Scripture records Jesus saying, *"Blessed are you, Peter, for flesh and blood has not revealed this to you, but My Father who is in heaven"* (Matthew 16:17). Just as God revealed to you that Jesus was the Christ, He desires to reveal the ability and power of Christ living in you. It is by the spirit of revelation that God will reveal to you the greatness of Christ in you. It takes the spirit of revelation to receive a spiritual understanding that Christ died as you, and it will take the spirit of revelation for you to gain the spiritual understanding of Christ living in you.

Paul said that he was in Arabia when God revealed Christ in him. It is the same for you during the wilderness seasons. There is barrenness, scarcity, and a lack of resources in the wilderness or desert. However, when you find yourself at the end of your own human ability you will be in a position to receive a revelation of the greatness of Christ in you. As long as you are trying to live independent of God's power and resources you are resisting Christ in you to meet your needs.

God told Israel he allowed them to hunger so that they would know, *"that man shall not live by bread alone, but by every word that proceeds from the mouth of the Lord"* (Deuteronomy 8:3). God wants you in the wilderness seasons to realize you do not have the knowledge, wisdom, strength, ability, or power to change the situation or fulfill God's purpose for your life. Jesus is the bread that you are to live upon. Jesus is the word of God and His spirit lives within you. You can feed upon His ability. You can draw upon His strength and power. You can do all things through Christ who strengthens you.

It was when Moses failed and fled after trusting in his own ability that he found himself sitting down by a well. (See Exodus 2:15) When you stop trusting in your own ability God can reveal the well of Christ's resources in you. Jesus said that He would be a fountain or well springing up within you. (See John 4:13-14) You do not have to continually experience the limitation of your body. Christ in you can provide you with divine ability and strength.

"But we have this treasure in earthen vessels, that the excellence of the power may be of God and not of us."

2 Corinthians 4:7

Christ is the treasure in your earthly body. This assures that anything in your life that meets the standard of God's blueprint is because of the power of Christ within you. As you began to accept Christ's death as your death then you will by faith be able to experience the power of Christ living in you. Your natural ability died with Christ. Your wisdom was crucified with Christ. Your knowledge was crucified with Christ. Your own strength died with Christ. Your resources for living died with Christ. However, if you do not consider these dead by faith then the power of Christ living in you will not be activated. Only as you stop trying to depend and live on your own resources and treasures will you be able to know by experience the treasure of Christ living in you. Then you can learn to know the mind of Christ. (See 1 Corinthians 2:16)

"The eyes of your understanding being enlightened; that you may know… what is the exceeding greatness of His power toward us who believe, according to the working of His mighty power which He worked in Christ when He raised Him from the dead and seated Him at His right hand in the heavenly places, far above all principality and power and might and dominion."

Ephesians 1:18-21

Jesus was raised for you. His resurrection was your resurrection. You were raised a new person with the exceeding greatness of His power available for your life. The same power displayed in the resurrection of Christ is the power to enable you to live a new life. His resurrection was your victory over anything. Nothing could withstand the power of His resurrection. Christ was raised far above all principality, power, might, and dominion. If you will yield to that same power living in you nothing can keep you from experiencing the life Jesus has made available for you. You are *"more than a conqueror through Him"* (Romans 8:37). God wants you to know the power of His resurrection in your life. (See Philippians 3:10) His power can lead you to always triumph over all things.

"Now thanks be to God who always leads us in triumph in Christ."

2 Corinthians 2:14

You have the same power that raised Christ from the dead and sat Him above all things dwelling on the inside of you. That is a reason for confidence! What can you face that Jesus has not already conquered? He wills to conqueror it again in your life as you trust in His ability and power living in you. You can experience the power of the resurrection daily in your life.

"Always carrying about in the body the dying of the Lord Jesus, that the life of Jesus also may be manifested in our body. For we who live are always delivered to death for Jesus' sake, that the life of Jesus also may be manifested in our mortal body."

2 Corinthians 4:10-11

When you take up your cross through faith you are carrying in your life the provisions of the death of Jesus. It is only as you remain in a place of accepting His death as your own death that you will see the life of Jesus being manifested in your daily walk with God. The more you through faith apply the death of Jesus' as your death, the more His life will be revealed in your body and walk with God. Your body will become an instrument for the will and behavior that is acceptable to God. You by faith believe that the old you has died and, at the same time, place faith in the greatness of Christ living in you to walk in victory.

"O wretched man that I am! Who will deliver me from this body of death? I thank God – through Jesus Christ our Lord."

Romans 7:24-25

Christ in you is your victory over the desires of your flesh or body. The power of the cross is Christ being able to dwell within you and empower you to not be controlled by the desires of your body. Thank God for the cross of Christ. Christ in you delivers you from having to obey the lust of your body.

"For those who live according to the flesh set their minds on the things of the flesh, but those who live according to the Spirit, the things of the Spirit."

Romans 8:5

As you set your mind upon the finished work of the cross and the power of Christ within, you will live according to the Spirit and not after the desires of the flesh. You have to reckon the power of Christ within you. In the moment of temptation you are to place faith in the fact that Christ is living in you. He is your help and strength to overcome any temptation. (See 1 Corinthians 10:13) Next time you are about to sin start thinking upon the fact that Christ is in you and see what happens. It is hard to go ahead and sin when you begin to acknowledge that Christ is in you. You do not have to fear temptation, the power of sin, or the desires of your flesh because *"greater is He that is in you"* (1 John 4:4). The power of Christ in you is greater than the flesh, the world, and the devil!

Here are some facts now that you are in Christ:

1. You have been joined to Christ.
    *"But he who is **joined to the Lord** is one spirit with Him"* (1 Corinthians 6:17).

    a) The Lord is your source for everything.
    b) You are to live out of your union with Christ.

2. You were made alive in Christ.
    *"But God, who is rich in mercy, because of His great love with which He loved us, even when we were dead in trespasses, **made us alive together** with Christ (by grace you have been saved),"* (Ephesians 2:4-5; Bold mine).

    a) You have new life in Christ.
    b) His life is your new life.

3. You were raised with Christ.

   *"But God, who is rich in mercy, because of His great love with which He loved us, even when we were dead in trespasses, made us alive together with Christ (by grace you have been saved), and **raised us up together**,"* (Ephesians 2:4-6; Bold mine).

   a) Evidence of your victory over all the past.
   b) You were raised with resurrection or overcoming power.

4. You were seated with Christ.
   *"But God, who is rich in mercy, because of His great love with which He loved us, even when we were dead in trespasses, made us alive together with Christ (by grace you have been saved), and raised us up together, and **made us sit together** in the heavenly places in Christ Jesus"* (Ephesians 2:4-6; Bold mine).

   a) The enemy is under your feet.
   b) God views you as ruling and reigning with Christ.
   c) You are seated in victory and in rest.

5. You are a joint heir with Christ.
   *"The Spirit Himself bears witness with our spirit that we are children of God, and if children, then heirs- heirs of God and **joint heirs with Christ**, if indeed we suffer with Him, that we may also be glorified together"* (Romans 8:16-17; Bold mine).

   a) You have received an inheritance in the kingdom of God.
   b) When His glory is revealed, yours will be revealed also.
   c) The suffering you experience in this life stores up more glory for you in the future.

The Law of the Spirit

"For the law of the Spirit of life in Christ Jesus has made me free from the law of sin and death."

Romans 8:2

163

Christ in you is the law or principle that sets you free from the law of sin that is in the members of your body. (See Romans 7:23) Christ living in you is the same thing as the law of the Spirit of life in Christ Jesus. The law of sin and death refers to the desires of your flesh or body. You must learn to follow the leading of the Spirit of God. This is to be the law that directs your life. You are to obey the Lord and not the desires of your body or flesh. If you do not learn to trust in the power of Christ living in you then you will continue to struggle with the desires and lusts of your flesh. It is only as you learn to yield to the ability of Christ in you that you will be able to experience victory over your flesh. When you resist the help of Christ in you then you are choosing to make a place for the law of sin and death to be activated in your body. Here are some of the characteristics that are the result of not depending on Christ in you.

"Now the works of the flesh are evident, which are: adultery, fornication, uncleanness, lewdness, idolatry, sorcery, hatred, contentions, jealousies, outbursts of wrath, selfish ambitions, dissensions, heresies, envy, murders, drunkenness, revelries, and the like."
Galatians 5:19-21

When you do not depend on the law of the Spirit you will be depending on your own ability or flesh. The works of the flesh listed above are the methods you will default to when you are not depending on the life of Christ inside of you. The works of the flesh are the ways in which you seek to achieve something in your life without allowing Christ to help you. When you depend on Christ on the inside you will not portray selfish ambition, hatred, outbursts of wrath, and the like.

It is sad to observe people who have been born again for many years but still depend on the methods of the flesh to manage living each day. You must learn to trust in the revelation of Christ living in you. You should not depend upon the flesh and manipulate people to try and get your desires fulfilled. You should not seek to intimidate people through loud outbursts of anger in order to get your way. Your life is not about you having your way any longer. The old you was crucified and you are to be living for the glory and will of God. You are not to depend on the ability of the flesh and revert to its methods. You are to learn to yield to the law of the Spirit on the inside of you. It is called the law of the Spirit of life because it is the way to experience the life that Jesus died to make available for you.

"I say then: Walk in the Spirit, and you shall not fulfill the lust of the flesh. For the flesh lusts against the Spirit, and the Spirit against the flesh; and these are contrary to one another, so that you do not do the things that you wish."

Galatians 5:16-17

Some of the struggles you are facing each day is not a matter of you desiring to sin. Transformation phase emphasized you allowing Christ to be Lord in your will and soul. However, even with Christ as Lord over the desires of your will it is possible for you to continue to not experience the complete victory that Christ has purchased for you. Without learning to walk in the Spirit you will continually commit works of the flesh. Walking in the Spirit is depending on the power of Christ in you. The Bible exhorts you to *"walk in the Spirit because you live in the Spirit"* (Galatians 5:25). You live in the Spirit because Christ lives in you.

To live in the Spirit means that because you are in right standing with God you can receive His power, help, and ability in your life. Living in the Spirit means you are living in a relationship with God. Your spirit has been joined to Christ and the resources of heaven. Remember, you lived in the realm of the flesh when you did not have a right relationship with God and therefore could not receive His power to help you live. You now live in the realm of God's empowerment and grace for your life, and because you live in the Spirit you are exhorted to also walk in the Spirit. Christ is in you, therefore, you should depend on His power and help as you walk through life each day! Walking in the Spirit is to experience the power of the law of the Spirit each moment.

Christ in you and the lust of your body are warring against each other. They will always be contrary to each other. You must learn to recognize the desires of your flesh and not get them confused with what you desire in the inner man. Your flesh will never want to serve God. The methods of your flesh or natural ability will always be opposed to the methods of Christ living in you. Learning to trust in the ability of Christ in you determines what you will experience each day. It is only as you trust in Christ's life within you that you give Him the opportunity to subdue the desires of your flesh. As you walk depending on Christ you will not fulfill the desires of the flesh. In fact, you will experience the power of the cross that crucified and rendered inoperative the lusts of your body. Then the real you, your spirit, will not succumb to the lusts of your flesh.

The same manner in which you experience the freedom that Christ purchased for your soul is to be the same way you experience freedom over the fleshly desires in your body. You must learn to trust in the provisions of Christ. Experiencing victory over the desires of your flesh is about learning to trust in the power of Christ living in you each moment, day by day. When you feel like responding to a person with an outburst of anger, you are to trust in Christ's power living in you. When you are feeling desires to lust after someone, you are to trust in Christ living in you. When you are not sure if you are going to be able to do something you would like to do then you are to trust in Christ to make it happen and not in the ability of the flesh to manipulate others. Learn to trust in Christ living in you for every situation you face.

"Therefore, brethren, we are debtors- not to the flesh, to live according to the flesh."

Romans 8:12

Walking in the Light

As you walk in the Spirit you will walk in the light. Walking in the light means that you are allowing the Spirit of God to lead you to obey what you know is right and what God has taught you so far on your spiritual journey. You will always be able to learn more truth and grow in your understanding of the specifics concerning God's will in your life. Therefore, on this journey God requires of you to obey what His Spirit has taught you concerning right and wrong conduct. This is what God asks of you. He does not expect you to change behaviors in your life that He has not yet made you aware of. However, He does expect you to obey what He has taught you, whether you learned them directly in your time with God or indirectly through hearing the preaching and teaching of the Word of God.

Have you ever wondered how there could be all kinds of wrong patterns of thinking, emotions, or behaviors in your life and at the same time you be unaware of them? You get up in the morning and live through the day with God's peace, joy, and freedom from oppression. The whole day you are unaware of things in your conduct that did not meet God's standard of acceptable behavior in His kingdom. This happens because you are walking in obedience to what you currently know to be right and wrong. James 4:17 states, *"Therefore, to him who knows to do good and does not do it, to him it is sin."* You only walk in the light as you obey what you know is right. When you disobey what you know to be right you sin. As you stay yielded to what God has taught you then you will continue to experience the joy of your salvation.

The Bible speaks of two categories of sin. There is known or deliberate sin. This is what the verse described. When you sin knowingly you are committing willful sin. However, there are also sins that you commit every day but are unaware of them because you have not been enlightened to know they are wrong. These sins are not willful acts of rebellion. To walk in the light and experience the joy of your salvation, God only expects of you to obey what you know.

"But if we walk in the light as He is in the light, we have fellowship with one another, and the blood of Jesus Christ His Son cleanses us from all sin."

1 John 1:7

Notice that you can walk in the light and still need the blood of Jesus Christ to cleanse you of sin. This cleansing refers to the sins that you are not aware that you do. When you sin unknowingly, and are unaware that you have done wrong, the blood of Jesus automatically provides cleansing for you. You do not have to repent of or confess this type of sin before you experience a cleansing because you are not even aware of the fact that you have done anything wrong. So walking in the light does not mean that you have learned to obey all of God's will for your life. Walking in the light means that you are obeying all of what you **know** to be right and wrong or God's will for your life. When you do this the Scripture says you fulfill what God expects of you. (See Romans 8:4)

As you walk in the light you are able to continue having fellowship with other believers. When you sin deliberately both your intimacy with Jesus Christ and His followers are hindered. Your fellowship with other believers is dependent on your fellowship with the Lord. Christ not only lives in you but He dwells in all His followers. When you resist the life of Christ on the inside, you also put yourself in a place of resisting Christ living in other believers. Walking in the light is significant to both your fellowship with the Lord and with His people. (See 1 Corinthians 5:11)

As you walk in the light of what you know to be right and wrong, God will continue to reveal other areas in your conduct that He wants to change. The key is allowing God to deal with what ever issue He wants to change and when He wants to change it. Therefore, keep your eyes on Christ and not your performance. Christ lives in you to lead you. As you follow the law of the Spirit you will continue to experience the life and resources of Christ in you. Remember, you are always to be led by the Lord; however, He chooses to communicate and confirm His will to you through different ways.

The Lord leads you by the written word. (2 Timothy 3:16; Hebrews 4:12-13) The Lord leads you by His voice. (See Hebrews 3:7; John 10:27; Acts 8:29) The Lord leads you by peace. (See Philippians 4:7; Isaiah 55:12; Psalm 23:2) The Lord leads you by circumstances. (See Psalm 32:8, 37:23; 2 Corinthians 2:12-13; Acts 9:23-31) The Lord can speak to you through the spiritual leaders that are over you. (See Hebrews 13:7, 17; 1 Corinthians 14:3; Psalm 77:20; 1 Timothy 4:14) This also includes godly counsel. (See Proverbs 11:14, 15:22; Acts 15:6) The Lord can lead you through the desires of your heart. (See Psalm 16:7, 37:4; Exodus 35:21; 2 Samuel 7:3) The Lord can lead through supernatural visions, dreams, etc. (See Acts 2:17, 10:3; Genesis 37:9; Ezekiel 1:1; 2 Corinthians 12:1) Remember, all of these must be submitted to the written word of God. It is not the leading of the Holy Spirit if it is contrary to the Scriptures.

Guard Against Legalism

"O foolish Galatians! Who has bewitched you that you should not obey the truth, before whose eyes Jesus Christ was clearly portrayed among you as crucified? This only I want to learn from you: Did you receive the Spirit by the works of the law, or by the hearing of faith? Are you so foolish? Having begun in the Spirit, are you now being made perfect by the flesh?"

Galatians 3:1-3

You must guard yourself from ever depending on your own self-effort. If you begin to trust in your own ability to live for God then you will be hindering the law of the Spirit in your life. You will then be unable to obey the truth. The only place you are to derive power from in order to obey the truth is through the indwelling presence of Christ. This Scripture speaks of believers who were bewitched and came under a wrong mentality. They took their attention off of the law of the Spirit within them. Their attention began to be focused on a list of commandments, or do's and don'ts, and then their own ability to keep them. Therefore, they were seeking to mature in Christ through their own ability. They had come under the spell of legalism. They had been clearly taught the power and finished work of the cross of Christ but still fell captive to legalism. People around them began to try and control their behavior by giving them a list of do's and don'ts. This legalistic teaching captured their minds from depending upon the leading and the power of Christ living in them as the means to growing in holiness.

You become legalistic when your focus is fixed on a list of do's and don'ts instead of Christ living in you. Legalism is when you depend on a list of do's and don'ts to change your behavior. The danger of legalism is it steals your strength to overcome the flesh because it takes your attention off of Christ and places the emphasis on your own behavior. Legalism is also dangerous because it emphasizes and is focused on your behavior despite what may be motivating you to perform certain behaviors. This is why religious people can read the Bible, assemble with other believers, pray; and nevertheless, still cuss you out if you do them wrong. Their motive for doing all those behaviors was not out of a sincere love for God.

When you focus on your behavior it actually leads to more sin. (See Romans 7:5) Focusing on your behavior leads to self-effort and trying harder after your sin to obey the laws or legalistic ways. You have fallen captive to trying through your own ability to control your behavior. This will never work! The more you focus on your behavior, or own ability, the more sin will result, and then the more laws or rules you will seek to add to your life to control your behavior. This is not what God intends for you! You will become so burdened with rules or laws that you will have not spiritual life. You have exchanged the power of Christ in you for a system of religious law-keeping. No amount of laws or commands can control your behavior other than the law of the Spirit of life in Christ Jesus.

You are only able to overcome the flesh by trusting in the power of Christ in you. Your conduct is to be changed only as the Spirit of God teaches and changes you. Any other method of trying to change your behavior is legalistic. If you depend on a list of do's and don'ts to inform you of what is right and wrong behavior you will only become aware of your own sinfulness because you will experience your inability to obey the list completely. Therefore, legalism occurs when you stop obeying and following the leading of Christ in you and focus on a list of do's and don'ts to direct your behavior.

Trying to live under a system of rules and laws always leads to the knowledge of sin. (See Romans 3:20) If you become focused on a list of do's and dont's, you will continue to sin and fail. Actually focusing on trying to obey a list of rules or commands will activate the desires of your flesh. (See Romans 7:5) Wrong focus will hinder the ability of Christ living in you and you will fall captive to the law of sin and death in the members of your body. It is legalism when you evaluate your love for God by following a list of laws or commands instead of by obeying the law of the Spirit of life within you.

Legalism is what religion is. Religion is adhering or practicing a set of beliefs or principles. You could become religious and never have any fellowship with Christ. If you start determining right behavior by following a list of commands instead of living out of your union with Christ, you have exchanged what God intended for legalism. When you walk in the Spirit you fulfill the requirements of God for your life. (See Romans 8:4) You do not need a list of commandments to determine what right behavior is for you. You just need to follow the Spirit of life within you. The Spirit of God is to be the one that deals with changing any behavior in your life. If you allow anything else to start determining how you evaluate your behavior or performance you are falling into legalism. This is how you can be bewitched and kept from obeying the truth. It is possible to read the Bible with a legalistic mentality. If you do this, you can read, memorize, and quote the Bible and still never experience the life Christ died to give you.

"Not that we are sufficient of ourselves to think of anything as being from ourselves, but our sufficiency is from God, who also made us sufficient as ministers of the new covenant, not of the letter, but of the Spirit; for the letter kills, but the Spirit gives life."
2 Corinthians 3:5-6

Without depending on the Holy Spirit to live for God, the words or letters in the Bible will kill your spiritual life. This is because you will never be able to obey the commands of God in your own ability. Christ living in you is the only sufficiency for obeying God. The letter refers to the commandments of God written in the Scriptures. You will never be able to fulfill them without depending on Christ living in you. It is only the Spirit that gives life. Your sufficiency for obeying God comes from the Spirit within you. The letters of the Bible cannot give you the power to obey what you read. This is why it is important to allow the law of the spirit to direct and guide your behavior.

If you try and use the letter to direct your behavior it will kill your spiritual life because only Christ living in you can change your behavior. Commands or a list of commands found in Scripture do not have the ability to change your behavior. It is only as you turn and depend on Christ living in you that you are able for your behavior to change and you experience freedom in your life. The ability of Christ living in you is the only way you will be able to live for God. The Scriptures are to cause you to depend more on the power of Christ living in you.

"You search the Scriptures, for in them you think you have eternal life; and these are they which testify to Me. But you are not willing to come to Me that you may have life."

John 5:39-40

The Scriptures testify concerning Christ. Therefore, the Scriptures are to lead you to trust in the power and ability of Christ within you. Christ provides life. Christ provides you with strength. Do not exchange the power of Christ for your own ability. Any time you only focus on a list of do's and don'ts it will cause you to become aware of your inability and blind you to the ability of Christ living in you.

This is the trap of legalism. It causes you to become focused on your behavior and performance. Then it shows you how sinful and unable you are to obey the laws. Legalism steals your joy. It will hold you in a continual pattern of self-effort, failure, and condemnation while causing you to resist the power of Christ available to you. You have died in Christ to a law-keeping system but you must continually guard yourself from such a mentality.

To be legalistic is to be focused on your self. To be legalistic is to reject the power of the cross. To be legalistic is to reject the power of Christ living in you. Legalism is based on self-effort, human ability, and pride. It is an offense to the cross of Christ and will become a stumbling block in your life. (See 1 Corinthians 1:22-23)

You will not mature spiritually through your own effort or striving. You will not overcome sin or the flesh through your own ability. You will not be able to control your behavior by making a list of do's and don'ts. Christ in you is your only hope. (See Colossians 1:27) You are to be focused on allowing Christ to live and direct your behavior. You are not to be dependent on a list of commandments to lead and guide you. You are to be focused on the power and ability of Christ to enable you to walk in the Spirit. As you do this you will "by reason of use, have your senses exercised to discern both good and evil" (Hebrews 5:14). Trust in Christ within you and not a system of law-keeping that falsely seeks to control your behavior.

Chapter 12

Christ Formed in You

"My little children, for whom I labor in birth again until Christ is formed in you."

Galatians 4:19

Christ lives in you so that He may be formed in you. Christ is to form your habits. Christ is to form your character. Now that you understand the importance of putting off the characteristics of your old man you must begin to display the characteristics of the new man. The characteristics of the new man refer both to your actions and what motivates them. In order for you to consistently put on the new man you must experience biblical formation. God's divine design for discipleship is for Christ to be formed in your behaviors and in your character in order for you to consistently display the new man. Without Christ being formed in both your behavior and character you will not display the new man. The new you is a person who is joined to Christ. It is out of that union that you are to have Christ formed in you in order to bear the fruit God has called you to.

Christ must be formed in the areas that have been set free from the characteristics of the old you. The deeds of Christ must also replace the deeds of your old man. The character of Christ must replace the character of the old you. This is why you must have the mind of Christ formed in your mind. You must have the desires and affections of Christ formed in your will. You must have the fruit of the Spirit formed in your emotions. Your actions and behaviors must also begin to reflect the image of the new creation that you have become in Christ. Though this process will continue throughout your life, God has designed for the greatest portion to be experienced now.

Modeling Community

"Brethren, join in following my example, and note those who so walk, as you have us for a pattern. For many walk, of whom I have told you often, and now tell you even weeping, that they are the enemies of the cross of Christ; whose end is destruction, whose god is their belly, and whose glory is in their shame- who set their mind on earthly things. For our citizenship is in heaven.

Philippians 3:17-20

The most prominent factor that facilitates your formation is the example of believers around you. The process of spiritual formation is similar to how you took on the habits of your earthly family and earthly culture as you observed and learned what was acceptable growing up. Paul told these believers that they had a pattern for conduct displayed before them. Paul, others, and the community of believers provided an example that was to be followed. This pattern was according to the standard and provisions of the cross and the culture of heaven, the city of God. Therefore, the community of believers modeled the culture of the kingdom of God.

The world around you does not demonstrate the pattern or culture of the kingdom of God. It is only as you fellowship with a modeling community of believers that you are able to observe the habits, customs, and values of the children of God. As you gather together with other believers in your local area you are a part of a modeling community of believers. As you move toward maturity in Christ you are able to observe and learn the habits, customs, values, and conduct of the community of believers. The believers within the community who are mature in Christ demonstrate by their life the culture of the kingdom of God. However, as you will learn, their ability to demonstrate the culture consistently is deeper than their ability to imitate what they have observed.

Many of the behaviors within the family of God and the culture of the kingdom of God are more caught than taught. You will automatically, through your fellowship with the community of believers, begin to display some of the habits and characteristics of the new man. The community will provide a model for you to follow. As you gather with the community of believers, they will model how to worship, how to pray, how to fast, how to give, and how to understand the Word of God.

"Remember those who rule over (lead) you, who have spoken the word of God to you, whose faith follow, considering the outcome of their conduct."

Hebrews 13:7

The life of leaders and mature believers provide an example of faith for you to follow. They model the acceptable behavior for the culture of the kingdom of God. As they live, you are able to observe and consider the outcome of their conduct. Their lives instruct the community of believers which in return lead and navigate you into the habits and behaviors you are to display.

"Now all who believed were together, and had all things in common, and sold their possessions and goods, and divided them among all, as anyone had need. So continuing daily with one accord in the temple, and breaking bread from house to house, they ate their food with gladness and simplicity of heart."

Acts 2:44-46

In the early days of the church the believers continued to fellowship with each other which led to them having all things in common. They were modeling and living as a true community of followers of Jesus Christ. They fellowshipped both through large gatherings that took place in the temple and also through smaller gatherings that met in their houses. Many behaviors and habits that you may overlook in the large gatherings will become apparent to you in the more intimate times of fellowship with other believers. You cannot experience God's plan for you and not continue to fellowship with the community of believers. You have, through Christ, become a part of a community of followers of Christ. It is in the modeling community that you learn about and fulfill God's purpose in His kingdom. This is why Ephesians 5:21 states you are to, *"submit to one another in the fear of God."*

In order for you to experience the biblical standard for Christian formation you must begin to evaluate the habits you have learned from the modeling community in the light of Scripture. This is the necessary path for you to experience biblical formation. Christ being formed in you is more than you just imitating what you have learned from the community. That was just the beginning of what true formation consists of. You must come to know the Biblical basis for the activity that you have come to model.

"Therefore lay aside all filthiness and overflow of wickedness, and receive with meekness the implanted word, which is able to save your souls."

James 1:21

The laying aside of filthiness and wickedness are the aspects of transformation phase. You put off the deeds and characteristics of the old you. Receiving with meekness the implanted word refers to the phase of formation. Notice it is more than just learning or hearing the Word that is able to save your soul. It is the implanted or engrafted Word that accomplishes Christ being formed in you. You can model the activity of the community of believers around you without necessarily having Christ formed in you. In order for Christ to be formed in you, the Word must first be received. This means that you must know the biblical basis and Scriptures that direct what you have caught through observing the modeling community that you are a part of. Therefore, for Christ, the Word of God, to be implanted in your soul you must not only portray acceptable behavior for the kingdom but also know the basis for why and what you do.

Without having the Word of God engrafted into your soul you will never be able to consistently model the culture you have observed. Without a deeper knowledge of the Word, when you are not around other people from the community of believers you will not have the ability to faithfully demonstrate the culture of the kingdom of God. This would be because you have just learned how to model or imitate the culture but the culture has not been formed in your soul. This is why many young believers no longer demonstrate the values, habits, or customs of kingdom culture when they leave the community to go to college. They never had Christ or the culture formed in their soul. Biblical formation is much deeper than just imitation. Your ability to model the culture of the kingdom comes from the Word being engrafted in your soul. Without the engrafted Word in your soul, whenever you are not with the community you will begin to model the values, habits, or customs of unbelievers around you.

"But be doers of the word, and not hearers only, deceiving yourselves. For if anyone is a hearer of the word and not a doer, he is like a man observing his natural face in a mirror; for he observes himself, goes away, and immediately forgets what kind of man he was."

James 1:22-24

For Christ to be formed in your soul after you have received the biblical basis for the characteristics of kingdom culture, you must obey what you know. Obedience completes the formation of Christ in your soul. It takes you knowing from Scripture both what to do and why you should do it concerning the customs of kingdom culture, and then obeying or acting on the basis of what Scripture teaches. Anything less will not lead to biblical formation.

Christ-Formed Habits

"Only let your conduct be worthy of the gospel of Christ."

Philippians 1:27

The old you died and was buried. As a new creation in Christ you are to put off your former conduct. Your old habits and behaviors are no longer to be demonstrated in your life. You are to replace them with new habits and behaviors that reflect the will of God for your life. Your conduct is to be worthy of what Christ has made possible for you. Old habits are to be replaced with new habits.

As you obey the directives for a child of God found in the Bible it will lead to Christ-formed habits. Through your obedience, the Word of God is being engrafted into your soul. The Holy Spirit uses the commands of Scripture to direct what you do and why you do it. Your habits are not to be based on what people have told you. They are to be based on the Word of God. The Word of God is to form your habits. It is only then that you truly have Christ-formed habits in your life.

You no longer hang out with people who drink or do drugs but instead hang out with people who go to the local assembly of believers. (See Hebrews 10:25) You no longer read romance novels but instead read the Bible. (See Matthew 4:4) You exchanged gambling for giving to the poor. (See Galatians 2:10) You no longer listen to music filled with cussing or sexually explicit language but listen to music that honors God. (See Mark 4:24) You no longer steal but are giving instead. (Acts 20:35) You no longer complain but are grateful to God for what you do have. (See Colossians 3:15) There are hundreds of possible habits that have changed in your life as you replaced old conduct with new conduct that is worthy of the gospel of Jesus Christ.

This I say, therefore, and testify in the Lord, that you should no longer walk as the rest of the Gentiles walk."

Ephesians 4:17

As your conduct and habits are conformed to those that honor God, you will no longer be living like the unbelievers around you everyday. Your walk will be different from theirs. Your conduct will not follow the pattern of the world but the pattern of God's people. You are no longer to act like the rest of the world. You do not follow them because they are heading in a direction different than where

God is leading you. You are a citizen of heaven and demonstrate good works. (See 1 Peter 1:11-12)

"As obedient children, not conforming yourselves to the former lusts, as in your ignorance; but as He who called you is holy, you also be holy in all your conduct, because it is written, 'Be holy, for I am holy.'"

1 Peter 1:14-16

As you experience formation your conduct will change. You will no longer participate in former lusts. You will no longer act like the person you use to be before you were born again. There were different behavioral sins in all of us before we received Christ. The wrong conduct that was in my life you may have never performed and had a struggle with. However, the point of the Scripture is that there were sinful conducts in all of our lives before we became a new creation. As you continue to experience formation in your spiritual development it will lead to new habits, behaviors, traditions, values, and conduct that are appropriate for your life as a child of God.

On earth you came from a family and were part of a culture. There were habits and conduct that you learned from them and that ended up being passed down into your life. Every family and culture has been influenced by Satan to some degree. The Apostle John clearly stated that *"the whole world lies under the sway of the wicked one"* (1 John 5:19). You grew up in a fallen world that does not reflect completely the conduct and culture of the kingdom of God. Your culture, simply put, is the way you do or live life. Your habits and conduct demonstrate the influence of the culture you received during your upbringing. The new behaviors and conduct you will need to have formed in your life will depend on the culture you were raised in.

Formation phase deals with receiving the new ways of God's family and the culture of the kingdom of God. All of your previous way of living must be submitted to the culture of the kingdom of God. This means that some things from the culture you were brought up in will have to be changed. Some will have to be completely surrendered and no longer be conducted in your life. (See Titus 1:12-13)

Others may still be allowed but now will be influenced by receiving new values and motives from the culture of the kingdom of God.

"And many who had believed came confessing and telling their deeds. Also, many of those who had practiced magic brought their books together and burned them in the sight of all. And they counted up the value of them, and it totaled fifty thousand pieces of silver. So the word of the Lord grew mightily and prevailed."

Acts 19:18-20

The believers in this story came from a culture where they practiced magic and read many books on the subject. The word "deeds" represents the behaviors, conduct, and practices of the culture they came from. Every deed in their life before they became a child of God that was contrary to the image of Christ or the kingdom of God had to be put off. The same is true for your life. (See Colossians 3:9, Acts 7:22, and Hebrews 11:27) Therefore, they brought all the books concerning magic together and burned them. When you submit every behavior and conduct in your life to the Lordship of Christ then the Word of God is prevailing mightily in your life. When you hold some of your cultures customs, traditions, and habits before the holiness of God, many will need to be burned in the fire.

"And about that time there arose a great commotion about the Way. For a certain man named Demetrius, a silversmith, who made silver shrines of Diana, brought no small profit to the craftsmen. He called them together with the workers of similar occupation, and said: 'Men, you know that we have our prosperity by this trade.'"

Acts 19:23-25

As you experience formation you may have to forsake your job or way of living for one that is acceptable for a child of God. A man named Demetrius made his living as an idol maker. His trade however was contrary to "the Way" or the culture of God's kingdom and family. All of your customs must be examined in light of God's Word and the acceptable behavior of God's children. (See Acts 15:22-29; 16:4-5)

You are called to be holy in all your conduct and habits. It is only as Christ is formed in your life that you will begin to see the changes in your walk. To put on the new man is to display the conduct of Christ. You now spend time praying, singing praises to God, inviting people to the assembly of believers, and many other habits that are to be in the life of every child of God. The way you talk will change. The way you walk will change and the direction you are heading will change. The way you spend your money will change. The friends you spend time with will change. This is Christ being formed in your habits and in all of your conduct. You are displaying the culture of the kingdom of God and God's family.

The Word of God sets some clear boundaries for acceptable behavior as a child of God. Paul said, *"You know what command-ments we gave you through the Lord Jesus"* (1 Thessalonians 4:2). However, within those boundaries usually the Bible does not speak specifically to certain details or situations that you will face. This is because you are to be led by the Spirit of God on the inside of you as to how to work out your salvation when facing specific questions that the Bible does not clearly answer. (See Philippians 2:12-13) You must remember, the Spirit of God will never lead you to do something that would be contrary to the boundaries that the Word of God does set. Let me say again, the Spirit of God will never lead you to do something that is not in agreement with verses found in the written Word of God. I say again- **never**!

Local Church Culture vs. Kingdom Culture

"But we command you, brethren, in the name of the Lord Jesus Christ, that you withdraw from every brother who walks disorderly and not according to the tradition which he received from us."
2 Thessalonians 3:6

There are customs or traditions that are commanded in Scripture. These traditions or behaviors are for every believer and for every local church to follow. They reflect the standard of the culture of the kingdom of God. When a person deliberately chooses to walk contrary to these commands given in Scripture, Paul says that believers are to withdraw from him. This is to help the person acknowledge their wrong, repent, and return to fellowshipping with the community of believers. Paul said the community is not to *"count him as an enemy, but admonish (warn) him as a brother"* (2 Thessalonians 3:15/ Parenthesis Mine; NKJV Marginal Reading).

The danger arises when you are not able to distinguish between the standard traditions for the culture of the kingdom and the traditions of your local church. Every local church has traditions or different customs that causes it to have unique characteristics from other local churches. Some churches use organs, others use electronic keyboards. Some churches receive the tithes and offerings in buckets while others have you bring them to the altar. Some churches use power point presentations while others use weekly bulletins. Some churches have an annual Christmas play and others do not. Some churches have a song during the offering and others do not. Some churches wear suits and others do not. Some churches spend thirty minutes singing and praising while others do not. All of these are examples of a local church's culture.

Local church culture is the way your congregation has decided to do things that the Bible does not set the standard for. Remember, the customs or traditions that the Word of God commands determines the culture of the kingdom of God and standards for every local church. On issues, such as those mentioned above, that the Word of God does not address, it is up to the leadership of the local church to determine. What they decide becomes traditions or distinct customs for that local church culture. Local church culture must never be emphasized over the standard for every church to obey the traditions and customs of the kingdom of God. Such an overbalance is unhealthy and leads to legalism.

"Then the scribes and Pharisees who were from Jerusalem came to Jesus saying, 'Why do Your disciples transgress the tradition of the elders? For they do not wash their hands when they eat bread.' He answered and said to them, 'Why do you also transgress the commandment of God because of your tradition?'"

Matthew 15:1-3

The leaders of the nation of Israel had established what was called the "tradition of the elders." These traditions were not commanded by the Scriptures but were established similar to a local church culture. The traditions were customs and practices that were set in place by the elders. The problem arises when these type of traditions become the focal point for what is considered acceptable behavior by God. The goal is for you to have Christ-formed habits not the traditions of men.

The traditions of men are not the standard for what is acceptable to God and the culture of the kingdom. The traditions of men are the standard of men not God. The people in the above verses were more concerned about their local church culture then they were the commandments of God. They sought to make sure everybody followed the tradition of the elders while at the same time they were not obeying the commandments of God. Local church culture is never to distract or keep you from obeying the commandments of God.

"He answered and said to them, 'Well did Isaiah prophesy of you hypocrites, as it is written: 'This people honors Me with their lips, but their heart is far from Me. And in vain they worship Me, teaching as doctrines the commandments of men.' For laying aside the commandment of God, you hold the tradition of men- the washing of pitchers and cups, and many other such things you do.' He said to them, 'All too well you reject the commandment of God, that you may keep your tradition.'"

Mark 7:6-9

Jesus exposed that these people had become religious. They cared more about **their** traditions and teachings being broken then they did the traditions and commandments of God. They had fallen captive to hypocrisy. They were honoring God with their lips but their hearts were far from God. They did not have Christ-formed habits but men-formed traditions. They laid aside the commandments of God for the traditions of men.

Local church culture must never become elevated or emphasized over the culture of the kingdom of God. Obeying the commandments of God should always take precedence in your heart over being so concerned about obeying the traditions or customs that men have created. You should never seek to get people to conform to the traditions of men while neglecting to teach them to obey the commandments of God. This makes the difference on whether you are basing your habits of the Word of God or on the traditions of men.

"Making the word of God of no effect through your tradition which you have handed down. And many such things you do."

Mark 7:13

Traditions and customs within a local church culture should never make the Word of God of no effect. The Word of God had lost its power in the lives of these people because they loved their traditions more than the commandments of God. You must not fall captive to trying to spread the culture of your local church instead of the culture and commands of the Word of God. To do so is to be religious and it is contrary to true maturity in Christ. Your main focus should be on handing down the commandments of God and the culture of the kingdom not the commandments of men and the culture of your local church.

If you care more about the culture of your local church than the culture of the kingdom of God you will begin to have a sectarian spirit. You will base your acceptance of people not on the standard of Scripture but by the standard of the traditions of men. Such an attitude is wrong and causes much harm to other people. Scripture is to always be your focus and not the traditions or teachings of men.

You must understand that the culture of your local church can change and should change with time. They can change because they are not standards set by Scripture but by men. The danger is when you are unwilling to let go of old traditions and replace them with new customs that will enable the local church to better obey the commands of God and reach people for Christ. The local church culture must never hinder the people of God from being able to fulfill the purposes and commands of God. Make sure you understand the difference between the culture of the kingdom of God and the traditions of your local church. God and the standard of Scripture set one and men set the other. Do you want to be a follower of men or a follower of God?

"Beware lest anyone cheat you through philosophy and empty deceit, according to the tradition of men, according to the basic principles of the world, and not according to Christ."

Colossians 2:8

Do not be cheated from experiencing what Christ has made possible. To fall captive and more in love with the traditions of men will keep you from reaching true maturity in Christ. Guard yourself from religious mentalities within people all around you. Allow your life to be a true demonstration of Christ-formed habits. Live for the standard of God not the standard of men. Love, for God always makes the difference concerning this issue.

"Knowing that you were not redeemed with corruptible things, like silver or gold, from your aimless conduct received by tradition from your fathers, but with the precious blood of Christ, as of a lamb without blemish and without spot."

1 Peter 1:18-19

Christ shed His blood and died to redeem you from aimless conduct. He has made it possible instead for you to have Christ-formed habits. Traditions of men can cause you to have nothing more than aimless conduct in your life. Aimless conduct is conduct that is not directed by the commandments of God but by the commandments of men. Determine to keep a right focus on the right things. Give more emphasis to having Christ-formed habits in your life.

Christ-Formed Character

Experiencing true formation is deeper than just having Christ-formed habits. You must also possess Christ-formed character. The formation of Christ in your character is extremely important. Christ-formed character makes the difference concerning what motivates you as you perform Christ-formed habits. You can have

Christ-formed habits but still have impure motives. Christ-formed character is to have Christ-formed motives. It is having the character of Christ as you perform Christ like habits that will enable you to walk as a new creation.

You are only displaying the new man when you have both Christ formed-habits and Christ-formed character. Biblical formation is what keeps you from just being or becoming religious. To have habits in your life that are directed and performed based on the Word of God, without having the character of Christ, will cause you to become religious. You are being religious when you follow or adhere to a set of beliefs or customs found in the Scriptures without having genuine intimacy with Jesus Christ and taking on His character. You can be religious and still imitate the culture of the kingdom of God to a certain point. However you will not be displaying or putting on the new man. Remember, you are only displaying the new man when you simultaneously have Christ-formed habits and are motivated by Christ-formed character.

"Having a form of godliness but denying its power. And from such people turn away!"

2 Timothy 3:5

Christ formation must include having the right motives and character in your life. Without Christ being formed in your character you will only have a form of godliness but no true power. A form of godliness lacks the life and power of Christ. A form of godliness is to settle for religious behavior without allowing the life of Christ to live through you. A form of godliness lacks the power to bring about lasting change in others. It takes the life and presence of Christ for true change to occur.

"Now as Jannes and Jambres resisted Moses, so do these also resist the truth: men of corrupt minds, disapproved concerning the faith; but they will progress no further, for their folly will be manifest to all, as theirs also was."

2 Timothy 3:8-9

Two religious men, Jannes and Jambres, could imitate the works of Moses up to a certain point. They had a form of religion but without the power and life of Christ. This form of godliness that does not manifest the power and life of Christ is the greatest enemy to the divine design for discipleship. Religious behavior becomes just an imitation of the true and genuine life that God has made possible. It is counterfeit religious behavior because it is performed without the presence and life of Christ living through a person. There is religious activity and there is Christ activity.

You must understand that being religious refers to all spiritual activity that is done outside of the presence, empowerment, and life of Christ. This means that all people who do not depend on the life of Christ to empower them for the spiritual activity they do are religious regardless of whether they call themselves Christian, Buddhist, Muslim, or Hindu. All religious activity that lacks the life of Christ is done in the flesh, regardless of what faith it is. Religious behavior is performed when the truth or Spirit of God is resisted. This type of religious activity is not approved as acceptable behavior for the kingdom of God nor is it true godliness. Religious activity will always eventually be exposed because it will not lead to further progress. True godliness or spiritual maturity can never be attained through religious activity. It is only by the life of Christ that true spiritual development can be attained.

"But you have carefully followed my doctrine, manner of life, purpose, faith, longsuffering, love, perseverance."
2 Timothy 3:10

Paul contrasted religious activity from what Timothy had learned to follow. Timothy had more than just a mere imitation. Timothy had received a Christ-formed manner of life and Christ-formed character. Timothy performed the biblical teachings that he had learned from the Apostle Paul with purpose, faith, and love. Timothy followed the doctrine and manner of life he was taught, because he possessed the right motives and character of Christ.

You would have a form of godliness if you continued to model the right behaviors and habits for a child of God without the

187

character, motive, and heart of Christ. Without such things, the life of Christ will not be manifested through what you do. Religious people can perform some of the same activities as persons who have had Christ formed in them but with a different motive and with a different outcome.

*"Bondservants, be obedient to those who are your masters according to the flesh, with fear and trembling, in sincerity of heart, as to Christ; not with eyeservice, as menpleasers, but as bondservants of Christ, **doing the will of God from the heart**, with goodwill doing service, as to the Lord, and not to men, knowing that whatever good anyone does, he will receive the same from the Lord, whether he is a slave or free."*

Ephesians 6:5-8 (Bold Mine.)

In the context of this passage the Apostle Paul is talking specifically about how Christians should work. However, the principle he gives applies to everything that you will do in life. Paul says that what you do is to be done for the Lord and not just for men. You are not to seek to please men but Christ. You are to do God's will for your life from your soul not just from your head. (The second word translated heart in the verse is the Greek word *"psuche,"* Greek for soul.) You are to do the will of God from a soul that has had Christ formed in it.

Activities, performances, and behaviors that are not done out of a Christ-formed soul are considered dead works. Dead works are religious works and are to be repented of. (See Hebrews 9:14) Anything that you do that is not motivated by the characteristics of Christ is considered a dead work. It is dead because the life of Christ is not motivating the behavior. Two believers can both feed the poor; however, one of them is acceptable behavior by the Father and the other is not. One will be rewarded at the judgment seat of Christ, the other will not.

Christ being formed in the soul makes the difference. When Christ is formed in the soul, what you do is motivated by sincerity and done out of love for the Lord. Religious behavior is what you do to be seen by men or with eye service. Religious behavior is not the fruit God is looking for in your life and it will never lead to lasting fruit in others. Jesus said that, *"The branch cannot bear fruit of itself, unless it abides in the vine, neither can you, unless you abide in Me...for without Me you can do nothing"* (John 15:4-5). You cannot do anything productive for God without Christ motivating and empowering you to perform it. However, good works done from a soul that has experienced formation will produce lasting fruit.

"It is the Spirit who gives life; the flesh profits nothing. The words that I speak to you are spirit, and they are life."

John 6:63

Also, without the formation of Christ in your soul you will be unable to perform behaviors that are commanded by the Word of God but are despised by the people around you. You will be susceptible to doing things to please men instead of Christ. You will be susceptible to peer pressure or the standards of people around you. Your motives and character effects how God views the behavior or good works that you begin to walk in. This is why it is necessary for you to allow the characteristics of Christ to be formed in your soul.

"Therefore, as the elect of God, holy and beloved, put on tender mercies, kindness, humility, meekness, longsuffering; bearing with one another, and forgiving one another, if anyone has a complaint against another; even as Christ forgave you, so you also must do. But above all these things put on love, which is the bond of perfection."

Colossians 3:12-14

Christ being formed in you pertains to you taking on the listed characteristics of Christ. Without having Christ formed in your soul you may do the rights things but for the wrong reasons. This would be living contrary to God's divine design for discipleship. Your spiritual development cannot stop after you have put off characteristics of the old you. You must have Christ formed in your soul in order to reach the end goal of maturity in Christ. Formation of your soul consists of both putting on the new man through your actions and also about having the right motives, attitudes, and character of Christ when you do it. Christianity is more than just changing your behavior. It is about possessing and having the character of Christ formed in your soul.

"But you know his proven character, that as a son with his father he served with me in the gospel."

Philippians 2:22

Christ-formed character is character that serves. Proven character is having a heart of a servant. Jesus said, *"But whoever desires to become great among you shall be your servant"* (Mark 10:34). You are to be willing to serve. There is a difference in serving and fulfilling your purpose in the kingdom of God. Serving is any activity for God where you are not ministering or leading others. Serving is helping someone else to fulfill their ministry and calling in the kingdom of God. You should have character that serves even though you are not ready yet to walk in your purpose or calling for the kingdom of God. Be a servant to someone around you like Timothy was to Paul! Serve God by serving them!

The Heart Matters

*"But the Lord said to Samuel, 'Do not look at his appearance or at his physical stature, because I have refused him. For the Lord does not see as man sees; for man looks at the outward appearance, but the **Lord looks at the heart**."*

1 Samuel 16:7 (Bold Mine.)

God looks at more than just the physical. When a believer performs a physical activity God looks at their heart. Experiencing formation is more than just having the right behaviors. The heart matters to God. When God sent the prophet Samuel to anoint the next King of Israel he warned him not to look merely at appearance. Religion looks only at the appearance of things where God looks at the heart of a matter. Man looks at the outward appearance of things while God is looking at the heart. This is a beautiful picture of the difference of religious activity verses Christ being formed in your soul.

*"Who is wise and understanding among you? Let him show by good conduct that his works are done in the meekness of wisdom. But if you have bitter envy and self –seeking (selfish ambition) **in your hearts**, do not boast and lie against the truth. This wisdom does not descend from above, but is earthly, sensual, demonic. For where envy and self-seeking exist, confusion and every evil thing are there. But the wisdom that is from above is first pure, then peaceable, gentle, willing to yield, full of mercy and good fruits, without partiality and without hypocrisy. Now the fruit of righteousness is sown in peace by those who make peace."*

James 3:13-18 (Parenthesis Mine.
NKJV Marginal Reading/ Bold Mine)

You are to have Christ-formed habits. However, your good conduct and works are to be done in the meekness of wisdom. Meekness is a part of the character of Christ that is to motivate your formed habits. In everything you do, God looks at your heart. Are you being motivated by envy or selfish ambition? Such motives and character traits are called demonic and earthly. You are to be motivated in your hearts by the character of Christ. Doing good works with selfish ambition in your heart is not acceptable behavior for the kingdom of God. Such motives invite every evil thing to operate. This is why religious people throughout the history of the world have done some of the most awful things. Christ-formed character makes the difference.

The fruit that is to come out of you being in right standing with God is to be sown in peace. The good works that have been made possible for you to perform because of your relationship with God are to be done with the character of Christ. They are not to be performed with an impure a heart. Your motives determine if your heart is pure. Good works are partial and hypocritical when they are done with an impure heart. It takes both Christ formed-habits and Christ-formed character in order for the fruits of righteousness to be sown in peace.

"Who can know it (the heart)? I, the Lord, search the heart, I test the mind, even to give to every man according to his ways, according to the fruit of his doings."

Jeremiah 9b-10

When God examines your spiritual life He takes a picture of your heart. The Bible uses the term "heart" most often to refer to your inner makeup. Your inner makeup consists of both your spirit and soul along with their functions and desires. Sometimes when the word "heart" is used it may refer to an aspect of your spirit, while other times it might refer to an aspect of your soul. This is why only God is able to completely know and examine your heart. As you spend time fellowshipping with the Lord, He will reveal and address any areas in your heart that should be dealt with.

The heart refers to the entire complexity of your inward workings. This is why you can have both pure desires and impure desires in your heart simultaneously. Your spirit desires to obey God and yet at the same time there may be areas in the affections of your soul or will that desire something impure. This is why the Psalmist said, *"Blessed are those...who seek Him with the whole heart"* (Psalm 119:2)! Therefore, your heart refers to all the inner makeup that determines how you live.

"As in water face reflects face, so a man's heart reveals the man."

Proverbs 27:19

Your heart reflects who you truly are as a person. Your heart reveals your true character. This is why your heart matters. You can work hard at trying to fool people by your good works but your heart still determines the type of character you possess. You might be able to imitate true godliness up to a certain point but eventually your heart will be revealed. This is why you should place such an emphasis on allowing Christ to be formed in your character.

"To be strengthened with might through His Spirit in the inner man, that Christ may dwell in your hearts through faith."

Ephesians 3:16b-17a

Paul prayed that the Spirit of God would strengthen the believers' inner man in order for them to have faith for Christ to dwell in their hearts. Your inner man is your born again spirit. This shows you that the heart refers to more than just your spirit. Your spirit is to be empowered by the law of the Spirit in order for you to by faith allow Christ to dwell in your heart. To have Christ dwell in your heart is to have Christ-formed character. The word "dwell" refers to Christ making His home in your heart. This is taking on His motives, values, thoughts, and so on. This is having your heart established.

"And may the Lord make you increase and abound in love to one another and to all, just as we do to you, so that He may establish your hearts blameless in holiness before our God and Father at the coming of our Lord Jesus Christ with all His saints."

1 Thessalonians 3:12-13

In order for your heart to be pure you must be motivated by love. Love is one of the primary characteristics of your life as you allow Christ to be formed in your heart. True holiness is not just about having the right conduct but allowing love to motivate what you do. All spiritual activity is to be motivated by love. (See 1 Corinthians 13)

"Now may our Lord Jesus Christ Himself, and our God and Father, who has loved us and given us everlasting consolation and good hope by grace, comfort your hearts and establish you in every good word and work."

2 Thessalonians 2:16-17

If you will allow God to deal with the issues of your heart He will establish in your life the character of Christ. Then every good word and work you do will be performed with Christ-formed character. You will be judged when the Lord returns, not just on what you have accomplished but also the motives of your heart. Remember, man looks at outward appearance but God looks at the heart. (See 1 Corinthians 4:4-5)

"Do not let your adornment be merely outward- arranging the hair, wearing gold, or putting on fine apparel- rather let it be the hidden person of the heart, with the incorruptible beauty of a gentle and quiet spirit, which is very precious in the sight of God."

1 Peter 3:3-4

Peter emphasizes that you should not focus only on outward things to the neglect of your heart. The hidden person of your heart refers to your character. A pure heart is what is precious and valuable in the sight of God when He observes your life. To be focused only on outward things is to be religious. You are also acting religious when you do something to receive praise from man. Religion seeks to please men while you are called to please God. (See Galatians 1:10) You must allow the character of Christ to be established in your heart. Then you will be experiencing what the Bible refers to as pure religion. (See James 1:27) Your heart does matter. Your heart and motives makes the difference. Will you choose to have a form of godliness or experience Christ-formed habits and Christ-formed character?

"Keep your heart with all diligence, for out of it spring the issues of life."

Proverbs 4:23

Chapter 13

Putting on the New Man

"Put on the new man which was created according to God, in true righteousness and holiness."

Ephesians 4:24

As you allow Christ to be formed in your soul it will enable you to put on the new man. In order to truly display the new man you must have Christ-formed character and Christ-formed habits. This means that you know why you are doing what you do, and you perform it with the character and motives of Christ. Biblical formation means that your activity is done with an understanding, purpose, meaning, and faith. Anything less is to settle for being religious and a form of godliness.

You have learned that in order for you to continue to be spiritually developed according to God's blueprint you must come to know the Biblical truths concerning what you learned and began to observe from the modeling community. You must know why the modeling community does what it does. You must know the Biblical basis for what the community does in order to withstand the customs of the world and in order for you to be able to teach others the culture of the kingdom of God.

"Therefore we do not lose heart. Even though our outward man is perishing, yet the inward man is being renewed day by day. For our light affliction, which is but for a moment, is working for us a far more exceeding and eternal weight of glory, while we do not look at the things which are seen, but at the things which are not seen. For the things which are seen are temporary, but the things which are not seen are eternal."

2 Corinthians 4:16-18

For you to display the new person you have become in Christ, your spirit needs to be strengthened or empowered each day. You will face things throughout your life that will afflict you and seek to distract you from what you should be focused on. The things you are dealing with and are able to see in your life are temporal. That which is seen is temporal while that which is unseen is eternal. You are a new person in Christ. Your spirit remains unseen but the change that has taken place nevertheless is eternal. Therefore, because of the temporal issues that you have to go through each day, your inward man needs to be renewed.

Your spirit is to be strengthened each day to withstand the pressures of life and the temporary difficulties that come and go in your life. Without your spirit being strengthened each day you will not be able to display who you are in Christ. Your inward man has to be strong enough each day to resist temptation, trample over depression, and remain free from anything that would seek to entangle you from displaying the new man. Your spirit being strengthened each day will greatly affect the amount of faith in your heart.

The significance of your faith in putting on the new man is the same as you putting off the old man. It is always through the law of faith that you are able to receive what Christ has freely made available for you through His finished work. The law of works has forever been fulfilled through the cross of Christ. (See Romans 3:27) You are to live and progress through the phases of spiritual development by faith. Paul quoted from the Old Testament stating, *"The just shall live by faith"* (Romans 1:17).

This chapter will cover many of the primary spiritual disciplines that should be in the life of every believer. You will learn the role each one plays in your ability to display the new man. Your ability to put on the new man is always related to your faith and strength within your spirit. It is extremely important that you view your involvement in these spiritual disciplines as methods for your faith to grow and to be strengthened and not through a works mentality. A works mentality seeks to earn what God will only give freely through His grace provided in Jesus Christ. People with a works mentality often think they can manipulate or force God to do something for them by their efforts.

Your efforts without faith are just dead religious works. God does not respond to your efforts but to your faith! Faith pleases God because it opens the door for God to move unhindered in your life. God rewards you when you diligently seek Him because your diligence is the direct result of your faith. In order for you to seek and spend time with God you must "believe that He is" (Hebrews 11:6). Believe that He is hearing you. Believe that He has provisions for you. Believe that He is your answer for your needs!

*"If then you were raised with Christ, **seek those things which are above**, where Christ is, sitting at the right hand of God."*
Colossians 3:1 (Bold Mine.)

Spiritual disciplines are ways for you to seek God and spend time with Him. They are opportunities for your faith to be developed and your spirit to be renewed. Your focus should always be on encountering the Lord through these times. You should not even focus on your spiritual development over encountering the presence of the Lord. Your spiritual development is a by product of spending time with the Lord. Christ is everything you need. Seek Him because He is your strength. Seek Christ, He is your maturity. Seek Christ, He is your victory. Seek Christ, He is your holiness. Remember the motives of your heart matters, even concerning your spiritual disciplines.

This chapter will also teach you basic principles from the Word of God concerning the spiritual disciplines. It is important for you to know the Biblical basis for these primary customs of the family of God. You will always be able to learn more in depth the more you engage in spiritual disciplines. However, what is necessary for formation phase is for you to have an adequate understanding of the biblical basis for the spiritual disciplines.

Through the Word of God

"And have put on the new man who is renewed in knowledge according to the image of Him who created him."
                                                                Colossians 3:10

The new you, your born again spirit, is renewed through knowledge. The word "renewed" means to be strengthened or receive new strength (Strong's #341). Your spirit receives new strength as you read the Word of God. The Word of God provides food and nourishment for you inner man. The Bible speaks of Scriptures as being milk, bread, solid food or meat, and food for you spirit. (See 1 Peter 2:2-3, Matthew 4:4, Hebrews 5:12-14, 1 Timothy 4:6)

It is in the Word of God that you learn who God is. As you behold the Lord you are seeing the image that you have been created after. To see the Lord is to see the new man. It is not just any knowledge that strengthens your spirit each day. It is knowledge of the person Jesus Christ, who is the image you have been created after. Remember, the new man was created in true righteousness and holiness according to the image of God. (See Ephesians 4:24)

"Now the Lord is the Spirit; and where the Spirit of the Lord is, there is liberty. But we all, with unveiled face, beholding as in a mirror the glory of the Lord, are being transformed into the same image from glory to glory, just as by the Spirit of the Lord."
                                                                2 Corinthians 3:17-18

The life of Jesus was built completely according to God's blueprint and you have been predestined to be conformed into the same image. As you spend time beholding the glory of the Lord you are actually seeing who you have been created to be. This is why beholding the glory of the Lord is like looking at your face in a mirror. A mirror reflects the object that is standing in front of it.

Therefore, the life and character of Christ reflects the image of the new creation.

Reading the Word of God is a way for you to fellowship with the Spirit of the Lord. It is then, through the Word of God, that the Lord is able to reveal to you who you have become through the new birth. As you see your reflection in Christ, your soul will be changed. You will be able to display more and more of the new man. From one glory to another glory your life will continue to reflect more and more of the person of Christ.

You must understand that to be in a relationship with Jesus Christ is to be in a relationship with His Spirit. The Lord is the Spirit and it is the Spirit of the Lord that causes you to experience freedom in your life. Your intimacy with the Spirit of the Lord determines if you are able to benefit from the written Word of God. It is impossible for the written Word of God to produce liberty in your life without you fellowshipping with the Holy Spirit. You cannot be resisting the Lordship of the Spirit in your life and at the same time expect to be changed by reading the Word of God.

"For the letter kills, but the Spirit gives life."

2 Corinthians 3:6

The spiritual discipline of reading the word of God is not to be a religious duty but a way for you by faith to fellowship with the Spirit of the Lord. To read the written Word of God without having fellowship with the Lord will not produce life or change in your life. You must constantly remind yourself that Christianity is about a relationship with Christ, not about just following a list of commandments from the written Word of God. You must approach your time reading the Word of God with a sincere heart and with faith. Read the Word of God in faith. Expect to fellowship with the Spirit of the Lord through your time in the Word of God. Listen for the Holy Spirit to apply the written Word of God to your life, your situation, and to your heart.

"So then faith comes by hearing, and hearing by the word of God."

Romans 10:17

It is through the Word of God that your faith can grow and be developed. This verse refers to the spoken or "rhema" word of God (Strong's #4487). It is through the spoken word of God that faith comes into your life. Faith comes when God takes a Scripture and speaks or applies it to your current situation. This means that the development of biblical faith is a product of your time fellowshipping with the Lord. It is impossible for your faith to grow and be developed while you are resisting the Holy Spirit in your life. Each day as you spend time reading the Bible you open up your heart for the Holy Spirit to apply and speak to you through the Scriptures.

Do you see how such an attitude is different than just reading the Bible with a works mentality? You can memorize and learn the Scriptures with your mind and still not increase your faith. It takes hearing the spoken word of God out of your time reading the Word of God for your faith to be developed and strengthened. There are no short cuts to putting on the new man. It is only a product of encountering the Lord through the written Scriptures. No fellowship with the Lord, no strong faith. No strong faith, no displaying the new man. You are to spend time reading the Bible with a mentality that seeks to provide the Lord opportunities to speak into your life and for Christ to be formed in your soul as you fellowship with Him.

"Open my eyes, that I may see wondrous things from Your law."
Psalm 119:18

It takes fellowshipping with the Lord in order for your eyes to be opened. Notice, the Psalmist knew that as he read the Scriptures he was dependant on the Lord to open his eyes. You must fellowship with the Lord as you read the Bible. If not, your eyes will not be opened.

"The entrance of Your words gives light; it gives understanding to the simple."
Psalm 119:130

It is the entrance of the Word of God that gives light. It is as you spend time with the Lord and He speaks to you through the Scriptures that light enters your heart. Faith is to come from your heart and not just from your mind. It is the engrafted word in your soul that makes the difference. The written Word of God must enter into your life through the Spirit of the Lord. This is whey the psalmist said, *"Revive me according to Your word"* and *"Strengthen me according to Your word"* (Psalm 119:25, 28). The written word alone cannot revive or strengthen you. It is as the Spirit of the Lord performs in your life what the Scriptures promise that makes the difference. He was asking the Lord to revive him according to what the Scripture promised. He was asking to be strengthened by the Lord according to what the Scripture had promised. This is the same approach you are to have as you read the written Word of God.

"For the word of God is living and powerful, and sharper than any two-edged sword, piercing even to the division of soul and spirit, and of joints and marrow, and is a discerner of the thoughts and intents of the heart. And there is no creature hidden from His sight, but all things are naked and open to the eyes of Him to whom we must give account."

Hebrews 4:12-13

Jesus Christ is the word of God and there is nothing hidden from His sight. (See John 1:14) It is through the written Scriptures that Jesus exposes the thoughts and intents of your heart. As you read the Word of God in faith while fellowshipping with the Lord, you are able to receive life and power. The Scriptures provide a way for the Lord to speak to you in every circumstance. Each day you can receive life and empowerment from the Lord through the written Word of God. Through the Scriptures the Lord can convict you, teach you, correct you, strengthen you, direct you, and so much more.

"All Scripture is given by inspiration of God, and is profitable for doctrine, for reproof, for correction, for instruction in righteous- ness, that the man of God may be complete, thoroughly equipped for every good work.

2 Timothy 3:16-17

All Scriptures were inspired by God. God influenced the individuals who recorded and wrote the Bible. There is nothing you can encounter in life that God has not already provided a Scripture for. Whatever it may be, God has a Scripture that He can use to speak through and apply to that situation. This is why the Bible is so wonderful. It has been inspired by God to provide a way for Him to communicate with you in all circumstances. God who inspired the Scriptures is the same Lord who then speaks to you through the Scriptures He inspired.

God uses the Scriptures for you profit. As the Spirit of the Lord applies the Scriptures to your life, you are able to be complete for the purposes God has for you in His kingdom. Scripture is used by the Lord to impart doctrine, reproof, correction, and instruction in righteousness in your life. Doctrine refers to receiving teaching or instruction. Reproof refers to having your convictions and things in your life tested or evaluated by the Lord. Correction refers to bringing your life and character back in line with God's blueprint for you. Instruction in righteousness refers to nurture through discipline that trains you to demonstrate through your conduct a life that reflects being in right standing with God. These purposes, that the Lord uses the Scripture for in your life, provide a great picture of the process of putting off the old man and putting on the new man.

*"That you may learn in **us not to think beyond what is written**, that none of you may be puffed up on behalf of one against the other."*
1 Corinthians 4:6 (Bold Mine.)

The written Word of God sets the boundaries for truth and the will of God for your life. Anything that contradicts Scripture is a lie. Jesus said, *"Sanctify them by Your truth, Your word is truth"* (John 17:17). Scripture provides a guideline for what you are to think about. You are not to think beyond what Scripture teaches.

If you think beyond what is written in Scripture it will lead to you becoming puffed up and set against another person. When you think beyond what is written you enter the realm of speculation and personal opinion. This is when you begin to hear people say, "Well I believe" or "I think" or "I feel" instead of "It is written." Jesus answered the voice of Satan every time with "It is written" not "I believe or feel." To think beyond what is written will cause pride and divide you from fellowshipping with other believers.

"Finally, brethren, farewell. Become complete. Be of good comfort, **be of one mind,** *live in peace; and the God of love and peace will be with you."*

2 Corinthians 13:11 (Bold Mine.)

Paul over and over again reminded believers in every city to be of one mind. (See Philippians 1:27, 2:2, 4:2; 1 Corinthians 1:10; Romans 15:6) It is the written Word of God that causes believers to be of one mind and have unity. The written Word of God becomes the sure foundation for what is true. The written Word gives you the ability to read, know, and be assured of what is true and right. You come across a person who says, "I believe this or that," then you can take them to the written word and show them it is contrary to what is written. Thank God you have a clear standard for truth and God's will for your life.

"Beware lest anyone cheat you through philosophy and empty deceit, according to the tradition of men, according to the basic principles of the world, and not according to Christ."

Colossians 2:8

Do not be cheated by thinking outside what is written in the Bible. Many people fall captive to deceiving spirits and doctrines of demons because they begin to listen or believe ideas that go beyond what is written in Scripture. (See 1 Timothy 4:1) The written Word of God is always to be your guideline to judge something. It is by the written Word of God that you are to *"test all things; hold fast what is good"* (1 Thessalonians 5:22).

Beloved, do not believe every spirit, but test the spirits, whether they are of God; because many false prophets have gone out into the world."

1 John 4:1

The written Word of God is the test. If something goes beyond what is written in Scripture then it is not from the Spirit of God. It is impossible for God to contradict what He has already spoken in the Bible. Thinking within what is written in Scripture is a very important guideline concerning dreams, visions, and other experiences. The Bible exhorts you not to focus and think upon experiences but upon what is written in the Scriptures. This is what Paul meant when he said, *"Let no one cheat you of your reward, taking delight in false humility and worship of angels, intruding into those things which he has not seen, vainly puffed up by his fleshly mind, and not holding fast to the Head"* (Colossians 2:18-19).

When you spend time reading the Bible it helps to guard your mind from false teachings and mentalities that are prevalent in the society all around you. This is one of the major importances of memorizing and learning Scripture. As you grow in your knowledge of the Bible it helps to guard your mind from false ideas, voices, spirits, and teachings. Remember, growing in biblical knowledge does not mean you are necessarily maturing in Christ. However, that in no way diminishes the importance of growing in the knowledge of Scripture. There must be a place for both in your life.

You should actively engage in memorizing Scripture. Such learning builds a fortress of protection around you mind. Peter told you to "gird up the loins of your mind, be sober" (1 Peter 1:13). You must deliberately protect your mind with studying and learning the written Word of God. There is to be a balance of maturing in Christ while growing in biblical knowledge. You are not to choose between one or the other, but to allow both of them to have the place the Bible says they should have in your life.

"Not to be soon shaken in mind or troubled, either by spirit or by word or by letter, as if from us."

2 Thessalonians 2:2

Growing in your knowledge of the Bible helps to protect you from being shaken in your mind. Knowledge of the written Word provides protection for your mind. Notice, Paul told the Thessalonians not to be shaken in mind or troubled by anything that is contrary to the written Word of God. The written Word of God makes you wise and provides assurance to withstand any spirit, word, letter, or idea that is contrary to truth. (See 2 Timothy 3:14-15)

"And you shall love the Lord your God with all your heart, with all your soul, with all your mind, and with all your strength."

Mark 12:30

Through Singing

"Be filled with the Spirit, speaking to one another in psalms and hymns and spiritual songs, singing and making melody in your heart to the Lord, giving thanks always for all things to God the Father in the name of our Lord Jesus Christ."

Ephesians 5:18-20

You can be filled with the Holy Spirit as you spend time singing and worshiping the Lord with your mouth. Through your singing you are to praise and give thanks to the Lord. As you are filled with the Spirit of God your faith will be strengthened. Your inner man will receive power that will enable you to walk in the spirit instead of having your flesh dictating your life. Singing to the Lord allows your mind to become focused on Him instead of your situations, circumstances, or failures.

"Serve the Lord with gladness; come before His presence with singing. Enter into His gates with thanksgiving, and into His courts with praise. Be thankful to Him, and bless His name."

Psalm 100:2, 4

You are to approach God with singing. You are to enter into His presence with thanksgiving and praise. As you spend time with the Lord each day you are to approach Him through singing which includes thanksgiving, praise, and blessing or worship. Thanksgiving is simply to give thanks to the Lord for what He has done in your life. It is rooted in the blessings you have received from God.

Thanksgiving is how you are to respond to what God did. Praise is to honor the Lord. Praise is responding to the Lord, His greatness, and His marvelous ways. Praise is rooted in who the Lord has been to you. Then the more you begin to encounter His manifest presence, it is to lead you to bless or worship His name. Blessing His name is to worship the Lord for who He is. This form of singing is rooted in the nature and personhood of God. This means that it is not rooted in anything pertaining to your life but is entirely focused on God.

"He is your praise, and He is your God, who has done for you these great and awesome things which your eyes have seen."

Deuteronomy 10:21

Jesus is your praise. He is the reason for you to praise with your mouth. As you sing to the Lord you begin to focus on His greatness and the many wonderful blessings He has given you. The more you praise Him for what He has done in your life the more you become aware of the many blessings you have already received from Him. Praise will always lead to more praise. Your faith will be strengthened as your recall and thank the Lord for all the many things He has already done in your life.

"The garment of praise for the spirit of heaviness."

Isaiah 61:3

There are many times you will get up in the morning and just feel heavy. Some mornings you might not feel the joy of your salvation, or victorious, or that God is with you. However, each day you are faced with a choice of whether or not you will put on the garment of praise. Singing to the Lord is an act of your will. David said, *"I will be glad and rejoice in You; I will sing praise to Your name, O Most High"* (Psalm 9:2). It is a choice to put on the garment of praise. Since Jesus is your praise, when you praise Him you are choosing to put on His presence like a garment.

"But You are holy, enthroned in the praises of Israel."

Psalm 22:3

When you praise the Lord you are making a place for His mani-fest presence to come and dwell. By focusing on the goodness of the Lord through your praise, instead of your problems, you are acknowledging that He is Lord over every circumstance. You are inviting His presence to come and sit upon your problems. Paul said, *"And the God of peace will crush Satan under your feet shortly"* (Romans 16:20). Whether you have to stand against the enemy or you are facing the common trials of life, your praise opens the door for the Lord to work on your behalf.

*"And when he had consulted with the people, he appointed those who should sing to the Lord, and who should praise the beauty of holiness, as they went out before the army and were saying: 'Praise the Lord, for His mercy endures forever.' Now **when they began to sing and to praise, the Lord set ambushes** against the people of Ammon, Moab, and Mount Seir, who had come against Judah; and they were defeated."*

2 Chronicles 20:21-22 (Bold Mine.)

As you praise the Lord, He defeats the plans of the enemy in your life. The Lord is your victory and deliverance. David said, *"The battle is the Lord's"* (1 Samuel 17:47). When you praise the Lord you are acknowledging His power and ability to defeat the enemy. Praising the Lord is a weapon. Praise binds the power of Satan. (See Psalm 149:5-8) Trust in the power of the Lord as you praise Him each day.

"Why are you cast down, O my soul? And why are you disquieted within me? Hope in God; for I shall yet praise Him, the help of my countenance and my God."

Psalm 42:11

Your soul or mind determines what you feel. You can get up each day and begin to dwell on your circumstances, or whatever it may be, and continue to experience your soul being down cast. Or you can do like the psalmist did and put your hope in God by praising Him. When you choose to minister to the Lord with praise you are demonstrating faith. As you reflect on His goodness your soul will begin to feel up lifted from the presence of the Lord.

"My heart is steadfast, O God, my heart is steadfast; I will sing and give praise."

Psalm 57:7

Praising the Lord helps your heart to be steadfast each day. As you praise the Lord you are submitting your heart to His Lordship. You are making a place in your heart for Christ to be enthroned. Your heart is established to obey and follow the Lord that day. As you praise Him, and thankfulness fills your heart, you desire to live worthy of Him each moment of the day. Your love for Christ is renewed as you acknowledge the many ways He has already demonstrated His love for you. Your heart must have already determined what it desires before the moment of temptation. Praising the Lord is a way for your heart to become steadfast in obeying the Lord. Your decision in the moment of temptation will be determined by what your heart was set on that morning.

"Therefore by Him let us continually offer the sacrifice of praise to God, that is, the fruit of our lips, giving thanks to His name."

Hebrews 13:15

When you make the choice to praise God it is an offering to God. Praise is to be the fruit of your lips. You are to praise the Lord with other believers in the congregation. The psalmist said, *"I will praise the Lord with my whole heart, in the assembly of the upright and in the congregation"* (Psalm 111:1). Singing and praising the Lord is to be a lifestyle for you. You should not just praise the Lord when you are gathered together with other believers but also on your own throughout each day

"I will bless the Lord at all times; His praise shall continually be in my mouth. My soul shall make its boast in the Lord."

Psalm 34:1-2

You are to bless or worship the Lord at all times. One way to worship the Lord at all times is for His praise to be continually in your mouth. He is worthy of receiving continual praise from your lips. His praise should be found continually in your mouth. As you praise the Lord your soul is boasting of the goodness of the Lord. You are boasting of all the wonderful things He has done in your life. You are declaring all of the benefits that He has given you.

The highest level of singing is when you worship or bless Him not for what He has done for you but because of who He is. This type of singing is focused on the nature of God instead of on His acts or deeds. This is when you bless Him because He is holy. You bless Him because He is righteous. You bless Him because He is love. You bless Him because you are commanded to. You give reverence to Him. The motivation and focus of this type of singing is completely rooted in God.

"Indeed it came to pass, when the trumpeters and singers were as one, to make one sound to be heard in praising and thanking the Lord, and when they lifted up their voice with the trumpets and cymbals and instruments of music, and praised the Lord, saying: 'For He is good, for His mercy endures forever,' that the house, the house of the Lord, was filled with a cloud, so that the priest could not continue (stand) ministering because of the cloud; for the glory of the Lord filled the house of God."
2 Chronicles 5:13-14 (Parenthesis Mine. NKJV Marginal Reading)

This level of singing often times leads to such an overwhelming manifestation of the glory or presence of the Lord. As the people were in one accord, focusing on the nature of the Lord the glory of God manifested. The manifest presence of God was so strong that the priest could not continue standing to minister because God had filled His house. You now are the house or temple of God. There may be times when His manifest presence is so strong in your life that you will be unable to stand. Remember all forms of singing have a place in your daily life and understand that singing is only one form of worship.

In the Old Testament there was a special group of people called the Levites who were set apart. The Scripture states they would *"stand every morning to thank and praise the Lord, and likewise at evening"* (1 Chronicles 23:30). How much more should you and I, who live after the finished work of Christ, continually have His praise in our mouth? Every morning put on Christ through your praise and continually be filled with His Spirit by singing unto the Lord. Paul said, *"Rejoice always"* (1 Thessalonians 5:16).

You can praise by clapping your hands. (See Psalm 47:1) You can praise with a shout. (See Psalm 95:1-2) You can praise Him by dancing. (See Psalm 149:3) You can praise Him with musical instruments. (See Psalm 150:4) You can praise Him with crying. (See Psalm 57:2) You can praise Him with uplifted hands. (See Psalm 134:2) You can praise Him with laughter. (See Psalm 126:2) You can praise Him with a joyful noise. (See Psalm 149:5) You can praise Him by bowing and kneeling. (See Psalm 95:6) You can praise Him with other tongues as the Spirit provides. (See Acts 10:46) You can sing by the Spirit or in tongues. (See 1 Corinthians 14:14-15) You can praise with a new song. (See Psalm 96:1) You can praise with a hymn or a psalm. (See Colossians 3:16)

"Blessed are those who dwell in Your house; they will still be praising You. Blessed is the man whose strength is in You, whose heart is set on pilgrimage. They go from strength to strength; each one appears before God in Zion."

Psalm 84:4-5, 7

Through Prayer

"Set your mind on things above, not on things on the earth."

Colossians 3:2

Prayer is one of the ways that you set your mind upon things above. It is through prayer that you are able to cast the earthly issues in your life before the Lord and become mindful of His resources and provisions. Prayer is simply talking and communicating with

God. Through Jesus you have access by the Holy Spirit to come into the Father's presence. (See Ephesians 2:18)

"For we do not have a High Priest who cannot sympathize with our weaknesses, but was in all points tempted as we are, yet without sin. Let us therefore come boldly to the throne of grace, that we may obtain mercy and find grace to help in time of need."

Hebrews 4:15-16

Jesus understands the weakness of your flesh. He understands the temptations you face each day. He was tempted in every way possible and yet remained sinless. Christ navigated successfully through every temptation He encountered. Through His experience of continual victory He is able to provide you with help for the temptations each day. It is through the finished work of Christ that you are able to come boldly before the throne of God. You are the righteousness of God and are able to approach God free from fear, condemnation, or guilt. Through Christ you have the right to come into God's presence and speak with Him.

You must understand that the throne of God is a throne of grace. Grace is God doing for you what you cannot do on your own. Grace is enablement that is provided by God. Grace is God enabling you to resist the flesh and temptation. Grace is God strengthening your spirit man. God's grace is to be more than just something you experienced when you were born again. God's grace is continually available for you life. God's grace is the strength and power you need for each day to experience victory over temptations. To receive God's grace is to receive the influence of His Spirit in your life.

You have access each day to come before the throne of God to receive grace or enablement that will help you in your time of need. The grace of God is sufficient for whatever you will face each day. (See 2 Corinthians 12:9) You need to position yourself each morning in prayer to receive the available grace that God has for you. David said, *"O God, You are my God; early will I seek You"* (Psalm 63:1). Prayer prepares your spirit for the day. As you fellowship with the Lord you are to draw from His strength and grace.

"Most assuredly, I say to you, whatever you ask the Father in My name He will give you."

John 16:23

You are to speak out loud or ask the Father when you pray. And it is in the name of Jesus that you are to ask the Father to answer your prayers. It is the name of Jesus that the Father responds to. *"Every spiritual blessing in the heavenly places"* has been made available for you through the finished work of Jesus Christ (Ephesians 1:3). The authority we have to receive these blessings and provisions is found in the name of Jesus. You must understand that self-pity, loud prayers, long prayers, or tears is not what causes God to answer your request. It is only by asking the Father in the name of Jesus that causes Him to respond to your prayers.

"Therefore I say to you, whatever things you ask when you pray, believe that you receive them, and you will have them."

Mark 11:24

God responds to your faith and to the authority of the name of Jesus. You do not have to try and manipulate God to answer your prayers. It is the Father's good pleasure for you to experience the provisions of the kingdom of God. (See Luke 12:32) God always desires for you to receive the things that He has freely given you in Christ. God does not want to withhold any good thing from you. You are to pray to the Father by faith and in the authority of the name of Jesus.

"For a testament is in force after men are dead, since it has no power at all while the testator lives. Therefore not even the first covenant was dedicated without blood."

Hebrews 9:17-18

When a person dies here on earth they leave a will or testament of what they desire to do with their belongings. The same was true for when Christ died. Through the blood and death of Jesus Christ, the Father established a new will or testament for mankind and the earth. The New Testament Scriptures reveal what Christ has given you and what belongs to you as a child of God. These Scriptures testify to what God willed for you to have and experience. Jesus shed His blood and died for you so that you could experience God's will for your life.

"What then shall we say to these things? If God is for us, who can be against us? He who did not spare His own Son, but delivered Him up for us all, how shall He not with Him also freely give us all things?"

Romans 8:31-32

God was willing to allow Christ to die. It was through this death that God made available to you the resources of heaven or the kingdom of God. Do you see the heart God has for you? If God allowed Christ to suffer so that He could establish a covenant or new will with you why would He then be reluctant for you to experience what He has for you? God is not reluctant. God desires to answer your prayers. God desires for you to spend time talking with Him. The fact that God did not spare His own Son demonstrates the fact that God wants to freely give you all that His will or word testifies about.

"Where do wars and fights come from among you? Do they not come from your desires for pleasure that war in your members? You lust and do not have. You murder and covet and cannot obtain. You fight and war. Yet you do not have because you do no ask."

James 4:1-2

You do not have to depend on the methods of your flesh to get what you need or desire. It is when you doubt the willingness of God to give you what Jesus left for you in His will that you begin to depend on your own ability or strength. Such wrong attitudes and perceptions keep you from boldly coming before the throne of grace to ask the Father. God is a perfect Father. (See Matthew 5:48) There are many things that God has provided for you that you will not experience if you remain unwilling to ask Him for them. How you perceive the Father will determine your reaction in your times of need. What have you read in "Jesus' will" that you do not have because you have been unwilling, scared, or hesitant to ask for?

"You ask and do not receive, because you ask amiss, that you may spend it on your pleasures."

James 4:3

There will also be times that you do not receive something even though you have asked the Father for it. The Father only responds to your faith when you ask in the name of Jesus. To ask in the name of Jesus means you are asking for the Father to do something for the sake of or on behalf of Jesus Christ. Remember the heart matters. When you ask for things out of selfishness or only for self-pleasure you are not asking in Jesus name. This would be asking the Father for something only because it benefits you or asking in your name. You are then just asking amiss or in a wrong manner.

What you ask the Father for is always to be for the sake of Christ. This means if you are asking for deliverance in your life you are to ask so that Christ will be magnified through it and as a result of it. To ask for something for Jesus' sake is to desire for Him to benefit from it. This means that through the Father answering your request it would result in Christ receiving glory, praise, and worship.

"Beloved, if our heart does not condemn us, we have confidence toward God. And whatever we ask we receive from Him, because we keep His commandments and do those things that are pleasing in His sight."

1 John 3:21-22

You are able to have confidence toward God when your heart does not condemn you. When there is selfishness or unforgiveness in your heart, your heart will condemn you. Jesus said, *"And whenever you stand praying, if you have anything against anyone, forgive him, that your Father in heaven may also forgive you your trespasses"* (Mark 11:25). If you are praying while holding on to bitterness, anger, or unforgiveness, it will keep you from receiving your requests. When you are not asking for the sake of Jesus but selfishly your heart will let you know. However, you can have confidence toward God when your heart does not condemn you.

"Now this is the confidence that we have in Him, that if we ask anything according to His will, He hears us. And if we know that He hears us, whatever we ask, we know that we have the petitions that we have asked of Him."

1 John 5:14-15

The basis for our confidence in prayer is always the will or testament of God. In the Scriptures we are able to read the will that Jesus left us after His death. Through finding God's will in the Word of God you are able to have confidence when you pray. You can have assurance that what you are asking for has been provided for you through the finished work of Christ. You can be confident that God desires to give you what you are asking for because you read it in His will. The result is you are able to boldly come before the throne of grace to make you petitions known according to the Word of God. *"Therefore, brethren, having boldness to enter the Holiest by the blood of Jesus"* (Hebrews 10:19).

Prayer comes out of your fellowship with the Lord through the Word of God and singing. In order for you to pray in faith you must know the will of God. This is another reason that spending time reading the Word of God is so valuable. Without knowing the Word of God you will not know what God has provided for you through the death of Jesus Christ. You can read and meditate on the promises of God until faith fills your heart to come before God and make your request known. Prayer is not to be wishful thinking. Prayer is established on the Word of God. You are ready to make your request known only when you have confidence that God will hear what you ask Him. Having this type of confidence is another way of expressing that you possess faith to receive God's will. (See Hebrews 11:1).

"Continue earnestly in prayer, being vigilant in it with thanksgiving."

Colossians 4:2

You must purpose in your heart to continue to pray. Prayer is to be filled with thanksgiving. As you spend time with God you will have moments of prayer and moments of thanksgiving that may lead to praise. Remember, spiritual disciplines are ways that you spend time fellowshipping with God. As with any relationship there are going to be times of spontaneity and times of structure. Jesus taught the disciples to pray by giving them a model prayer. (See Matthew 6:9-13) For centuries believers have also used the many psalms to provide a structure to their prayers. You should also pray earnestly with your heart as you face specific situations in life and throughout each day. There is a place for both structured prayers and free flowing heart felt prayers.

It is important to spend time fellowshipping with God in the morning in order to put on the new man. However, like worshipping the Lord with your praise, you should also pray throughout the day. Paul said, *"Rejoice always, pray without ceasing"* (1 Thessalonians 5:16-17). You are also to pray or communicate with God in your heart throughout the day.

"You will keep him in perfect peace, whose mind is stayed on You, because he trusts in You. Trust in the Lord forever, for in Yah, the Lord, is everlasting strength."

Isaiah 26:3-4

As you pray your mind is stayed or fixed on the Lord. This is keeping your heart and attitude trusting in the Lord in every moment of the day. Such communion with the Lord will keep you in perfect peace. This peace will guard your life each day.

"Be anxious for nothing, but in everything by prayer and supplication, with thanksgiving, let your requests be made known to God; and the peace of God, which surpasses all understanding, will guard your hearts and minds through Christ Jesus."

Philippians 4:6-7

Spending time with the Lord in prayer allows the peace of God to rule in your heart and mind. It is in prayer that you are able to rid your heart of anxiety and worry. The peace of God can fill your life and give you a calm assurance that surpasses your own understanding that everything is going to be all right. Such peace will help protect you in the moments of temptation. It will also provide you with continual strength as you draw from His presence on the inside of you.

"He gives power to the weak, and to those who have no might He increases strength. But those who wait on the Lord shall renew their strength; they shall mount up with wings like eagles, they shall run and not be weary, they shall walk and not faint."

Isaiah 40:29, 31

When you seek God in prayer you are waiting on the Lord. This time of fellowshipping with the Lord causes the strength of your inward man to be renewed. This deposit of strength will allow you to walk worthy of the Lord each day. You can run the race of being conformed to the image of Christ and not be weary. You will also be able, in the future, to take your place of authority and purpose in the kingdom of God. This is why prayer plays such an important role in your ability to display the new man in your life. You are able to encounter the presence of the Lord and be strengthened in your inward man.

There are different kinds of prayer. Paul said, *"Take...the sword of the Spirit, which is the word of God; praying always with all prayer and supplication in the Spirit"* (Ephesians 6:17-18). Supplication refers to earnest and heartfelt passion in your prayers. When you make your requests known to God you are petitioning in prayer. This is what is called the prayer of petition. (See 1 John 5:14-15) There is also the prayer of faith which is closely related to the prayer of petition. (See James 5:15 and Mark 11:23-24) Other times you may intercede or pray for God's will on behalf of another person. (See 1 Timothy 2:1-2) The prayer of consecration is when you are not sure of what God's will is. (See Luke 22:42) There is the prayer of commitment when you cast your cares and concerns on the Lord. (See 1 Peter 5:7) There is the prayer of agreement with other believers. (See Matthew 18:18-20) There is praying in the spirit or in tongues. (See 1 Corinthians 14:14-15) There is corporate prayer or praying in one accord with a group of believers in your local church. (See Acts 4:23-24)

"And when you pray, you shall not be like the hypocrites. For they love to pray standing in the synagogues and on the corners of the streets, that they may be seen by men. Assuredly, I say to you, they have their reward. But you, when you pray, go into your room, and when you have shut the door, pray to your Father who is in the secret place; and your Father who sees in secret will reward you openly. And when you pray, do not use vain repetitions as the heathen do. For they think that they will be heard for their many words. Therefore do not be like them. For your Father knows the things you have need of before you ask Him."

Matthew 6:5-8

Through Confession

"That the sharing of your faith may become effective by the acknowl-edgement of every good thing which is in you in Christ Jesus."

Philemon 1:6

Basically confession is acknowledgement. When you confess God's Word you are agreeing with Him. You are choosing to acknowledge that the Word of God is true despite any circumstances or situations. As you acknowledge every good thing that you have been given in Christ, your faith will become effective. The word effective means to become active, operative, or powerful (Strong's # 1756). Confessing the Word of God will cause your faith to be ener-gized. The more your faith is energized the more you will actively experience and live out the truth that you are confessing.

Faith comes by hearing the Word of God. As you confess the Word of God you are putting yourself in a position for your faith to grow and be strengthened. You must understand that your tongue is linked to your heart. The Scripture states, *"If anyone...does not bridle his tongue but deceives his own heart"* (James 1:26). However, when you confess the Word of God, you are guarding your heart from deception.

"For with the heart one believes unto righteousness, and with the mouth confession is made unto salvation."

Romans 10:10

When you believed the gospel of Jesus Christ in your heart it led you to confess Him as your Lord and Savior. It was when you believed in your heart and confessed with your mouth that you were able to experience the salvation Christ has made possible for you. This also is a principle for your spiritual journey. Your confession is to be a result of your faith. Confessing is not a religious work but is to be a demonstration of your faith in the Word of God.

"And since we have the same spirit of faith, according to what is written, 'I believed and therefore I spoke,' we also believe and therefore speak."

2 Corinthians 4:13

A manifestation of the spirit of faith is speaking the Word of God. This is why confession is a direct result of your times in the written Word and singing. As you spend time learning and acknowledging what God has given you in Christ, faith fills your heart. As your heart is filled with the spirit of faith it will led you to confess what you have come to believe. This is why confessing the Word of God is an aspect of prayer. Your confidence in prayer comes from the written Word of God and this will lead you to confess the promises of God for your life.

"For He Himself has said, 'I will never leave you nor forsake you.' So we may boldly say: 'The Lord is my helper; I will not fear, what can man do to me?'"

Hebrews 13:5-6

When the writer of Hebrews focused on the promise of God it led him to boldly declare the Word of God over his situation. Your time with the Lord each morning should lead you to declaring the promises of God over your life. You should remind yourself every morning that you are a new creation in Christ. The old you was crucified, died, and buried never to rise again. Remind yourself that all things regarding your identity have become new in Christ. You are a child of God and have been created in true righteousness and holiness. Such acknowledgment will strengthen your inner man and enable you to put on the new man each day. Go ahead and declare the good news over your life each day. Acknowledge every good thing you have in Christ. Acknowledge what you have for your family. Acknowledge what you have to live godly. Acknowledge what you have to direct your steps. Acknowledge what you have for your future. Acknowledge what you have for your finances.

"Whoever guards his mouth and tongue keeps his soul from troubles."

Proverbs 21:23

By simply guarding your mouth and what your tongue speaks you are able to keep your soul from some troubles. Remember, your soul determines what you feel or experience each day. Confessing the Word of God will keep your soul from unnecessary troubles. The Word of God is active and powerful. As you speak the Word of God over your circumstances it has the power to bring everything in line with the will of God.

When you read the Psalms you will notice time and time again how they end declaring the will of God over their situations. Confession should never seek to deny the circumstances or what you may be feeling or experiencing. However, it does seek to speak the promises and will of God over those things. The psalmist never denied their reality or feelings but they always ended up placing their experience under the authority of the Word of God. Feelings and situations are temporary but the Word of God contains the unchangeable truths for your life. You should in faith profess what you have in Christ. It is your faith in the Word of God that activates and releases the power of God to change whatever you may be facing.

"Death and life are in the power of the tongue, and those who love it will eat its fruit."

Proverbs 18:21

You have already learned that one sin that will keep you from reaching your personal promise land is complaining. This is because the tongue has great power in your life. It has the ability to release death or life over your situations and experience. You will eat the fruit of what you speak. Those who complained in the wilderness attracted the destroyer. (See 1 Corinthians 10:10) Complaining will never release the power to bring any circumstance in line with the will of God. To complain is to use the power of the tongue to release more death or destruction over what you are going through. This is why confessing the Word of God is so powerful. When you allow the capability of your tongue to release God to come and work on your behalf eventually you will eat the fruit of what God's Word will produce.

"For as the rain comes down, and the snow from heaven, and do not return there, but water the earth, and make it bring forth and bud. That it may give seed to the sower and bread to the eater, so shall My word be that goes forth from My mouth; it shall not return to Me void, but it shall accomplish what I please, and it shall prosper in the thing for which I sent it."

Isaiah 55:10-11

The Word of God has been provided for you to continually confess what you have been freely given. The Word of God is like seed. It has the power to produce what it was given for. When you confess the Word of God in faith you are using the seed that God has provided for you. If you don't like what you are experiencing in life then you can start sowing God's seed to receive a new crop. God's word has the power to accomplish what it was given for. Your tongue has the power to sow God's seed into your life and circumstances. If you will hold fast to your confession of the Word of God you will eventually reap what the Word says. (See Galatians 6:9)

For all the promises of God in Him are Yes, and in Him Amen, to the glory of God through us."

2 Corinthians 1:20

Speak and pray the Word of God over your life each day. The promises of God are yes for your life. By your confessions you can sow the Word of God and therefore determine some of your future harvest or experience in life. The promises of God are sure and amen. To "amen" something you hear is to confess that it is true and faithful. You are agreeing by faith to what you heard and that you desire it to be fulfilled as stated. Confess the promises of God over your life each day as you spend time in His presence and then go about displaying the new man you have become in Christ.

Through Giving

"And remember the words of the Lord Jesus, that He said, 'It is more blessed to give than to receive.'"

Acts 20:35

Jesus spoke on giving. He expected every believer to give. In Matthew 6:2 Jesus spoke about, *"When you give or do a charitable deed."* Giving is a manifestation of the new man. This is because God is a giver and you have been created according to His image through the new birth. God so loved the world that He gave Jesus. (See John 3:16) Therefore, when you give with the right motives you are putting on display the new man you have become in Christ.

When you understand and receive what God has freely given you through Christ it helps establish you in the grace of giving. Giving is considered a grace because it is a result of the work of God in your life. God, through Christ, enables you to give and to do so with a giving heart. (See 2 Corinthians 8:7) Giving is related to more than just your money. It is related to any type of giving. You may be giving food, clothes, shelter or giving love, mercy, and forgiveness. All giving done with a right heart is a display of the new man.

"No one can serve two masters; for either he will hate the one and love the other, or else he will be loyal to the one and despise the other. You cannot serve God and mammon (riches).

Matthew 6:24 (Parenthesis Mine. NKJV Marginal Reading)

The magnitude of you faithfully giving of your money to the Lord can be seen in this verse. Jesus said it is impossible to serve both God and money. You are not able to faithfully serve two masters. At some point you will only be able to be loyal to one over the other. It is impossible for you to love money and at the same time faithfully love and obey God. This is one of the reasons so many people get angry over the topic of money. When you teach on money and giving you are attacking their god.

Money has a strange ability to control the hearts of people. As you give faithfully you are protecting your heart from falling captive to the love of money. The love of money has led to many evils outside and inside the church. When a person begins to serve money instead of God, their flesh is capable of doing all kinds of evil. The apostle Paul also warned of this very thing.

"For the love of money is a root of all kinds of evil, for which some have strayed from the faith in their greediness, and pierced themselves through with many sorrows."

1 Timothy 6:10

The Bible takes the topic of money serious. Why? Because the love of money causes one to stray from the faith. You cannot serve both money and God. People with money are commanded *"not to be haughty nor to trust in uncertain riches but in the living God"* (1 Timothy 6:18). If you allow it, money has the capability to draw your heart away from God. Giving is an expression of the character of Christ. When you read through the Bible and the life of Jesus you see continually the giving nature of God.

Your attitude toward money is a reflection of your heart. This is the clear teaching of Scripture. The reason you must understand what the Bible teaches concerning money is because without it you will be unable to display an aspect of Christ being formed in you. A record of how you spend your money is a record of the condition of your heart. Jesus said, *"For where your treasure is, there your heart will be also"* (Matthew 6:21). The Bible teaches that you are to be a faithful steward with the money that God entrusts into your hands.

"And so it was that when he returned, having received the kingdom, he then commanded these servants, to whom he had given the money, to be called to him, that he might know how much every man had gained by trading."

Luke 19:15

The money you have has come from God. David said, *"For all things come from You, and of Your own we have given You"* (1 Chronicles 29:14). He has blessed you with the ability to work and to make money. The Scripture also states, *"The earth is the Lord's, and all it fullness"* (Psalm 24:1). This world and the things in the world belong to God. Jesus is Lord and King over all the earth. His Kingdom reigns over everything, even your pocketbook. You will give an account to the Lord for how you have handled the money that He has given you. This is the point of the story there in Luke chapter nineteen. Jesus also said in another place concerning the topic of money, *"Therefore if you have not been faithful in the unrighteous mammon, who will commit to your trust the true riches"* (Luke 16:11)?

How you handle the money God has given you is a matter of your heart. It is a matter of your character. When you demonstrate responsibility and faithfulness with your money it proves that you will act the same with other things and in other circumstances. *"He who is faithful in what is least is faithful also in much; and he who is unjust in what is least is unjust also in much"* (Luke 16:10). This principle is always true because it flows from your character. Faithfully giving money is a result of having Christ-formed character.

There are three types of giving that involve your money: the tithe, the offering, and giving to the poor. The tithe is giving ten percent of all your income to your local congregation. Let me start by saying that the tithe is for the New Testament church. The principle of the tithe was established by God four hundred and thirty years before God gave the Old Covenant or Law of Moses. (See Galatians 3:17)

"For this Melchizedek, king of Salem, priest of the Most High God, who met Abraham returned from the slaughter of the kings and blessed him, to whom also Abraham gave a tenth part of all..."

Hebrews 7:1-2

Abraham tithed hundreds of years before the Old Covenant. Abraham gave his tithes in obedience to God. A priest of God named Melchizedek was the person who received them. Melchizedek was a type or representation of Christ. (See Hebrews 7:15) You must understand that when you give the tithe you are giving it to God even though a person collects it from you. The Scripture states, *"Here mortal men receive tithes"* (Hebrews 7:8).

One of the points of this chapter in Hebrews is to demonstrate how the Levites, who were required by God to receive the tithes under the Old Covenant, tithed through Abraham to this person named Melchizedek who obviously represented something greater than the Law of Moses. Therefore, how much more should we tithe to Christ and His kingdom. The tithe is a principle that God established throughout the Old Testament books of the Bible. This is why there are not many verses in the letters written to the church that deal with the topic of tithing. It is the same as the topic of using musical instruments to worship God. The principle was already established in the Old Testament Scriptures and therefore the letters written to the church did not need to present and cover the topic in depth.

"Will a man rob God? Yet you have robbed Me!' But you say, 'In what way have we robbed You?' 'In tithes and offerings. You are cursed with a curse, for you have robbed Me, even this whole nation. Bring all the tithes into the storehouse, that there may be food in My house, and try Me now in this,' says the Lord of hosts; 'and all nations will call you blessed, for you will be a delightful land,' says the Lord of hosts."

Malachi 3:8-12

You rob God if you withhold the tithe. God has given you every dollar you have but He allows you to keep ninety percent of it. The other ten percent or tithe however, you are commanded to give back to the Lord. The tithe is considered a devoted or holy thing. (See Joshua 7:11) If you keep money that is to be devoted to the Lord it will not benefit you but will become a curse instead. Tithes are to be given to the storehouse or your local assembly. It is the tithe that allows the church to be able and fulfill its purpose on the earth.

Any money you give above your tithe is called on offering. There are both freewill offerings and commanded offerings. A commanded offering is when the Lord leads and speaks to you to give money to something that is connected to God's body or church. The nation of Israel had also robbed God by not obeying His voice when He spoke to them to give offerings. You must not resist God when He desires to channel the money He has given you for another purpose of His.

"But this I say: He who sows sparingly will also reap sparingly, and he who sows bountifully will also reap bountifully. So let each one give as he purposes in his heart, not grudgingly or of necessity; for God loves a cheerful giver."

2 Corinthians 9:6-7

The principles in the above verses relate to a free will offering. (See also Leviticus 1:3, 19:5) Notice it says you can give as you purpose in your heart. The tithe is commanded but a free will offering is something you give freely from the desires in your heart. A free will offering should be given not out of necessity, obligation, or grudgingly. You are to give a free will offering cheerfully. If you give a small free will offering you will reap a small harvest. If you give a large free will offering you will reap a large harvest. The amount of financial blessings that will come from a free will offering is determined by the amount sown. You should be *"ready to give, willing to share"* at all times (1 Timothy 6:18).

"If there is among you a poor man of your brethren, within any of the gates in your land which the Lord your God is giving you, you shall not harden your heart nor shut your hand from your poor

brother, but you shall open your hand wide to him and willingly lend him sufficient for his need, whatever he needs… You shall surely give to him, and your heart should not be grieved when you give to him, because for this thing the Lord your God will bless you in all your works and in all to which you put your hand. For the poor will never cease from the land; therefore I command you, saying, 'You shall open your hand wide to your brother, to your poor and your needy, in your land.'"

Deuteronomy 15:7-8, 10-11

The other way you should give with your money is to the poor. You are to open your hand wide and willingly to those in need. The Bible says that in this age, the poor will always be among us. You are commanded to use your money to help the poor. Your heart should be open and sensitive to the poor around you. This is one of the reasons we are commanded to work. *"Rather let him labor, working with his hands what is good, that he may have something to give him who has need"* (Ephesians 4:28). Your money is to be used to honor God and bless those in need.

"He who oppresses the poor reproaches his Maker, but he who honors Him has mercy on the needy."

Proverbs 14:31

"He who gives to the poor will not lack, but he who hides his eyes will have many curses."

Proverbs 28:27

"He who has pity on the poor lends to the Lord, and He will pay back what he has given."

Proverbs 19:17

"He who has a generous eye will be blessed, for he gives of his bread to the poor."

Proverbs 22:9

Through Fasting

"If then you were raised with Christ, seek those things which are above, where Christ is, sitting at the right hand of God."

Colossians 3:1

One of the ways you are to seek the things that are above is through fasting. Biblical fasting is when you abstain from food or liquid for a godly purpose. Jesus expected all of His followers to fast. In Matthew 6:16 Jesus said, *"Moreover, when you fast."* In Matthew 9:15 He also said, *"Can the friends of the bridegroom mourn as long as the bridegroom is with them? But the days will come when the bridegroom will be taken away from them, and then they will fast."* The disciples were not required to fast while Jesus was with them in person. However, He said that after He is taken away from them that then they will fast.

"So when they had appointed elders in every church, and prayed with fasting, they commended them to the Lord in whom they had believed."

Acts 14:23

Every early church fasted. When elders were appointed to lead a church they were commissioned by prayer and fasting. Fasting is a spiritual discipline that you at times should add to your praying and giving. Jesus spoke of all three of these disciplines in Matthew chapter six. Concerning each discipline He said, *"when you"* (Matthew 6:2, 5, 16). Therefore, Jesus expected for all three disciplines to be in the life of every believer. Fasting also plays a role in your ability to put on the new man just like prayer and giving does. It was after Jesus fasted for forty days that He *"returned in the power of the Spirit"* (Luke 4:14).

When you fast you are choosing to lay aside one of the necessary physical needs of your life. Through fasting you are demonstrating by faith, *"Man shall not live by bread alone, but by every word of God"* (Luke 4:4). You are acknowledging that you cannot live by food alone in this life. Fasting is humbling yourself before God and acknowledging your need for Him in your life. When you fast it is to position yourself under the authority of the Word of God and His will for your life.

"Then I proclaimed a fast there at the river of Ahava, that we might humble ourselves before our God, to seek from Him the right way for us and our little ones and all our possessions."

Ezra 8:21

Fasting is a way to seek the Lord. Whether you need direction, deliverance, divine wisdom, or provisions, fasting is positioning yourself in a manner that will release the power of God in your life. James 4:10 states, *"Humble yourselves in the sight of the Lord, and He will lift you up."* Fasting is about having an attitude of humility before God. Such temporary discomfort is worth having God lift you up out of what you are going through.

"So He said to them, 'This kind can come out by nothing but prayer and fasting.'"

Mark 9:29

There are some bondages that are unable to be broken without adding fasting to prayer. The disciples of Jesus were unable to cast out a demon spirit in a boy. Jesus said it took prayer and fasting in order for the breakthrough to come. The gospel of Matthew's account relates the statement to the amount of faith a person can attain. Fasting will break off your life any strongholds that you have been unable to get free from. One of the reasons for this is that fasting allows your inner man to be strengthened and for your faith to grow.

Fasting helps your focus and attention to be fixed on the things of heaven or the spirit. Because of this, it helps your spirit to become sensitive to the Spirit of God. You will become more aware of things in your life that grieve Him, and to His voice when He speaks. When you fast you are afflicting your soul. (See Isaiah 58:5) This allows your spirit man to become free from any entanglements you have allowed in your soul.

"Now, therefore,' says the Lord, 'Turn to Me with all your heart, with fasting, with weeping, and with mourning.' So rend your heart and not your garments; return to the Lord your God."

Joel 2:12-13

If you ever fall captive to sin you should fast. Through fasting you can humble yourself before God and receive His mercy and deliverance from any bondage you have allowed in your life. (See 1 Samuel 7:6) Fasting allows your heart to be dealt with. Any places you have hardened and given to sin should be surrendered back to the Lordship of Christ. The Lord says, *"Is this not the fast that I have chosen: To loose the bonds of wickedness. To undo the heavy burdens, to let the oppressed go free, and that you break every yoke"* (Isaiah 58:6)?

Fasting is the most intense way for you to humble yourself and seek God. When your hunger for God is greater than your hunger for food you should fast. Or when your need for God to move in your life is greater than a full belly you should fast. In the Bible, fasting is most often mentioned when a person or persons were facing an overwhelming circumstance or had an enormous need.

"Moreover, when you fast, do not be like the hypocrites, with a sad countenance. For they disfigure their faces that they may appear to men to be fasting. Assuredly, I say to you, they have their reward. But when, you fast, anoint your head and wash your face, so that you do not appear to men to be fasting, but to your Father who is in the secret place; and your Father who sees in secret will reward you openly."

Matthew 6:16-18

Fasting purifies your body of harmful toxins. This is why when you fast you should make sure to keep good hygiene. You also are to take care of your appearance so that you do not appear to people to be fasting. The motives of your heart are important when you fast. The heart always matters. Jesus, in this context, is speaking concerning a private fast. During private fast you are not to purposefully make others aware of the fact that you are fasting. To do so is to lose the rewards or breakthroughs that would have come from humbling yourself before the Lord.

There are private fast and public fast. A public fast is also a corporate fast. This is when a group of believers or a local congregation is fasting together. Such fasting is not private but openly declared among those that have been called to fast. Most of the fast mentioned in the Bible were public fast. The nation of Israel had corporate fasts throughout the year. There are times when local assemblies will declare a corporate fast.

A complete fast is when you abstain from water and food. (See Acts 9:9) This type of fast should not be done by you for longer than three days. A full fast is abstaining from all food. (See 1 Samuel 28:20) A partial fast or half fast is from sun-up to sundown or from 6 a.m. to 3 p.m. (See 2 Samuel 3:35 and Acts 10:3, 30) There are two Daniel fasts. The first Daniel fast is to eat vegetables and drink only water. (See Daniel 1:12) The second type of Daniel fast is to eat no pleasant (desirable) food, no meat, and drink no wine. (See Daniel 10:2-3)

The Bible speaks concerning a 1 day fast. (See 1 Samuel 7:6) A 3 day fast. (See Acts 9:9) A 7 day fast. (See 1 Samuel 31:13) A 10 day fast. (See Daniel 1:12) A 14 day fast. (See Acts 27:33) A 21 day fast. (See Daniel 10:2-3) And a 40 day fast. (See Matthew 4:2)

Ultimately Through Obedience

"Since you have purified your souls in obeying the truth through the Spirit in sincere love of the brethren, love one another fervently with a pure heart."

1 Peter 1:22

You put on the new man ultimately through your obedience to the Lord. Your soul is purified only as you obey the truth through the Spirit. I love how the Scriptures are so specific. You must not just obey the truth, but you must obey the truth through the Spirit. This speaks concerning the difference between having a form of godliness without the power, and also the difference between religious behavior and Christ-formed habits.

It is through the Spirit that your motivation for obeying the truth is cleansed. The Holy Spirit influences you to be sincere and have fervent love toward other believers. Paul said in Romans 5:8, *"The love of God has been poured out in our hearts by the Holy Spirit who was given to us."* As you continue to yield to the Holy Spirit and obey the truth through the Spirit your heart will remain pure.

You are not to depend upon your own ability to obey the truth. Your natural ability and flesh have been crucified with Christ. (See Galatians 5:24) Therefore, you are not to seek to live by them. God does not need, nor does He want, your self-effort. The cross of Christ is the wisdom of God so *"that no flesh should glory in His presence"* (1 Corinthians 1:29). God has provided within you the law of the Spirit of life so that you can obey Him through the Holy Spirit. Christ in you is the well of provision you need in order to obey the truth. (See Colossians 1:27)

It is your obedience through the Spirit that purifies your soul and maintains the purity of your heart. Love, generated by the Spirit within you, is to be the main motivator for all you do. Paul said, *"Love is the fulfillment of the law"* (Romans 13:10). Participating in the spiritual disciplines without the motivation of love for God and love for His people will not enable you to put on the new man. The term "new man" includes Christ-like behavior, motives, character, and obedience. The "new man" is the display of the person of Christ and all that He is. When you put on the new man you are displaying who you have become in Christ. Without the motivation of love whatever you do will *"profit you nothing"* (1 Corinthians 13:3). Paul also prayed that your love for people would continue to abound in order that your heart would be established in holiness. (See 1 Thessalonians 3:12-13) This is what it means for your heart to be blameless before the Lord.

"Has the Lord as great delight in burnt offerings and sacrifices, as in obeying the voice of the Lord? Behold, to obey is better than sacrifice."

1 Samuel 15:22

God desires your obedience more than your sacrifice. Your obedience reveals that Christ is sanctified as Lord in your will. Your sacrifices do not necessarily reveal the same. You can be resisting the Lordship of Christ in your will while still making sacrifices for the Lord. You can sacrifice time praying, time reading the Word of God, and time singing praises to God but be resisting what God has commanded you to do. You can sacrifice of your money and give to God and still not be yielding to the Lordship of Christ in your life. God desires your obedience to His voice rather than just having your sacrifices.

When you perform such sacrifices you must understand that you are still dictating what you do. You decide how much time you are going to sacrifice to pray, or to read the Word, or to worship. You decide how much money you are going to sacrifice. Such sacrifices do not require you to have surrendered your will to the voice of the Lord. It is impossible to experience and live out the Lordship of Christ without having to obey His voice. How you respond to the voice of the Lord is the true test of who is actually leading your life and decisions. It is easy to obey the voice of the Lord when you desire to do what He is asking of you. However, how do you respond when you are asked to do something that is contrary to your desires or will?

"For You do not desire sacrifice, or else I would give it; you do not delight in burnt offering. The sacrifices of God are a broken spirit, a broken and a contrite heart- these, O God, You will not despise."
Psalm 51:16-17

The sacrifice that God desires is your will being submitted to His. This is what is meant by: a broken spirit or contrite heart. Think of being broken as when a wild horse has to be broken by its owner. The horse's freedom and will has to become submitted to the will and desires of its owner. The same is true for your relationship with Christ. You are broken when you are not dictating your life and decisions but are submitted and obeying the voice of the Lord. Having a heart of obedience it what honors God. It is what God values. Also, this is the obedience that purifies your soul. Your soul is purified as you obey God, not because it benefits you but you obey Him for His benefit.

"These people draw near to Me with their mouth, and honor Me with their lips, but their heart is far from me."

Matthew 15:8

Sacrifices without obedience are equivalent to lip service. Lip service is any activity you seek to perform for God while deliberately resisting His Lordship in areas of your will. Lip service is being religious because it is resisting fellowshipping with the Spirit of the Lord. You cannot enjoy intimacy and fellowship with the Spirit of the Lord if you are rebelling against His voice. Such resistance is hardening and closing your heart to the Lord's right to control and direct the affairs of your life.

As you participate in the spiritual disciplines you must keep a broken and contrite heart. When you do not remain in a position of obeying the voice of the Lord you will lack the life and presence of the Holy Spirit for any sacrifices you perform. God is after your heart, and He only truly has it as you continue to obey His voice. Singing praises to God while deliberately rebelling against the voice of the Lord is lip service. It is lip service because your heart is far from obeying the Lord.

The many spiritual disciplines discussed in this chapter will only benefit you in putting on the new man as you remain obedient to the voice of the Lord. You can be more diligent than other believers in the spiritual disciplines and still not have Christ formed in your soul because you are harboring areas of disobedience in your life. Obedience by the Holy Spirit is the ultimate factor for your ability to live out who you are in Christ. Stay submitted and surrendered to the voice of the Lord. Choose each day to allow the fear of the Lord to remain in your heart. Give God the rightful place He deserves in your heart and will.

"And He died for all, that those who live should live no longer for themselves, but for Him who died for them and rose again."

2 Corinthians 5:15

Chapter 14

Built Up In Christ

"As you therefore have received Christ Jesus the Lord, so walk in Him, rooted and built up in Him and established in the faith, as you have been taught, abounding in it with thanksgiving."

Colossians 2:6-7

When you consistently walk each day displaying the new man, then Christ has been formed in you. You are rooted and built up in Christ and therefore, have become established in Him. You are established in the faith, in the character of Christ, and in your daily habits. Reaching this place in your spiritual development should cause you to abound with thanksgiving. You are no longer struggling with major bondages and sins. You have learned to depend upon the life of Christ within you each day to overcome the flesh, world, and devil. The character of Christ is being displayed in your life. You have reached a place of stability in your walk with Christ.

The life of Christ that was once just rooted in your spirit has now become formed in your soul. His life is now built in you. Your life portrays the stability of the person of Christ. You have allowed the characteristics of His life to grow more and more on the inside. Now the inward change consistently affects your daily walk. You live by faith each moment, trusting in the life of the Son of God to be revealed through you.

"Be sober, be vigilant; because your adversary the devil walks about like a roaring lion, seeking whom he may devour. Resist him, steadfast in the faith, knowing that the same sufferings are experienced by your brotherhood in the world. But may the God of all grace who called us to His eternal glory by Christ Jesus, after you have suffered a while, perfect, establish, strengthen, and settle you."

1 Peter 5:10

You have learned to resist the devil. You have become steadfast in the faith. You have gone through suffering and seasons of allowing Christ to be formed in you, and now you have become established and settled in your walk with Christ. The word translated "establish" comes from the Greek word *"sterizo"* which carries the idea of being stable, fixed, strengthened, made firm, and firmly placed (Strong's # 4741). Before Christ was formed in your life you were unable to consistently walk in the new man. You were *"by reason of use having your senses exercised to discern both good and evil"* (Hebrews 5:14).

Now your walk has become fixed and firm. You now have become trained to discern how to display Christ when facing different situations. You know who you are in Christ and live accordingly each day. You have been taught how to display the new man. You have become built up in Christ. Christ has been formed in you.

"That He may establish your hearts blameless in holiness before our God and Father at the coming of our Lord Jesus Christ with all His saints."

1 Thessalonians 3:13

Being established in the faith and in the character of Christ does not mean you are sinless and have reached the goal of maturity in Christ. However, it does mean that you have reached a place in your spiritual development where you have put off the old man and put on the new man. Your entire life has become submitted to the Word of God and what God has done for you in Christ. Your life, as a whole, is characterized as a believer who is not constantly tossed to and fro in their walk with Christ. Your heart is blameless before

God. You are walking in the light of what you know to be right. Your heart has been established in holiness and you have sanctified Christ as Lord in your will. You have established your heart for the coming of the Lord. (See James 5:8)

Being established means that you have learned to live by faith through every circumstance. You have learned not to allow your emotions and situations to cause you to become unsettled. You have seen the faithfulness of God time and time again and know that you are able to trust Him with all things. You have learned to allow the Word of God to settle you in every circumstance.

"Now to Him who is able to establish you according to my gospel and the preaching of Jesus Christ, according to the revelation of the mystery kept secret since the world began."

Romans 16:25

You have allowed the Lord to establish you. You have applied the relevant divisions of Scripture to your life in order for you to become built up in Christ. You have learned how to put off the old man and put on the new man through the finished work of Christ. The mystery of Christ in you is now an every day experience that empowers you to display the new man. Christ in you has now become Christ formed in you. You are now built up in Christ or established in Him.

"Brethren, join in following my example, and note those who so walk, as you have us for a pattern. For many walk, of whom I have told you often, and now tell you even weeping, that they are the enemies of the cross of Christ: whose end is destruction, whose god is their belly, and whose glory is in their shame- who set their mind on earthly things."

Philippians 3:17-19

You have been built so far according to the pattern or blueprint of God for your life. You are following in the footsteps of those who modeled the pattern. Your god is not your own fleshly appetites but Christ and His will for your life. You have set your mind on the things above and not on the temporary pleasures of earthly things. You are not an enemy to the power of the cross but have embraced its capability for your life. You are walking worthy of the Lord and His cross.

Walking Worthy

"As you know how we exhorted, and comforted, and charged every one of you, as a father does his own children, that you walk worthy of God who calls you into His own kingdom and glory."

1 Thessalonians 2:12

When you are built up in Christ you are able to walk worthy of the kingdom of God. Walking worthy of the Lord means that you reflect the culture of the kingdom of God in your behavior and life. Your habits and character manifest the new man. You are now walking through life demonstrating the person you became the moment you were born again. It is impossible to walk worthy of the Lord without experiencing the restoration of your soul. In order for you to walk worthy of the Lord, you have learned in your mind what the acceptable behavior is for a child of God. You have learned to surrender your will to the will of Christ.

"And he who does not take his cross and follow after Me is not worthy of Me."

Matthew 10:38

You have taken up your cross and followed after the Lord. You have allowed Him to lead you through the foundation phase, transformation phase, and formation phase. You have learned to deny your will and obey the voice of the Lord. You are no longer living each day for selfish desires but for the glory of God. You are walking worthy of the Lord. You are walking worthy of what the Lord made possible for you through His finished work. You have allowed His grace and Word to run swiftly in your life. (See 2 Thessalonians 3:1)

You have yielded your soul to the power of the cross in order for Christ to be formed in you. You are living no longer for your self but for the One who died on the cross for you. The love of God, demonstrated through the cross of Christ, has led you to embrace your own cross. You, like Paul, proclaim each day, *"I have been crucified with Christ; it is no longer I who live, but Christ lives in me"* (Galatians 2:20).

"I, therefore, the prisoner of the Lord, beseech you to walk worthy of the calling with which you were called."

Ephesians 4:1

From one prisoner to another, Paul exhorts you to walk worthy of the Lord. You are now living as a bondservant of Christ. Your will and walk has become submitted to the Lord. This is part of what you were called to. You were transferred out of the authority of sin and Satan into the kingdom of Jesus Christ. You were called out of darkness into the marvelous light of Christ's reign. Christ is your king and you are his subject. You live for His purpose and delight. You have been called to be a representative of the kingdom of God and the heavenly city.

"And do not be conformed to this world, but be transformed by the renewing of your mind, that you may prove what is that good and acceptable and perfect will of God."

Romans 12:2

Through the renewing of your mind you have come to know what the good and acceptable will of God is. You have come to demonstrate acceptable behavior for the kingdom of God. Your mind is now set upon the things above, not the things of this earth. You think upon that which his true, noble, just, pure, lovely, and of good report. (See Philippians 4:8) You live no longer for temporary pleasures but for eternity. You are willing to deny yourself in order for the life of Christ to be manifested in your life. You are mindful of the things of the Spirit instead of the things of the flesh. You have come to find out the ways and thoughts of the Lord. (See Isaiah 55:8-9)

"For you were once darkness, but now you are light in the Lord. Walk as children of light (for the fruit of the Spirit is in all goodness, righteousness, and truth), finding out what is acceptable to the Lord."

Ephesians 5:8-10

You have now found out and are displaying what is acceptable to the Lord. You are no longer just light in the Lord but you are also walking as a child of light. Your behavior has lined up with your identity in Christ. Due to the life of Christ on the inside of you the fruit of the Spirit is now growing and being produced in your life. You are now experiencing the fruit that is a result of the root of Christ dwelling in your spirit. In Galatians 5:22-23 we are told, *"But the fruit of the Spirit is love, joy, peace, longsuffering, kindness, goodness, faithfulness, gentleness, self-control."* Christ is now able to produce such characteristics in your life because the major hindrances in your soul have been removed and the character of Christ has replaced them. You are now experiencing more love, joy, and peace in your soul. You have come to experience the fruit of His life in your emotions.

"Therefore we make it our aim, whether present or absent, to be well pleasing to Him."

2 Corinthians 5:9

The words "well pleasing" are translated from the exact Greek word that was translated as "acceptable" in the two previous verses (Strong's # 2101). You are well pleasing to the Lord when you are demonstrating acceptable behavior for the kingdom of God. Now that you have become established you must continue to keep this as your aim as you live each day. Your life is acceptable to the Lord because you remained yielded to the Holy Spirit and allowed Christ to be formed in your soul. You have not resisted the process of sanctification in your soul. Walking worthy of the Lord, having acceptable behavior, and being well pleasing to Him are all different ways that the Scripture expresses that same truth.

"Finally then, brethren, we urge and exhort in the Lord Jesus that you should abound more and more, just as you received from us how you ought to walk and to please God; for you know what commandments we gave you through the Lord Jesus."

1 Thessalonians 4:1-2

You have remained yielded to the Lord and have allowed Him to work in your soul what is well pleasing in His sight. You live according to the commandments given by the Lord Jesus. A renewed mind and a crucified will leads to pleasing the Lord. You have embraced the will of God for your spiritual development. You have not refused to acknowledge that God has called you to holiness, and that the cross of Christ has made it possible. You have identified and appropriated the power of the cross for your life. Your inner man rules over your body and you have yielded your members to be instruments of holiness. (See Romans 6:19)

Paul concludes the above verses saying:

"For this is the will of God your sanctification: that you should abstain from sexual immorality; that each of you should know how to possess his own vessel in sanctification and honor, not in passion of lust, like the Gentiles who do not know God...For God did not call us to uncleanness, but in holiness. Therefore he who rejects this does not reject man, but God, who has also given us His Holy Spirit."

1 Thessalonians 4:3-8

Fully Pleasing

*"That you may walk worthy of the Lord, fully pleasing Him, **being fruitful in every good work** and increasing in the knowledge of God."*

Colossians 1:10 (Bold Mine.)

You are now ready to move into the next phase of spiritual development. Now that Christ has been formed in you He is ready to live through you. Since you are walking worthy of the Lord you should now learn how to fully please Him. God is fully pleased as you bear fruit for the kingdom of God while living worthy of the Lord. You have been called to fruitfulness in the kingdom of God. You have been called and created to perform good works. (See Ephesians 2:10)

*"I call to remembrance the genuine (unhypocritical) faith that is in you, which dwelt first in your grandmother Lois and your mother Eunice, and I am persuaded is in you also. **Therefore**, I remind you to stir up the gift of God which is in you through the laying on of my hands."*

2 Timothy 1:5-6 (Parenthesis Mine.
NKJV Marginal Reading; Bold Mine)

It was because of the genuine faith that dwelt in Timothy that Paul reminded him to stir up the gift of God in his life. It is having Christ formed in you that qualifies you to stir up your gifts of God and begin to walk in the good works that God has predetermined for you. You have gone through the character preparation in order to have the stability to fulfill your purpose. You have been built for a purpose related to the kingdom of God.

The blueprint for discipleship is that you first walk worthy of your calling before you begin to fulfill your purpose in the kingdom of God. God values character over charisma or your gifting. Being built up in Christ qualifies you to move forward in your specific calling in the kingdom of God. God does not want unsanctified good works. He desires the gifts you have been given to be used with the character and motives of Christ. Launching into your purpose without having been built up in Christ would cause you to fall apart spiritually.

"But thanks be to God, who gives us the victory through our Lord Jesus Christ. Therefore, my beloved brethren, be steadfast, immovable, always abounding in the work of the Lord, knowing that your labor is not in vain in the Lord."

1 Corinthians 15:57-58

Now that you are experiencing the victory you have through Christ, you are to begin abounding in the work of the Lord. The work of the Lord is different than just serving or helping. The work of the Lord refers to the ministry and purpose that God has called and gifted you to perform for the kingdom of God. As you remain steadfast and immovable in Christ, you are to continue to labor, bearing fruit for God's kingdom.

"If you keep My commandments, you will abide in My love, just as I have kept My Father's commandments and abide in His love. These things I have spoken to you, that My joy may remain in you, and that your joy may be full."

John 15:10-11

You will experience the joy of the Lord to the fullest as you fulfill your purpose in the kingdom of God while walking worthy of the Lord. God will give you His joy as your walk fully pleasing to Him and this will cause your joy to become full. You must not stop now in your spiritual development. You must continue to run the race. (See 1 Corinthians 9:24) You must continue to move forward in the divine design of discipleship.

Many believers become dry and do not experience the joy of the Lord because they remain inactive in their purpose. They come to service after service but have not stepped out into the good works that God has preplanned for them. They are built up in Christ but have stopped yielding to what the Holy Spirit wants to do next in their life. Maybe they are distracted by the busyness of their life. However, the kingdom of God should be your priority. (See Matthew 6:33) If you stop short of God's divine design for your life you will not continue to experience the joy and fruit of the Spirit in your emotions. Many believers are unfilled because they have not continued in the next phase of their spiritual development. Choose not to be a person like that!

Section IV.

Impartation Phase – Christ Lives through You

Phase
Introduction

Impartation phase is connected to the second pair of elementary teachings of Christ specifically the laying on of hands. It is during impartation phase that believers are to begin to align themselves for their purpose in the kingdom of God. The doctrine of laying on of hands in this phase pertains to a believer being released to operate in his or her gifting.

The last pair of elementary teachings of Christ also pertain to this phase. The doctrines of the resurrection of the dead and eternal judgment speak to the third age in the experience of believers. It is at the end of impartation phase that believers, through their service, should seek to lay up for themselves rewards in the millennial reign of Christ.

A believer is to be in the spiritual growth stage of a young man or woman in the faith during the entire impartation phase. Impartation phase deals primarily with the body because of its focus on a believer's service for the kingdom of God. The primary division of truth that is relevant for this phase is the gospel of the kingdom. The primary method that facilitates spiritual growth for impartation phase is mentoring. Please see the chart on the next page!

Three Ages Elementary Teachings of Christ Represent	Spiritual Growth Stages	Phases for Discipleship	Primary Division of Truth	Primary "M" Facilitates Growth for Phase
Age 1 Transferring Kingdoms *Repentance from Dead Works and Faith toward God*	Babes	I. Foundation 1 Cor.3:11 (Spirit)	Gospel of Jesus Christ, Elementary Teachings of Christ Overview	Ministry of the Word
	Little Children		Gospel of Grace, Paul's Gospel, Word Of Righteousness	
Age 2 Life in God's Kingdom *Doctrine of Baptisms and Laying on of Hands*	Little Children	II.Transformation Rom. 12:2 (Soul)	Revelation of the Mystery	My Role
	Children			
	Children	III.Formation Gal.4:19 (Soul)	Revelation of the Mystery	Modeling Community
	Young Men			
Age 3 Life in the Millennium *Rewards for Resurrection and Judgment*	Young Men	IV.Impartation Matt.10:7-8 (Body)	Gospel of the Kingdom	Mentoring
	Father	V.Multiplication John17:6-8,20 (Entire Person)	Whole Counsel of Scripture	All the M's

Chapter 15

The Kingdom of God

"Come, you blessed of My Father, inherit the kingdom prepared for you from the foundation of the world."

Matthew 25:34b

The kingdom of God refers to the rule of God upon heaven, the earth, and its inhabitants. The idea for the kingdom of God originated before the foundation of the world. The kingdom of God was a part of the eternal purpose of God that was accomplished in Christ Jesus. (Ephesians 3:11) When God created the first male and female He blessed them and gave them dominion over the works of His hands. (See Genesis 1:28 & Psalm 8:6) However, due to Adam and Eve's rebellion they lost their ability to operate in the kingdom because their relationship with God was broken.

This is why throughout the Bible the Scriptures speaking of the kingdom of God primarily deal with the earth and its inhabitants. It was on earth that the rule of God was resisted while it continued to exist in heaven. This is why Jesus taught the disciples to pray, *"Your kingdom come, Your will be done on earth as it is in heaven"* (Matthew 6:10). Then what was lost was eventually restored through the Christ, Jesus of Nazareth.

"According to the working of His mighty power which He worked in Christ when He raised Him from the dead and seated Him at His right hand in the heavenly places, far above all principality and power and might and dominion, and every name that is named, not only in this age but also in that which is to come. And He put all things under His feet."

Ephesians 1:19-22

When God raised Jesus from the dead He seated Him far above all powers and put all things under His feet. Jesus is the King of the Kingdom of God. Jesus Christ has been given all authority and rule over the earth and its inhabitants. Future judgment has also been committed to Jesus Christ. (See Acts 17:30-31)

"God has delivered us from the power of darkness and conveyed (transferred) us into the kingdom of the Son of His love, in whom we have redemption through His blood, the forgiveness of sins."

Colossians 1:13-14

As a born again believer you have been transferred into the kingdom of God through Jesus Christ. You must understand that the cross of Christ that provided your redemption and forgiveness of sins made it possible for you to enter the kingdom of God and live under the rule of God through Christ. The cross was grace for a purpose! It was grace that was provided for you in order for you to fulfill your purpose that is attached to the kingdom of God. The free gift of righteousness through the finished work of Christ was provided for you to be able to operate in and experience the kingdom or rule of God. The truths contained in Paul's gospel, and the revelation of the mystery, have given you the ability to fulfill God's desire regarding the kingdom.

"Who gave Himself for us, that He might redeem us from every lawless deed and purify for Himself His own special people, zealous for good works."

Titus 2:14

Part of the purpose of God from the beginning was for mankind to operate in partnership with their Creator. Mankind was to be an extension or vessel for the authority and rule of God to be enforced upon the earth and its inhabitants. Jesus gave Himself in order for you to be redeemed from every lawless deed, be purified, and be zealous for good works. Do you see that the grace of God, demonstrated through the finished work of Christ, was for a purpose? Do you see a purpose bigger than you just experiencing the forgiveness of your sins? Yes, the forgiveness of your sins was a necessary step, but it was provided in order for you to fulfill your purpose that is connected to the kingdom of God.

If you receive the forgiveness of your sins, are purified, and then stop short of becoming zealous for good works, you miss the divine design of discipleship. Jesus gave Himself for us that we would be redeemed from our sin, purified, and zealous for good works. Now that you have been through the foundation phase, transformation phase, and formation phase, it is time, through good works, to impart the kingdom of God to the world and people all around you. God has changed you in order for your life to be a vessel for His kingdom and an instrument that brings Him glory. The gospel of God is grace provided for His purpose not just for your benefit.

"And this I pray... that you may approve the things that are excellent, that you may be sincere and without offense till the day of Christ, being filled with the fruits of righteousness which are by Jesus Christ, to the glory and praise of God.

Philippians 1:9-11

As Christ lives through you, the good works that He has predestined for you will be performed. These good works are the fruits of righteousness. These good works are the result of God's grace that enabled you to come into right standing with Him. They are good works that come out of fellowshipping with the Lord. They are produced because of the life of Christ living through you, and are for the glory and praise of God.

You live under the Lordship of Christ and He has assigned you to a kingdom purpose. It is a purpose that is related to the increase of His government and rule. It is not for selfish gain or self promotion. It is not for you to build a name for yourself or your own little kingdom. Your kingdom assignment is for His glory and for His namesake. Lastly, it will only be experienced as you remain under God's order.

Authority of the Kingdom

"Therefore God also has highly exalted Him and given Him the name which is above every name, that at the name of Jesus every knee should bow, of those in heaven, and of those on earth, and of those under the earth, and that every tongue should confess that Jesus Christ is Lord, to the glory of God the Father.
Philippians 2:9-11

Jesus is Lord over all. There is nothing that has not been subjected to Him. The name of Jesus is above every name. His authority is over the name of circumstances. His authority is over the name of depression. His authority is over the names of demons. His authority extends to heaven, the earth, and under the earth. Paul said in Ephesians 1:22, *"God put all things under His feet."* Jesus, during His ministry, demonstrated the continual authority of the kingdom that He was given by the Father. He went about everywhere preaching the kingdom of God. Jesus declared the authority of the kingdom over all things and every name.

"Then Jesus went about all the cities and villages, teaching in their synagogues, preaching the gospel of the kingdom, and healing every sickness and every disease among the people."
Matthew 9:35

Jesus went about the cities and villages healing every sickness and every disease. The preaching of the gospel of the kingdom is the demonstration that all things have been placed under His feet. Whenever you read in the Gospels that the gospel of the kingdom was preached, you would find it was accompanied by the demonstration of God's reign being enforced. All circumstances and situations that were the result of mankind stepping out of their place of dominion were changed. The blind received their sight. The lame were made to walk. The storms were calmed. Fish retrieved lost money. The poor received provisions. The dead were raised. The sick and brokenhearted were healed. Jesus, operating as a man, under the reign of God was defeating all that was contrary to the kingdom of God.

The Body of Christ

"Now, therefore, you are no longer strangers and foreigners, but fellow citizens with the saints and members of the household of God, ... in whom the whole building, being fitted together, grows into a holy temple in the Lord, in whom you also are being built together for a dwelling place of God in the Spirit."

Ephesians 2:19, 21-22

God no longer dwells in a building. He does not live in a physical temple. The people of God make up the temple of the Lord. The church is not the building you meet in with other believers. The church is the group of believers who meet in the building. As a believer you are part of the new temple of the Lord.

"But you are a chosen generation, a royal priesthood, a holy nation, His own special people, that you may proclaim the praises of Him who called you out of darkness into His marvelous light; who once were not a people but are now the people of God, who had not obtained mercy but now have obtained mercy."

1 Peter 2:9-10

The body of Christ is God's new temple and new nation. In the Old Testament, God chose and set apart the nation of Israel to be a light to the nations. The nation of Israel possessed, under the Old Covenant, a special place above all people. They were a special treasure to God and were to be a kingdom of priests and a holy nation. (See Exodus 19:5-6) This purpose and place in the plan of God was not offered under the Old Covenant to any nation other than the Jews.

"Also today the Lord has proclaimed you to be His special people, just as He promised you, that you should keep all His command-ments, and that He will set you high above all nations which He has made, in praise, in name, and in honor, and that you may be a holy people to the Lord your God, just as He has spoken."

Deuteronomy 26:18-19

The nation of Israel was given a special place concerning the kingdom of God. As Israel remained submitted to God they would be set high above all the people of the earth. This place of elevation was so Israel could display God's rule upon the earth and their lives. Their testimony was to draw the other nations of the world to see the need to submit to God's right to rule their lives. Notice it was only if Israel obeyed and kept all God's commands that they would be able to take their place in the kingdom. This is exactly what we saw in the beginning of creation with Adam and Eve. God was working continually to restore His original intention concerning the kingdom.

"Therefore I say to you, the kingdom of God will be taken from you and given to a nation bearing the fruits of it."

Matthew 21:43

However, after hundreds of years of rebelling against the Spirit of God, killing the servants God sent them, breaking the Old Covenant, they ultimately rejected and killed the Son of God. Due to their continual disobedience to the Old Covenant, Jesus said the kingdom of God would be taken from the nation of Israel and given to another nation that would bear the fruits worthy of it. The body of Christ is the new nation that Jesus was referring to. Through His finished work, Jesus established a New Covenant and a new nation that would be a light to the nations.

"There is neither Jew nor Greek, there is neither slave nor free, there is neither male nor female; for you are all one in Christ Jesus."

Galatians 3:28

This new nation, the body of Christ, is made up of neither Jew nor Greek because we are all one in Christ. Every believer has become a new man or a new creation in Christ. The body of Christ therefore, has become the corporate new man or new kind of humanity. Paul said, *"For as in Adam all die, even so in Christ all shall be made alive"* (1 Corinthians 15:22). The old creation or humanity descending from Adam shall all die. The new creation or humanity descending from Christ shall all be made alive. God viewed the old you both individually and corporately. God viewed you corporately as a part of the old creation stemming from the first man, Adam. Now as a child of God you are a part of the new creation and your life is hidden in the last Adam, Jesus Christ. (See 1 Corinthians 15:45 and Colossians 3:3)

Jesus Christ was the last head or originator of a group of humanity called the body of Christ. The body of Christ is God's new temple, new nation, and new man or new humanity. Paul said, *"Now you are the body of Christ, and members individually"* (1 Corinthians 12:27). God now views you individually as a new creation in Christ and also as a part of the body of Christ.

This is extremely important to understand. Your assignment in the kingdom of God is both an individual calling as well as a part of the overall purpose of the body of Christ. This means you can not be an extension of the kingdom of God and not stay connected to the body of Christ. As a child of God you have been brought into a relationship with Christ and His body or people.

Under the New Covenant, it is through the body of Christ that the rule of God is to be displayed upon the earth and its inhabitants. The body of Christ is in partnership with God to be a vessel of the kingdom of God. Again, God's grace, provided through Christ, was for His purpose regarding the kingdom to be fulfilled. This is why throughout the New Testament teachings believers who have engaged in sanctification are continually exhorted to maintain good works. Just as you live through your body and engage the world around you, Jesus desires to live through His body and impact this world with the authority of His kingdom.

"But if I cast out demons by the Spirit of God, surely the kingdom of God has come upon you."

Matthew 12:28

It is the Spirit of the Lord that administers the Lordship of Jesus Christ. When Jesus cast out demons by the Spirit of God, the rule of God had come upon the individuals' lives. The same is true for the body of Christ. As we remain yielded to the Spirit of God, we manifest the rule of God upon people's lives. The body of Christ has been set apart and called to administer the kingdom of God by the power of the Holy Spirit upon the earth and its inhabitants.

"For He has not put the world to come, of which we speak, in subjection to angels. But one testified in a certain place, saying:
'What is man that You are mindful of him, or the son of man that You take care of him? You have made him a little lower than the angels; You have crowned him with glory and honor, And set him over the works of Your hands. You have put all things in subjection under his feet.'
*For in that He put all in subjection under him, He left nothing that is not put under him. **But now we do not yet see all things put under him. But we see Jesus...**"*

Hebrews 2:5-9 (Bold Mine.)

Jesus has become King over all the earth and its inhabitants. Jesus has conquered sin, death, Satan, and hell. He has defeated all the works of darkness. He has had all things be put in subjection under His feet. However, we do not yet see the manifestation that all things have been put under him. He has defeated all things, but we have not yet seen all things be made subject to His victory and Lordship. Jesus has defeated every disease and sickness but we have not yet seen all cancer become submitted to Him.

During this time of tension, the body of Christ is to see Jesus. As we fix our eyes on Jesus, despite our surroundings, our circumstances, and the things we encounter on the earth, we will be able to behold His victory and Lordship over all. It is "through faith and patience" that we are able to enter into the experience of God's promises.

The victory has been won by Christ over all things contrary to the kingdom of God. Jesus Christ has now commissioned His body to apply His victory and rule upon the earth and its inhabitants. When the body of Christ continues to see the finished work of Christ, we are able to be the instrument that enforces the victory that Jesus has already accomplished.

Armor of the Kingdom

"Put on the whole armor of God, that you may be able to stand against the wiles of the devil."

Ephesians 6:11

The body of Christ is to stand against the enemy. We are to stand against sin. We are to stand against poverty. We are to stand against injustice. We are to stand against sickness. We are to stand against bondages and hindrances that seek to hinder people from experiencing God's purpose for their life. We are to stand against everything that is contrary to the kingdom of God.

Paul, in the book of Ephesians, presents in order the phases of spiritual development. He used the terms: sit, walk, and stand. The first three chapters of Ephesians speak concerning your need to sit and learn your new position and identity in Christ which coincides with the foundation phase. Then, beginning at chapter four Paul begins to speak about the walk and character of believers which corresponds with the transformation and formation phases. Lastly, Paul ends the letter speaking of believers standing against the enemy which matches with the impartation phase. You are first to sit and then learn to walk before you begin to fulfill your purpose in the kingdom of God by standing against the works of Satan in the world and in lives of other people.

"Nor give place to the devil."

Ephesians 4:27

As a child of God, you always have authority over the devil in your own life. This is what the above Scripture speaks about. You do not have to give any place to the devil in your life. You have the ability through Christ to resist the devil. The Bible states, *"Therefore submit to God. Resist the devil and he will flee from you"* (James 4:7). As you stay submitted, surrendered to God, and resisting the devil he will flee from you. You are the gatekeeper for your own life.

There are times that your spirit man becomes overwhelmed by the issues you are facing in your life and soul. This is when you at times need to be comforted, upheld, and strengthened by God's grace supplied through other believers. (See 1 Thessalonians 5:14, Galatians 6:9, Hebrews 12:3) This supply of grace strengthens your spirit to stand up and resist the works of the devil against your life. Other times you may have given place to the devil and are in need of being restored. (See Galatians 6:1) Always remember the enemy has no legal right to enter your life unless you open the door to him. Choose to resist the devil. Choose to not give him any place in your personal life.

As a believer, your ability to operate in the authority of the kingdom towards others and in society is determined by several factors. First, you must have been taught who you are in Christ and have been established in spiritual understanding. Secondly, you must have allowed Christ to be formed in your soul. You must always remember that it is Christ living through you that enables the kingdom of God to be manifested toward the world and people around you. If you have not allowed Christ to be formed in your soul, it will hinder His authority and life from being able to live through you. Walking obediently to the Lord and remaining yielded is a key factor in actively advancing the kingdom of God around you.

"Therefore take up the whole armor of God, that you may be able to withstand in the evil day, and having done all, to stand. Stand therefore, having girded your waist with truth, having put on the breastplate of righteousness, and having shod your feet with the preparation of the gospel of peace; above all, taking the shield of faith with which you will be able to quench all the fiery darts of the wicked one. And take the helmet of salvation, and the sword of the

Spirit, which is the word of God; praying always with all prayer and supplication in the Spirit."

Ephesians 6:13

It is after you have "done all" that you are to stand against everything that is contrary to the rule and kingdom of God. Notice that part of the "doing all" is taking up the whole armor of God. The word translated "done" comes from the Greek word *"katergazomai"* which also carries the idea of being rendered fit for a thing (Strong's # 2716). Therefore, when you are rendered fit, have worked out your own salvation, and lastly put on the whole armor of God, you are ready to stand against the works of the devil around you. You have to first defeat and have the areas in your own life submitted to the authority of Christ before you can begin to stand against the issues in other people's life and within society. This is why Paul said, *"And being ready to punish all disobedience when your obedience is fulfilled"* (2 Corinthians 10:6).

Observe that the armor of God lists topics that you have encountered during the phases of your spiritual development. You have learned the importance of the second elementary teaching of Christ which is faith toward God. It is by faith that you are able to quench all the fiery darts of the enemy. Through your faith, the Spirit of the Lord is able to raise up a standard against the flood of the enemy. Your faith is the victory that has overcome the world. (See 1 John 5:4)

Your mind is to be protected by the helmet of salvation. Through the Word of God and the witness of the Holy Spirit, you can have peace of mind concerning your salvation. Your mind has been delivered from the authority and torment of the devil. You do not have to listen to his condemnation and accusations based on your past before Christ. Allow your mind to be guarded with the helmet of salvation.

You are to put on the breastplate of righteousness. You must continually remind yourself of the truths contained in the doctrine of righteousness. You are to be confident that you are in right standing with God through faith in Christ. You know that Christ has become your righteousness. Because of the shed blood of Christ you are able to approach the throne of God boldly, make known your request, and spend time with your heavenly Father. Thank God for the finished work of Jesus Christ; and that it does not need for you to add anything to it!

As a child of God you are to stand with your life centered on the truth of God's Word. Your waist is to be girded with the faithfulness of God. Never has one word of God failed to accomplish what it was sent forth to produce. Your waist represents the center of the body. Your life is to be surrounded and directed by truth. The truth of God's Word enables you to remain balanced. Have your waist girded with truth as your stand against the works of the enemy.

Your ability to stand against the enemy will flow out of your intimacy with the Father. You are to pray always with all types of prayer as you resist the works of the enemy. In formation phase the different kinds of prayer were addressed. There is a place for each type of prayer as you encounter different attacks and situations in your life. You are to draw near to God and put your cares into His hands. Regardless of what you face you must purpose to persevere in prayer.

A piece of the armor of God is having your feet prepared to advance the gospel of peace. Your feet are not destined to be aimless or self-guided. Your feet are to be bound with preparation. You are not to go forward in your kingdom purpose without having your course set and directed by godly preparation. You must be prepared in order to share the gospel of peace with others. The kingdom advances through believers who have been prepared with the gospel of peace.

"For the weapons of our warfare are not carnal but mighty in God for pulling down strongholds."

2 Corinthians 10:4

The body of Christ does not depend on carnal weapons. It is not by our own ability but by the Spirit of the Lord that we are to stand against the enemy. (See Zechariah 4:6) The sword of the Holy Spirit is the Word of God. You are to speak the word of God by faith. As you do, the sword of the Lord will prevail against the already defeated enemy. The Spirit of God will always respond to faith in the Word of God that is demonstrated through our speech.

"To the intent that now the manifold wisdom of God might be made known by the church to the principalities and powers in the heavenly places, according to the eternal purpose which He accomplished in Christ Jesus our Lord."

Ephesians 3:10-11

The purpose of God from the beginning carried the intent that His wisdom would be known by and through the church. The word "purpose" is translated from the Greek word *"prothesis"* which carries the meaning of setting forth something for viewing (Strong's # 4286). It also is the same word used for the showbread that was placed in the holy place under the Old Covenant. Therefore, God's intention for the body of Christ is to show forth or display His wisdom by manifesting the life and kingdom of Christ through us. As the body of Christ, "having done all," stands against the works of the enemy, we will see the victory of Christ revealed. Remember, Satan and his kingdom have already been defeated but we, as the body of Christ, are responsible to enforce the victory that Christ has won.

Chapter 16

The Law of the Kingdom

"Where the word of a king is, there is power; and who may say to him, 'What are you doing?'"

Ecclesiastes 8:4

Jesus Christ is your King and He has established the law of the kingdom. As you remain obedient to this law you are able to experience the power of the kingdom. Jesus Christ has set you free from sin and bondages in order for you to become His bondservant or slave. Throughout the book of Acts, we read of the power of the kingdom being manifested and it was administered primarily by those who referred to themselves as bondservants of Christ. Peter, Paul, Epaphras, and Jude all understood that there was power in the word of the King. The law of the Kingdom is to hear the words of the King.

"Assuredly, I say to you, there are some standing here who shall not taste death till they see the Son of Man coming in His kingdom.' Now after six days Jesus took Peter, James, and John his brother, led them up on a high mountain by themselves...And behold, Moses and Elijah appeared to them, talking with Him. Then Peter answered and said to Jesus, 'Lord, it is good for us to be here; if You wish, let us make here three tabernacles: one for You, one for Moses, and one

for Elijah.' While he was still speaking, behold, a bright cloud over-
shadowed them; and suddenly a voice came out of the cloud, saying,
*'This is My beloved Son, in whom I am well pleased, **Hear Him!**'"*
Matthew 16:28-17:1-5 (Bold Mine.)

It was on Mount Sinai where God spoke and gave to Moses the Old Testament Law. It was on this high mountain that the Law of the Kingdom was given. Jesus referred to what happened in this text as Peter, James, and John seeing *"the Son of Man coming in His kingdom."* It was during this manifestation of His kingdom that the Father said we are to *"hear Him."* Therefore, the Law of the kingdom is to hear Him.

In the kingdom, God has only ordained for the King of Kings to be heard. It was while Peter was still expressing his thoughts, opinions, plans, and words that they were overshadowed by the command to hear Christ. As a child of God you do not live in a democracy but in a kingdom. Jesus Christ, as King of the kingdom, must be heard and obeyed. What Jesus has spoken and is speaking is the law of the kingdom. Everything in our life and in the activity of the body of Christ must be submitted to this law of hearing Him.

"The Lord your God will raise up for you a Prophet like me from
*your midst, from your brethren, **Him you shall hear**."*
Deuteronomy 18:15 (Bold Mine.)

Under the Old Covenant, God informed Moses and the nation of Israel that He would raise up a Prophet, like Moses, that they should hear and obey. Jesus Christ is the Prophet that God promised to raise up. Therefore, it is Christ the King that you must hear and obey. I love how the law of hearing Him directs the body of Christ toward an intimate relationship with Christ. Biblical Christianity is far more than trying to follow a list of written rules. It is experiencing a vibrant relationship with the living King.

Since you are commanded to hear Christ you must first find out what He spoke while He was here on the earth. The Father has sought to direct every person's attention to Christ and to any commands He may have given. As you hear what He has said and is saying, you will be at the same time obeying the law of the kingdom by hearing the Law of Christ.

Relationship to the Law of Moses

"Therefore, my brethren, you also have become dead to the law (of Moses) through the body of Christ, that you may be married to another- to Him who was raised from the dead, that we should bear fruit to God."

Romans 7:4 (Parenthesis Mine.)

When you died with Christ you also died to the Law of Moses or *"the law of commandments contained in ordinances"* (Ephesians 2:15). As a child of God under the New Covenant you are not to be led by a list of rules or commandments contained in ordinances. You have died to a system of law-keeping in order for you to be married or joined to Christ. You no longer have a relationship with the Law of Moses. This is what it means to have become dead to the law.

Your relationship with God is not to be founded upon the letter of the law. Paul said, *"The letter kills, but the Spirit gives life"* (2 Corinthians 3:6). The letter of the law is not to direct your behavior or judgments each day. As a new creation in Christ under the New Covenant a new law has been established. You are under the law of the kingdom.

As you spend intimate time with the Lord, He will speak to you. You have not been joined to a piece of paper containing commandments but to the living Son of God. It is as you obey what He speaks to you that you receive His power to bear fruit to God. This is how your good works stem from Him and are performed for His glory. The hundred and twenty believers on the Day of Pentecost were endued with power as they obeyed the command to wait. The ten lepers were cleansed *"as they went"* in obedience to His word (Luke 17:14). It was when the man with the withered hand obeyed the King's command that *"his hand was restored"* (Mark 3:5). Where the word of the King is there is power!

"For though I am free from all men, I have made myself a servant to all, that I might win the more; and to the Jews I became as a Jew, that I might win Jews; to those who are under the law, as under the law (though not being myself under the law), that I might win those who are under the law; to those who are without law, as without law (not being without law toward God, but under law toward Christ), that I might win those who are without law."

1 Corinthians 9:19-21 (Marginal Reading NKJV.)

Notice Paul was very clear that he was not under the Law of Moses. There were times out of love when he became like the Jew in order to reach them for Christ. However, like every believer he had died to the Old Testament Law through Christ and yet was not without a law to direct his life. Paul acknowledged that toward God he was under the law of Christ. The same is true for your life. The law of the kingdom is to hear Him. The law of Christ is what the New Testament refers to the command He gave while on earth. The Law of Moses was the Old Covenant. The law of Christ is for the New Covenant.

The Law of Christ

"Bear one another's burdens, and so fulfill the law of Christ."

Galatians 6:2

It should not be surprising that the law of Christ directs our lives towards others. When Jesus came it was not *"to be served, but to serve, and to give His life a ransom for many"* (Mark 10:45). We do not give our life for a ransom; however, we are to lay down our selfish desires in order to be a vessel for Christ to live through toward others. Jesus paid the ransom but He does need His body to disperse to others the provisions of His finished work. We are to serve others by allowing Christ to be manifested through us.

Commanded to Love

"This is My commandment, that you love one another as I have loved you."

John 15:12

Jesus has commanded His followers to love one another. The love that He has shown you is to become the model for how you are to treat others. You are commanded to love as He has loved. When you truly have heard Him you are aware that He has given the command to love. Loving others is not to be an option for you when convenient but a command that is to direct your entire life.

"Teacher, which is the great commandment in the law?' Jesus said to him, 'You shall love the Lord your God with all your heart, with all your soul, and will all your mind. This is the first and great commandment. And the second is like it: 'You shall love your neighbor as yourself.' On these two commandments hang all the Law and the Prophets.'"

Matthew 22:36-40

Jesus ministered under the Old Covenant. So when a lawyer asked Him what the greatest commandment was under it, He spoke of loving God with your entire being and the second as loving your neighbor as yourself. The demonstration of what obedience to these top two commandments would be like is the essence of the Ten Commandments. The Law of Moses contained the entire commandments, statutes, and judgments of what a life of love was to look like under the Old Covenant. In order for people to know what they should do, they had to consult the letter or written Covenant. (See 2 Corinthians 3:6-7)

"A new commandment I give to you, that you love one another; as I have loved you, that you also love one another. By this all will know that you are My disciples, if you have love for one another."

John 13:34-35

267

Under the New Covenant, the law of the kingdom is a new commandment and a new style of living. As the Apostle John mentioned, it is a new commandment but it has also stemmed from the two greatest commandments under the Old Covenant. (See 1 John 2:7-8) It is new because you are now to love as Christ loved you. In the Old Covenant you were to love others as you loved yourself. The Old Covenant was preoccupied with self focus because it was to reveal man's sinfulness. (See Romans 3:20) The New Covenant is preoccupied with focus on Christ.

"And this is His commandment: that we should believe on the name of His Son Jesus Christ and love one another, as He gave us commandment."

1 John 3:23

The commandment of God the Father is to believe on His Son Jesus Christ. (Remember, the Biblical definition of "believe" includes responding through repentance and sincere faith that leads to the fruit of confessing Christ as Lord with both your mouth and through water baptism.) If a person claims to love God, the Father, then he or she must love His Son. Then once a person has believed on Christ and come into a relationship with Him, they are to obey His commandment to love one another. If a person claims to love Jesus then he or she must love His followers. The commandment of the Father is to believe on the Son and the commandment of the Son is to love those who believe. This is why the Apostle John said we are to *"love one another, as He (Jesus) gave us commandment" (1 John 3:23/ Parenthesis Mine)*.

"The love of God has been poured out in our hearts by the Holy Spirit who was given to us."

Romans 5:5

This verse sheds light on the new system of living under the New Covenant. As a child of God, when you were given the Holy Spirit the love of God was poured into your heart. You do not have to consult "the letter" or a list of rules in order to know what love would look like. You now, because of the new birth and the indwelling presence of the Holy Spirit, have the law of the New Testament written upon your heart and mind. (See Hebrews 8:7-13)

"That the righteous requirement of the law (Old Testament) might be fulfilled in us who do not walk according to the flesh but according to the Spirit."

Romans 8:4 (Parenthesis Mine.)

Though you are dead to the law there remain righteous requirements that you could find under the Old Covenant that do apply to the children of God. This is because God's nature, or what He has determined evil or holy, always remains the same. (See James 1:17) So, even though you are dead to the law and its sacrificial system was fulfilled by Christ, the moral truth it contained continues to exist under the New Covenant. As you walk according to the Spirit your behavior will reflect the acceptable behavior for the kingdom of God. This acceptable behavior meets the requirements for God's eternal standard of what is right and wrong.

"Owe no one anything except to love one another, for he who loves another has fulfilled the law. For the commandments, 'You shall not commit adultery,' 'You shall not murder,' 'You shall not steal,' 'You shall not bear false witness,' 'You shall not covet,' and if there is any other commandment, are all summed up in this saying, namely, 'You shall love your neighbor as yourself.' Love does no harm to a neighbor; therefore love is the fulfillment of the law."

Romans 13:8-10

When you walk according to the Spirit you do not commit adultery, steal, lie, or break any of the Ten Commandments of the Old Covenant. So as you, through the indwelling Spirit, walk in love you meet God's standard requirements for right behavior. This moral standard is unchanging; therefore, it existed under the Old Covenant and exists under the New Covenant. Walking in love fulfills God's moral standard for right and wrong behavior. The Old Covenant has served its purpose and has become obsolete. (See Hebrews 8:13)

However, as you obey the command of Christ to love under the New Covenant you fulfill God's righteous standard which was also contained in the old.

"Though I speak with the tongues of men and of angels, but have not love, I have become sounding brass or a clanging cymbal. And though I have the gift of prophecy, and understand all mysteries and all knowledge, and though I have all faith, so that I could remove mountains, but have not love, I am nothing. And though I bestow all my goods to feed the poor, and though I give my body to be burned, but have not love, it profits me nothing."

1 Corinthians 13:1-3

Love is to be the motivation for all you perform. God values, not only what you do for the kingdom, but why you do it. Your talents, resources, and gifting are to be used with a heart full of love. Speaking in tongues does you no good if you do not have love ruling in your heart. Operating in the gifts of the kingdom is meaningless without love. The body of Christ is to be motivated and clothed in the love of God.

As you begin to navigate further through impartation phase never forget the importance of love. Your purpose in the kingdom of God is to be fulfilled with a heart full of love, not selfish ambition. Your pride and ego is to give place to the love of God. Good works without love is nothing more than religious behavior. It is a form without the substance of the life of Christ. Love is to be the driving force behind the activity for the kingdom of God. Love is to be the motivation for the gifts of the kingdom. Your service is to flow from love, not any unrenewed mentalities. Faith is to work by love. (See Galatians 5:6) Prophecy is to work by love. All the gifts of the Spirit are to be performed by love.

Jesus Christ gave the commandment for His followers to love when He was on earth. This is what He has already commanded that you are to hear Him about. Jesus said, *"By this all will know that you are My disciples, if you have love for one another"* (John 13:35). When you are truly hearing Him you will be directed into the love of God.

"But concerning brotherly love you have no need that I should write to you, for you yourselves are taught by God to love one another."

1 Thessalonians 4:9

Some might wonder why this section on love is not closer to the beginning of the book. The answer is in the Scripture quoted above. When it comes to the topic of love new believers do not need another person to teach them about it. This is because new believers are taught directly by God how to walk in love. This is the only thing I have found in Scripture that states that God directly teaches His children. Therefore, when it comes to love He does not need His ministers or mature believers to instruct the young in faith in the way of love.

When God seeks to teach His children on other topics related to their spiritual development He may accomplish it both indirectly and directly. It is indirectly when He uses other believers as vessels to teach and instruct the young in faith and those growing toward maturity. However, Paul said every believer has the experience of being taught directly by God to love one another. With other topics, some believers may be taught indirectly while others believers, on the same issue, were taught directly. Nevertheless, when it comes to the topic of love, every believer has the experience of being taught directly by God.

A new believer does not have to be instructed or told to love others because they have become partakers of the divine nature. As a new creation in Christ they have been created to love. (See 1 John 5:1) Also, the love of God has been poured out in their hearts by the Holy Spirit. The law of Christ has been written upon their heart and mind by the Holy Spirit. Then believers throughout their life should be reminded, exhorted, and encouraged to keep the main thing the main thing: The command to love.

The Spoken Command

"Therefore, as the Holy Spirit says: 'Today, if you will hear His voice, do not harden your hearts as in the rebellion.'"

Hebrews 3:7-8a

The Lord still speaks to His people. Jesus said, *"My sheep hear my voice"* (John 10:27). The law of the kingdom to hear Him also includes what He has currently spoken to you. To harden your heart and rebel against His spoken command concerning the situation you may find yourself in equals lawlessness. This type of resistance is rebelling against the law of Christ.

"Christ also loved the church and gave Himself for her, that He might sanctify and cleanse her with the washing of water by the word."

Ephesians 5:25b-26

The word translated "word" is from the Greek word *"rhema"* which carries the idea of the spoken word or living voice (Strong's #4487). Notice that Christ washes the church through the spoken word or command. Out of your relationship with the Lord He will begin to speak to areas in your life that are hindering you from moving forward in your spiritual development. As you grow in your intimacy with the Lord, you will become more acquainted with His voice. The Scripture speaks of this process as learning to discern what the right decisions are for your life. (See Hebrews 5:14)

"It is the Spirit who gives life; the flesh profits nothing. The words that I speak to you are spirit, and they are life."

John 6:63

There will be numerous times in your life when you face a situation that the Bible does not specifically give you the answer for. For example, you cannot find in the Bible who you should marry. You cannot find in the Bible what job you should take. You cannot find in the Bible what city you are to live in. You cannot find in the Bible if you should invest money in a company. However, with each of these examples there are guidelines and principles that the Bible does give that sets some boundaries. Nevertheless, within the Biblical boundaries you need to hear Him concerning your situation. You need the spoken command.

The life of Jesus is experienced as you hear and obey the words that He speaks to you by His Spirit. The Lord's words are spirit and they are life. His spoken command to your spirit can provide what your own ability could never accomplish or foresee. This is the abundant life that Jesus has made available for you. A life led and guided by His spoken command. One major word of caution that must be understood is the voice of the Lord would never contradict the principles, guidelines, and boundaries already provided in the Bible. Any voice or guidance that is contrary to what boundaries the Bible does provide is not the voice of the Lord. You must *"test the spirits"* (1 John 4:1).

"For as many as are led by the Spirit of God, these are sons of God."

Romans 8:14

The word translated "sons" is the Greek word *"huios"* (Strong's #5207). In this context it is used to describe you manifesting by your character that you are a child of God (Vine's Dictionary). This is similar to how Jesus used it in the Sermon on the Mount. (See Matthew 5:9, 44-45) A manifestation of spiritual development is learning to be led by the Spirit of God. You are to grow in your ability to know and discern the Spirit's leading every moment, every day, and for every major decision. Learn to hear and be led by the Holy Spirit for He only repeats what He hears the King speak. (See John 16:12-14) Lastly, you might want to read again Chapter 11.

Chapter 17

Empowered for the Kingdom

*"But you shall receive power when the **Holy Spirit has come upon you**; and you shall be witnesses to Me in Jerusalem, and in all Judea and Samaria, and to the end of the earth."*

Acts 1:8 (Bold Mine.)

Jesus reminded the disciples before His ascension that the Holy Spirit would come upon them. The Holy Spirit coming upon them would enable them to be His witnesses and to administer the kingdom of God on the earth.

Since our warfare is not against flesh and blood we need a supernatural empowerment from God in order to stand against the supernatural forces of Satan. Throughout the book of Acts we read of the kingdom of God advancing through the vessels that had been empowered by the Holy Spirit. A measure of the empowerment that Jesus received following His water baptism had then been transferred to His disciples. (See Matthew 3:16 & Acts 10:38)

*"And being assembled together with them, He commanded them not to depart from Jerusalem, but to wait for the **Promise of the Father**, 'which,' He said, 'you have heard from Me; for John truly baptized with water, but you shall be **baptized with Holy Spirit** not many days from now.'"*

Acts 1:4-5 (Bold Mine.)

Jesus referred to this one experience in Acts chapter one in three different ways. In verse four as the *"Promise of the Father."* In verse five as *"being baptized with the Holy Spirit."* In verse eight as receiving power *"when the Holy Spirit has come upon you."* Notice that Jesus in this conversation with the disciples, right before His ascension, made it clear that the disciples have already heard and been instructed about this experience by Him beforehand. So let us first look to the Scriptures concerning this experience when described as the "Promise of the Father."

The Promise of the Father

*"And the Scripture foreseeing that God would justify the Gentiles by faith, preached the gospel to Abraham beforehand, saying, 'In you all the nations shall be blessed.'… Christ has redeemed us from the curse of the law… that the blessing of Abraham might come upon the Gentiles in Christ Jesus, that we might receive **the promise** of the Spirit through faith."*

Galatians 3:8,13a,14 (Bold Mine.)

The promise of the Father to His children is specifically the baptism with the Holy Spirit or also as the Scripture refers to it as receiving power when the Holy Spirit comes upon you. This promise was originally spoken to Abraham and was included in what is referred to as the covenant of promise. (See Galatians 3:17) This covenant of promise that God gave to Abraham was that through His seed or lineage all nations would be blessed. Paul said that the essence of the gospel was preached to Abraham through the phrase *"in you all the nations shall be **blessed**"* (Bold Mine). The promise of the Father was included in that phrase and is therefore a part of the blessing!

"Now to Abraham and his Seed were the promises made. He does not say, 'And to seeds,' as of many, but as of one, 'And to your Seed,' who is Christ."

Galatians 3:16

The Seed of Abraham was and is a reference to Christ. Therefore, it is through Christ that all the nations can be blessed. By believing in Christ, and coming into union with Him, you are able to experience the "blessing of Abraham" or the promises that were made to him in the covenant of promise. This covenant of promise included both the gift of righteousness and the gift of the Holy Spirit.

"And if you are Christ's, then you are Abraham's seed, and heirs according to the promise."

Galatians 3:29

Another aspect of the covenant of promise to Abraham was that his seed would be heir of the world. Paul said that *"the promise that he would be the heir of the world"* was received by faith (Romans 4:13). In Christ you are Abraham's seed and have become a joint heir of this world. This is what it means to be a joint heir with Christ. (Romans 8:17) In Christ, you have received an inheritance of land in the kingdom of God. God desires for His kingdom to come to this earth.

The promise of righteousness is connected to being able to receive the promise of the Holy Spirit. The promise of receiving the Holy Spirit is connected to being able to receive the promise of being a joint heir of this world. You have become righteous in Christ in order to be empowered. You then are empowered in order to be a joint heir of this world. As a joint heir in Christ you are to enforce the rule of God upon the earth and its inhabitants. Speaking about this earth, God promised Abraham that his *"descendants shall possess the gate of their enemies"* (Genesis 22:17b). What Adam had lost in the garden was promised to be restored to Abraham. Once again in partnership with God mankind would have dominion over the earth and subdue it. (Genesis 1:28)

Through the new birth you are able to be blessed or receive the blessing that God promised to the Seed of Abraham. You must understand that according to the Scriptures the terms to *"be blessed"* or the *"blessing of Abraham"* includes receiving the promised Spirit. The person who has been justified by faith and become a child of God has been brought into a position where they are able *"to receive the promise of the Spirit."* And receiving this empowerment by the Holy Spirit is for the advancement of the kingdom of God.

*"This Jesus God has raised up, of which we are all witnesses. Therefore being exalted to the right hand of God, and having **received from the Father the promise of the Holy Spirit**, He poured out this which you now see and hear... Then Peter said to them, 'Repent, and let every one of you be baptized in the name of Jesus Christ for the remission of sins; and you shall **receive the gift of the Holy Spirit**. For **the promise** is to you and to your children, and to all who are afar off, as many as the Lord our God will call.'"*

Acts 2:38-39 (Bold Mine.)

In this text, the promise of the Father, or being baptized with the Holy Spirit, is referred to as the gift of the Holy Spirit. After Jesus was exalted to the right hand of God He received the ability to pour out the promise of the Father. The Apostle John said before Jesus' death, *"The Holy Spirit was not yet given, because Jesus was not yet glorified"* (John 7:39). Now the question must be asked: Did any person before, or even during the lifetime of Jesus, have any experiences or fellowship with the Holy Spirit? The answer is yes! There are numerous examples throughout the Scriptures of this. One took place in the days of Moses.

"Then the Lord came down in the cloud, and spoke to him, and took of the Spirit that was upon him, and placed the same upon the seventy elders; and it happened, when the Spirit rested upon them, that they prophesied."

Numbers 11:25

So, if the Holy Spirit had been clearly active before Jesus ascended then how was He not yet given? The Holy Spirit had not yet been given in His New Testament role and ministry. Therefore, in Acts and other verses when the Scriptures speak of receiving the Holy Spirit, it is in this sense that it does so. Jesus said, *"However, when He, the Spirit of truth, has come"* (John 16:13a). So, does this mean that the Spirit of truth had no previous activity? No! Again,

278

Jesus is saying to the disciples that the Holy Spirit had not come in His full and complete roll under the New Covenant. This could not happen until the finished work of Jesus was accomplished. Therefore, as a child of God living after the ascension of Jesus Christ you can receive the Holy Spirit in His full role and ministry for your life.

Before I continue, I must stress that great is the mystery of godliness or the nature of the Godhead. (See 1 Timothy 3:16) It is because of this mystery that many people stumble as they try to depend upon their own understanding. You must purpose in your heart to allow your mind to accept both what the Scripture addresses and does not address. This is what it means to think within what the Scripture says and reveals. (See 1 Corinthians 4:6)

There are times you must accept the limitations of both what your mind can understand and what the Scripture addresses. For instance, many people get hung up on this topic because they constantly try to figure out questions related to "how." The problem with this is that the Scriptures do not always explain things to the satisfaction of your natural mind. Therefore, it requires you to accept by faith what the Scriptures do say and provide answers for, regardless, of whether the reasonings of your natural mind have been satisfied or not.

Jesus was born of the Spirit from the moment of conception. (See Luke 1:35) And being born of the Spirit, Jesus increased in wisdom and in favor with God and men (Luke 2:52). However, in some new sense the Holy Spirit descended upon Jesus later in life after His water baptism. The gospel of Matthew says, *"When He had been baptized, Jesus came up immediately from the water; and behold, the heavens were opened to Him, and John saw the Spirit of God descending like a dove and alighting upon Him"* (Matthew 3:16).

The life of Jesus provides a parallel and a pattern for your own experience. When you repented and placed faith in Christ, you received Him and were born again by the Spirit. (See John 3:3-8) By being born of the Spirit you are also able to grow in your spiritual development. (See Galatians 4:19) Nevertheless, there still remains for you, in some new sense, an encounter with the Holy Spirit for your life.

"And He was handed the book of the prophet Isaiah. And when He had opened the book, He found the place where it was written:

'The Spirit of the Lord is upon Me, because he has anointed Me to preach the gospel to the poor; He has sent Me to heal the brokenhearted, to proclaim liberty to the captives and recovery of sight to the blind, to set at liberty those who are oppressed; to proclaim the acceptable year of the Lord.'"

Luke 4:17-18

It was only after this occurrence that Jesus said the above prophecy was fulfilled. Jesus connected the Holy Spirit coming upon Him to receiving an empowerment for ministry. He was empowered to preach, to heal the brokenhearted, to proclaim liberty, recovery of both physical and spiritual sight, to set the oppressed free, and to proclaim the acceptable year of the Lord. We would not dare to say that Jesus did not have the Holy Spirit before this experience. Nevertheless, Jesus said that it was when the Holy Spirit descended upon Him that He was anointed for ministry. It was only after this incident that we have record of Jesus performing miracles.

"How God anointed Jesus of Nazareth with the Holy Spirit and with power, who went about doing good and healing all who were oppressed by the devil, for God was with Him."

Acts 10:38

Jesus was born of the Holy Spirit but it was later when God anointed Him with the Holy Spirit. It was after He received this anointing that He *"went about doing good and healing all who were oppressed by the devil."* The same was true for the disciples who were in the upper room on the Day of Pentecost. It was after the Holy Spirit came upon them that they went about performing miracles and advancing the kingdom of God. Peter explained the Holy Spirit coming upon them as a fulfillment to what God had promised in the Old Testament.

*"But this is what was spoken by the prophet Joel: 'And it shall come to pass in the last days, says God, that **I will pour out of My Spirit***

280

*on all flesh; your sons and your daughters shall prophesy, your young men shall see visions, your old men shall dream dreams, and on My menservants and on My maidservants **I will pour out My Spirit** in those days; and they shall prophesy.'"*

Acts 2:16-18 (Bold Mine.)

The promise of the Father was that He would pour out His Spirit upon all flesh. What had only been the temporary experience of some under the Old Covenant would now be available to every child of God. Regardless of a persons gender, God had promised to permanently pour out His Spirit and empower them to advance the kingdom of God. This outpouring of God's Spirit was to enable all the servants of God to flow in the supernatural power of God. Peter said that what took place on the Day of Pentecost was a fulfillment of what God spoke by the prophet Joel. This is the same thing Jesus called: the Promise of the Father, being baptized with the Spirit, and receiving power when the Holy Spirit has come upon you.

"If you then, being evil, know how to give good gifts to your children, how much more will your heavenly Father give the Holy Spirit to those who ask Him!"

Luke 11:13

Empowerment for the kingdom of God is promised by the Father to His children. Notice the Father is extremely willing to give the Holy Spirit to His children who ask Him. Again, you must understand that when the Scripture speaks of receiving the Holy Spirit it almost always uses this phrase in the sense of receiving Him in His complete role and ministry under the New Covenant. It is only those who have already become children of God through the new birth that are able to receive the outpouring of God's Spirit. (See John 14:15-17)

One Baptism, Two Aspects

*"Moreover, brethren, I do not want you to be unaware that all our fathers were under the cloud all passed through the sea, all were **baptized into Moses** in the cloud and in the sea."*

1 Corinthians 10:1-2 (Bold Mine.)

The relationship between the children of Israel and Moses is a type of your relationship with Christ. All of the children of Israel were *"baptized into Moses."* This phrase speaks of there being one baptism. However, notice that it was *"in the cloud and in the sea"* that the children of Israel were baptized into Moses. Therefore, there were two aspects or experiences of their being baptized into Moses. This is the same for you as a believer in Christ.

*"There is one body and one Spirit, just as you were called in one hope of your calling; one Lord, one faith, **one baptism**; one God and father of all, who is above all, and through all, and in you all."*

Ephesians 4:4-6 (Bold Mine.)

The Apostle Paul states very clearly that there is "one baptism" for the believer in Christ. Yet, Scripture also clearly speaks of both water baptism and being baptized in the Holy Spirit. This "one baptism" Paul refers to is regarding being baptized in the body of Christ. It is the same as the example of the children of Israel being baptized into Moses.

"For as many of you as were baptized into Christ have put on Christ."

Galatians 3:27

When you repented and received Christ you became a part of the body of Christ. You were immersed into the provisions of the work of Christ. The old you were buried with Christ and you became a new creation in Christ. You were born again as a person descending from the lineage of Christ. You then became a person who was "in Christ." You had been, supernaturally through the new birth, baptized into Christ. You, through your faith in the working of God, became identified with the death, burial, and resurrection of Jesus Christ. You are in Christ and Christ is in you. (See Galatians 2:20)

*"Moreover, brethren, I do not want you to be unaware that all our fathers were under the cloud all passed through the sea, all were baptized into Moses **in the cloud and in the sea.**"*

1 Corinthians 10:1-2 (Bold Mine.)

The two aspects of you having been baptized into Christ are water baptism and Holy Spirit baptism. The Old Testament type for the children of Israel was the cloud and the sea. The cloud was a type of the baptism of the Holy Spirit for the child of God. The sea was a type of water baptism under the New Covenant. The children of Israel being baptized into Moses in the sea is a reference to the Red Sea crossing. In chapter three we discussed the need for you as a believer in Christ to be water baptized. Therefore, let us continue in this chapter to discuss the baptism of the Holy Spirit.

*"Then the **cloud covered the tabernacle of meeting**, and **the glory of the Lord filled the tabernacle**. And Moses was not able to enter the tabernacle of meeting, because the cloud rested above it, and the glory of the Lord filled the tabernacle. Whenever the cloud was taken up from above the tabernacle, the children of Israel would go onward in all their journeys. But if the cloud was not taken up, then they did not journey till the day that it was taken up. For the **cloud of the Lord** was above the tabernacle by day, and fire was over it by night, in the sight of all the house of Israel, through all their journeys."*

Exodus 40:34-38 (Bold Mine.)

The cloud was the manifest presence of the Lord among the people of Israel. It guided them in their journeys toward the promise land. It was a source of protection for them both in the daytime and in the night. In the day, the presence of the Lord manifested as a cloud covering them from the scorching heat of the sun. In the dark, the presence of the Lord was a fire that kept them warm and also provided light as they walked. The cloud of the Lord and its provisions is an example (or Old Testament typology) of being baptized with the Holy Spirit under the New Testament.

It was Paul who wrote that there was one baptism and who also correlated it with the example of the children of Israel being baptized into Moses in the cloud and in the sea. The Scriptures are clear and do not contradict themselves. There is one baptism into Christ but it is appropriated in the two aspects of water baptism and in being baptized with Holy Spirit. Just as being water baptized is a distinct experience from being born again so is being baptized with the Holy Spirit. (See Appendix)

The doctrine of baptisms and the specific teaching on the baptism in the Holy Spirit are rooted in the Old Testament Scriptures. This is important to remember when seeking to understand what is written in the New Testament concerning it. The Old Testament types provide details, descriptions, and pictures that are consistent with those who received the baptism in the Holy Spirit after the ascension of Jesus.

Baptized with the Holy Spirit

"I indeed baptize you with water unto repentance, but He who is coming after me is mightier than I, whose sandals I am not worthy to carry. He will baptize you with the Holy Spirit and fire."
Matthew 3:11

John the Baptist preached that the One who would come after him would baptize people with the Holy Spirit and fire. The picture John paints for his hearers is the same picture the Scriptures present concerning the pillar of cloud and fire that came upon the nation of Israel. All four of the gospels refer to the fact that it is Jesus who would baptize people with the Holy Spirit. John the Baptist was told that the person who he saw the Spirit descending and remaining upon was the One who baptized with the Holy Spirit. (See John 1:32-33)

This is why Jesus pointed to the blind seeing, the lame walking, the lepers being cleansed, the deaf hearing, the dead raised, and the preaching of the gospel by Him to give John assurance that He was the Messiah. (See Luke 7:18-22) Only a person whom the Spirit had remained upon would be able to continually administer the kingdom of God upon the earth. Also, only He could be the person who would baptize others with the Holy Spirit and fire. What God did, when He took the Spirit upon Moses and put it upon the seventy elders, would now be available through Christ on a greater scale. A measure of the same anointing that God placed upon Jesus is now available to be put upon every child of God under the New Covenant. (See Ephesians 4:7) As Peter said, *"For the promise is to you and to your children, and to all who are afar off, as many as the Lord our God will call"* (Acts 2:39).

"When the Day of Pentecost had fully come, they were all with one accord in one place. And suddenly there came a sound from heaven, as of a rushing mighty wind, and it filled the whole house where they were sitting. Then there appeared to them divided tongues, as of fire, and one sat upon each of them. And they were all filled with the Holy Spirit and began to speak with other tongues, as the Spirit gave them utterance."

Acts 2:1-4

This account was the fulfillment of what Jesus had commanded the disciples to wait for. The whole house was filled with the power of the Holy Spirit and they were all filled with the Holy Spirit and began to speak with other tongues. Jesus said, *"For out of the abundance of the heart the mouth speaks"* (Matthew 12:34). As the disciples' hearts were filled with the presence of the Holy Spirit, it flowed out of their mouth through tongues as the Spirit gave them utterance. Tongues were the manifestation of their hearts initially being filled with the Holy Spirit. The Spirit gave them the utterances or words and they did the speaking.

The picture here of this outpouring is the same as when the cloud of His presence covered and filled the temple on the day that the tabernacle of Moses was raised. (See Exodus 40:34-38) Now, under the New Testament the new temple of God had been established and was being covered and filled with the Holy Spirit. The picture is both the Holy Spirit coming upon the believers and also filling them on the inside. In this text, the promise of the Father, being baptized with the Holy Spirit, and receiving power when the Holy Spirit comes upon you is described as the disciples being surrounded by His presence and experiencing the initial infilling of the Holy Spirit.

"Now when the apostles who were at Jerusalem heard that Samaria had received the word of God, they sent Peter and John to them, who, when they had come down, prayed for them that they might receive the Holy Spirit. For as yet He had fallen upon none of them. They had only been baptized in the name of the Lord Jesus. Then they laid hands on them, and they received the Holy Spirit."

Acts 8:14-17

In this text the believers in Samaria had already received the Word of God and been water baptized through the ministry of Philip. They had received Christ and been born again but had not yet been baptized in the Holy Spirit. They had become partakers of Christ. (See Hebrews 3:14) Just like Christ was anointed with the Holy Spirit, Christ in them now needed to be baptized with the Holy Spirit. They had already received the second person of the Godhead, Jesus Christ. However, they had not received the third person of the Godhead in His full New Testament role and ministry. They needed in this sense, to become partakers of the Holy Spirit. (See Hebrews 6:4b)

This Scripture again demonstrates that being born again, being water baptized, and being baptized in the Holy Spirit are separate experiences. It was not until Peter and John came to Samaria and laid hands on them that they received the Holy Spirit. Remember, the phrase used here of receiving the Holy Spirit is speaking of receiving Him in His complete role and ministry under the New Covenant. It is talking about receiving the baptism in the Holy Spirit. The picture that is used of the Holy Spirit falling upon them coincides with the prophecy of Joel that God would pour out of His Spirit upon all flesh.

"And as I began to speak, the Holy Spirit fell upon them, as upon us at the beginning. Then I remembered the word of the Lord, how

He said, 'John indeed baptized with water, but you shall be baptized with the Holy Spirit.' If therefore God gave them the same gift as He gave us when we believed on the Lord Jesus Christ, who was I that I could withstand God?'"

Acts 11:15-17

Peter, in this text, is giving an account of what happened when he preached to the household of Cornelius in Caesarea. As Peter was still preaching the gospel, the Holy Spirit fell upon this group of Gentiles in the same manner as He did with him on the Day of Pentecost. Peter connected what happened in this story to the words of the Lord concerning being baptized with the Holy Spirit. They had received the same gift of being baptized with the Holy Spirit as those in the upper room did on the day of Pentecost. Peter knew they had been baptized with the Holy Spirit because he *"heard them speak with tongues and magnify God"* (Acts 10:46). The evidence that they had received the baptism in the Holy Spirit was when Peter heard them speaking in tongues.

"Paul...finding some disciples said to them, 'Did you receive the Holy Spirit when you believed?' So they said to him, 'We have not so much as heard whether there is a Holy Spirit.' And he said to them, 'Into what then were you baptized? So they said, 'Into John's baptism.' Then Paul said, 'John indeed baptized with a baptism of repentance, saying to the people that they should believe on Him who would come after him, that is, on Christ Jesus.' When they heard this, they were baptized in the name of the Lord Jesus. And when Paul had laid hands on them, the Holy Spirit came upon them, and they spoke with tongues and prophesied."

Acts 19:1-6

Notice that Paul joined the question of whether these disciples had received the Holy Spirit to a question concerning what they had been baptized into. This again shows that the phrase of "receiving the Holy Spirit" is used by the Apostles and the Scriptures to refer to being baptized with the Holy Spirit. Also for Paul to ask if they received the Holy Spirit when they believed demonstrates again that it is something distinct from being born again. Even if a person is baptized with the Holy Spirit at the moment of being born again, like the household of Cornelius, they still remain two distinct biblical experiences regardless of when it is received.

Paul found out that these disciples had not yet been born again. They had only received the water baptism of John for repentance. John's water baptism was a baptism of preparation. It prepared people by turning them from their sinful lives and looking expectantly toward their coming Savior. Paul pointed these disciples to believe in Christ. After they had believed they were water baptized in obedience to the gospel. Then Paul laid hands on them and the Holy Spirit came upon them and they spoke with tongues and prophesied.

Notice that in every account of people being baptized with the Holy Spirit it was a distinct experience from being born again and being water baptized. These stories in the book of Acts completely coincide with the Old Testament types and prophecies that we have looked at. The promise of the Father which is being baptized with the Holy Spirit is for you. (See Acts 2:39) The same initial evidence of speaking in tongues is for you when you are baptized with the Holy Spirit. Most of the doctrine and teaching regarding being baptized with the Holy Spirit was established previously in the Old Testament. What we read in the book of Acts is people experiencing something that had already been established and taught by the Old Testament Scriptures.

In the Old Testament, only select individuals experience the Holy Spirit coming upon them. However, this experience was only temporary in duration. The Holy Spirit would come upon a person for a specific purpose and then He would leave. Now under the New Testament every child of God can have the Holy Spirit come upon them and remain permanently like He did upon Jesus. This empowerment by the Holy Spirit is for you to be able to administer the kingdom of God upon earth and its inhabitants. You will be empowered to stand against the works of the devil.

Receive

1. Being baptized with the Holy Spirit is for you if you have become a child of God. (John 14:17)

2. Receiving the baptism with the Holy Spirit is offered to you as a promise from God the Father. (Acts 2:39)

3. Therefore, you can only receive by faith. (Galatians 3:14 & Romans 4:4-5; 11:6)

4. You are to ask God to be baptized with the Holy Spirit. (Luke 11:13)

5. Jesus is the One who baptizes you with the Holy Spirit. (John 1:33)

6. Many times it is received by faith through the laying on of hands. (Acts 8:17)

7. Through being baptized with the Holy Spirit you will receive the anointing upon, and the initial infilling within, with the evidence of speaking in tongues. (Acts 1:8, 2:2-4, 10:44-46, 19:6)

8. The Holy Spirit will provide the utterance but you must do the speaking. (Acts 2:4)

Chapter 18

Sharing the Kingdom

"First, I thank my God through Jesus Christ for you all, that your faith is spoken of throughout the whole world."

Romans 1:8

Your faith should be shared and not kept a secret. The faith of the believers in Rome was spoken about throughout the whole world. Your faith also should be spoken about in the world you encounter each day. At home, at family gatherings, and at your work, your faith should be shared. Jesus said, *"You are the light of the world. A city that is set on a hill cannot be hidden"* (Matthew 5:14). The fact that Christ lives in you and that you have had Christ formed in you will cause your life to be a demonstration of your faith and the kingdom of God. You have been empowered by the Holy Spirit to be a witness.

The sharing of your faith should be visible through both your deeds and your words. You cannot separate the two when discussing the topic of sharing your faith. You have faith in certain truths and are to communicate those truths to others. However, biblical faith also affects the way you live. The Scripture states, *"For as the body without the spirit is dead, so faith without works is dead also"* (James 2:26). Without having both of those in your life, the communication of your faith will not be as effective for the kingdom of God. Also, much damage has been done in the name of Christ because people have not shared their faith by both their deeds and their words.

People need more than religion. Many people are seeking for something. Though they do not know exactly what they are looking for, they do know they need something more than just a piece of paper with beliefs that they are to accept and adhere to mentally. They need the power of Christ to change them. They need a new life. They need forgiveness, peace, and a relationship with God. This is clearly more than just words. This is why the Apostle Paul said, *"For the kingdom of God is not in word but in power"* (1 Corinthians 4:20). Sharing the kingdom and our faith in Christ must consist of communicating the gospel by our transformed life and with the words that testify of the person who can also change them.

People need to be able to observe the gospel of Jesus Christ. They need to be able to observe the culture of the kingdom of God. People need to see the life of Jesus living through you. Your life should make people thirsty with curiosity and questions. Jesus said, *"You are the salt of the earth"* (Matthew 5:13). As they begin to think, ponder, and meditate on what they are observing, it will begin to affect their heart.

"For out of the abundance of the heart the mouth speaks."
Matthew 12:34

When their heart is filled with questions then eventually those questions will flow out of their mouth. This is extremely important because their heart has to be prepared for the hearing of the gospel. Jesus shared how the heart is like the earth. The good ground speaks of the heart that has been prepared. It is a heart that is responding to what the Spirit of God is doing in their life. It is a heart that is open and seeking. The result of such a heart is that when the person hears the words of the gospel they understand it and indeed bear fruit. (See Matthew 13:18-23)

The sharing of your faith through your deeds and words will always lead to different responses. The responses of people are determined by the condition of their heart. You must remember that when some respond negatively, they are not rejecting you but Christ.

Jesus said, *"He who hears you hears Me, he who rejects you rejects Me, and he who rejects Me rejects Him who sent Me"* (Luke 10:16). Remember, this rejection can manifest against your lifestyle and against the words of truth. Paul said a man named Alexander greatly resisted his words. (See 2 Timothy 4:15).

"I planted, Apollos watered, but God gave the increase."
1 Corinthians 3:6

Sharing your faith sometimes leads to a person being planted in the kingdom of God, while other times you are watering the condition of their heart. Sometimes it leads to persecution. Peter said, *"Yet if anyone suffers as a Christian, let him not be ashamed, but let him glorify God in this matter"* (1 Peter 4:16). However, you should never focus only on the responses of people around you. Remaining obedient to God should be your focus. You must learn to depend on the discernment of the Holy Spirit concerning the people around you. God knows the hearts of all mankind. (See 2 Chronicles 6:30) And their heart determines how the Holy Spirit is working in their life.

"Therefore He says: 'God resists the proud, but gives grace to the humble.'"
James 4:6

It is impossible for you to bear fruit for God without the Spirit of God doing the work through you. You have to follow the leading of the Holy Spirit when you share your faith with words. There are some people God is resisting because of their pride. These types of people are hardened toward God. They have closed their hearts and ears to the voice of the Lord. However, it amazes me how many people go ahead without the leading of the Spirit of God and try to witness to them. Listen, your own self-effort in evangelizing will not be productive for the kingdom of God. It is only the Spirit that can give life; therefore, you must follow His leading.

You must understand that you need to be sensitive to where people are in their response to the work of the Holy Spirit in their life. You can tell when you are forcing a conversation and are sharing your faith in your own ability. The conversation will lead to nothing edifying. The person will not be open to what you are sharing because their heart is in a state of resisting God. They are not open or yielded to the influence of the Holy Spirit. The discussion will cause you to become irritated or angry because the grace of the Lord is not leading you. There is a difference between a person who is open and seeking, than someone who is hardened and resisting. You will save yourself much frustration if you learn to follow the leading of the Spirit instead of depending on your own self effort.

"Let them alone. They are blind leaders of the blind. And if the blind leaders of the blind. And if the blind leads the blind, both will fall into a ditch."

Matthew 15:14

Jesus told the disciples to leave certain people alone. Why? They had chosen to shut their heart to the influence of the Holy Spirit. They were blind because of their own hardened heart. (See Ephesians 4:18-19) These people need prayer, not the hearing of your words. They had already resisted the words that had been shared with them numerous times. Judgment is what lies ahead for people like this. This is why sometimes people like this go through such a horrible incident. This is an act of the mercy of God to soften their heart to His call and influence.

This is what happened for the majority of the city of Jerusalem. Jesus spoke or prayed over them, *"How often I wanted to gather your children together, as a hen gathers her chicks under her wings, but you were not willing"* (Matthew 23:37). Then they experienced judgment when the city was destroyed in 70 A.D. When you read through the Gospels you will notice that Jesus did not witness to all people the same. He discerned where they were at spiritually. Were they seeking or were they resisting? Were they religious or were they a broken sinner? Each heart needs to be ministered to differently. The more you follow the Holy Spirit the more you will have the wisdom to say the necessary words to reach the current condition of their heart.

Prayer is a way that people's heart can come again under the influence of the Holy Spirit. As you intercede on their behalf you are asking mercy and grace to flow from the throne of God into their life. As you trust in the Lord you will learn to become more and more sensitive on how the Holy Spirit desires to use you in the lives of the people around you. There are people all around you who are open to the work of the Lord in their hearts. If you will remain open, God will use you to speak into their life the words of salvation.

By Deed

"You are our epistle written in our hearts, known and read by all men; clearly you are an epistle of Christ, ministered by us, written not with ink but by the Spirit of the living God, not on tablets of stone but on tablets of flesh, that is, of the heart."
2 Corinthians 3:2-3

Paul told the believers at Corinth that they were a living epistle known and read by all men. Clearly Paul viewed sharing the kingdom, as being more than just words. Your life and deeds are observed and evaluated by all the people you spend time with. Since you have navigated through the previous phases of spiritual development people should notice the change that Christ has produced in your deeds and walk. Through your Christ-like actions the power of the cross is proclaimed to those who knew you before. You have put off the deeds of the old man and now your family, friends, and co-workers are encountering the deeds of the new man you have become in Christ.

"Exhort bondservants to be obedient to their own masters, to be well pleasing in all things, not answering back, not pilfering, but showing all good fidelity (honesty), that they may adorn the doctrine of God our Savior in all things."
Titus 2:9-10 (Parenthesis Mine. NKJV Marginal Reading)

Possessing biblical doctrine is more than just mental assent. True doctrine is a lifestyle that is in accordance with acceptable behavior for the kingdom of God. Paul instructed Titus to exhort the believers to be obedient to their bosses. As a child of God, your character is to be different from the unbelievers you work with. You are not to be argumentative, disruptive, or lazy on the job. By your deeds people are to view the gospel of Jesus Christ that *"is the power of God to salvation"* (Romans 1:16).

"Let as many bondservants as are under the yoke count their own masters worthy of all honor, so that the name of God and His doctrine may not be blasphemed."

1 Timothy 6:1

Sharing the kingdom through your words while your conduct is contrary to the character of Christ will bring reproach upon the name of Christ. Wrong deeds and wrong character among unbelievers gives place for the doctrine of God to be blasphemed. Such actions give place for doubt and confusion to attack the minds of unbelievers. This is because unbelievers need to view that God can perform for them what He has promised in His Word. As you allow Christ to live through you, they will be able to see a consistency with what you say and do. This is the only way to ensure that the name and doctrine of God is not spoken evil of. Paul said that *"the obedience of your confession to the gospel"* will lead people to glorify God (2 Corinthians 9:13).

Signs of the Kingdom

"And we are His witnesses to these things, and so also is the Holy Spirit whom God has given to those who obey Him."

Acts 5:32

You have been empowered with the Holy Spirit in order to bear witness of the kingdom of God. Jesus said that *"signs will follow those who have believed"* (Mark 16:17). A vital aspect of sharing the kingdom through your deeds is manifesting the signs of the kingdom. The Holy Spirit has anointed you to lay hands on the sick, cast out demons, and bring God's will in heaven upon the earth.

"And as you go, preach, saying, 'The kingdom of heaven is at hand.'
Heal the sick, cleanse the lepers, raise the dead, cast out demons.
Freely you have received, freely give."

Matthew 10:7-8 (Bold Mine.)

When Jesus sent out the twelve he told them to declare that the kingdom is being manifested through the sick being healed, the lepers being cleansed, the dead coming to life, and demons being cast out. This verse gives the essence of impartation phase. The anointing and ministry of the Holy Spirit that you have freely received from Christ you are to freely give its benefits to others. The anointing of God that breaks every yoke is what you have to impart and give to others.

*"Then Peter said, 'Silver and gold I do not have, but **what I do have I give you**: In the name of Jesus Christ of Nazareth, rise up and walk.' And he took him by the right hand and lifted him up, and immediately his feet and ankle bones received strength."*

Acts 3:6-7 (Bold Mine.)

Peter gave the lame man what he had to give: the anointing of God. In the authority of the name of Jesus Christ and by the power of the Holy Spirit this man received strength and immediately began to walk for the first time in his life. Peter demonstrated the kingdom through this deed. He shared the kingdom with someone who desperately needed it. What he had freely received, he freely gave to this lame man. This is the heart of sharing the kingdom through the signs of the kingdom. He gave and administered the kingdom of God upon that which was contrary to God's will.

Through the finished work of the cross you have been able to be empowered for the kingdom. The anointing you have received is in order for the Lord to minister to others through you. Your deeds should share the reality of the kingdom, both in your godly character and in manifesting the signs of its presence. The purpose of the anointing coming upon Jesus is the same purpose it has come upon you. Choose to be a vessel to impart the anointing you have received upon those that are hungry and in need. (See Luke 4:18)

By Word

"But sanctify the Lord God in your hearts, and always by ready to give a defense to everyone who asks you a reason for the hope that is in you, with meekness and fear."

1 Peter 3:15

This Scripture shows the importance of experiencing the phases of transformation and formation. In order for you to truly be ready to give a defense of the faith, Christ must be sanctified as Lord in your heart. Therefore, it is apparent that Scripture exhorts you to share of the kingdom through your words, that flow out of your godly character and your obedience to Christ. The rule of Christ in your will and heart is the true preparation for sharing your faith by word.

There are many times we are too timid to share our faith through our words because we have allowed compromise to root in our heart. These little foxes hinder the boldness of the Holy Spirit in our life. In times such as this, your conscience seeks to accuse you and keep you from feeling able to share your faith. This is why you are exhorted to always be ready. You never know when the Lord has arranged an opportunity for you to share your faith with another person.

"Walk in wisdom toward those who are outside, redeeming the time. Let your speech always be with grace, seasoned with salt, that you may know how you ought to answer each one."

Colossians 4:5-6

Your speech has power. It has the power to influence those that hear what you speak. Ideas, thoughts, doubts, negativity, and comfort can all be transferred through your words. This is why you are exhorted to always have your speech release grace. Your words should release God's influence upon those you speak with. Notice that you walk in wisdom toward unbelievers by having been prepared to know how you should answer them.

"How then shall they call on Him in whom they have not believed? And how shall they believe in Him of whom they have not heard? And how shall they hear without a preacher?"

Romans 10:14

This is an amazing verse. It shows the value of believers who are ready at all times to share the gospel through their words. This is the main method that God has ordained for people to be born again. Paul said, *"it pleased God through the foolishness of the message preached to save those who believe"* (1 Corinthians 1:21). Sharing the kingdom through your deeds and through signs prepare people's hearts for the moment of hearing.

Unbelievers must hear and understand the gospel of Christ in order to believe. They are unable to call upon what they have not heard. Your mouth is a tool of God for salvation. You, as a child of God on this earth, have the ability to speak the words by which people can be saved. The angel told Cornelius to call for Peter *"who will tell you words by which you and all your household will be saved"* (Acts 11:14).

"And since we have the same spirit of faith, according to what is written, 'I believe and therefore I spoke,' we also believe and therefore speak."

2 Corinthians 4:13

When you believe something it is like putting water to boil; eventually it is going to move you to action. The apostle Paul spoke because he believed. When you believe that you have the words of salvation that can release the power of God and snatch a person from the grasp of sin you will speak. The spirit of faith or presence of the Lord wants to be imparted into others through your words. I pray you will become bolder each day *"to speak the word without fear"* (Philippians 1:14). As you pray, ask *"that God would open to you a door for the word, to speak the mystery of Christ"* (Colossians 4:3).

Chapter 19

Mentored for the Kingdom

"Two are better than one, because they have a good reward for their labor."

Ecclesiastes 4:9

The primary method that facilitates your spiritual development during the impartation phase is being mentored. A spiritual mentor is someone that is more mature than you in the things of God, that is used by God to impart into your life. By having a mentor, you are able to submit to the counsel, wisdom, and guidance of a seasoned man or woman of God for your purpose in the kingdom. You can learn from a mentor's mistakes instead of having to repeat them. Proverbs 19:20 states, *"Listen to counsel and receive instruction, that you may be wise in your latter days."* A mentor can help teach and direct you in the things of God. You can learn from them how to flow in the power of the Holy Spirit and maximize the gifts of God you have been given. Two are better than one!

"Counsel in the heart of man is like deep water, but a man of understanding will draw it out."

Proverbs 20:5

Spiritual mentors are used by God to help draw out what He has put within you. There are many things that a mentor will be able to see about you that you will not be able to discern yourself. Moments spent with a mentor allows someone who has walked with the Lord longer than you to speak concerning what you are facing. A good mentor is a person of understanding that will draw out your greatest potential for the kingdom of God.

"For this reason I am sending to you Timothy, my son whom I love, who is faithful in the Lord. He will remind you of my way of life in Christ Jesus, which agrees with what I teach everywhere in every church."
1 Corinthians 4:17

Timothy was a spiritual son to the Apostle Paul. Paul took Timothy under his wings and mentored him in the kingdom of God. Timothy was brought to a place in his life where he was able to faithfully remind believers of the ways of Christ that Paul taught in every church. Timothy was trained in his purpose for the kingdom of God by Paul. Paul imparted to Timothy the knowledge, experience, and wisdom that he had gained in his years of ministering the kingdom of God.

I hope that you will begin to ask God to connect you to a spiritual mentor that can help equip you for your purpose in the kingdom. God has mature believers all around you that have already navigated through and encountered what He has called for you to do. No mentor is perfect. However, a mentor will empower you in the things of God to go further than you could every reach on your own. Believe today that God is turning the spiritual *"hearts of the fathers to the children, and the hearts of the children to their fathers"* (Malachi 4:6).

Accountability

"Then the apostles gathered to Jesus and told Him all things, both what they had done and what they had taught. And He said to them, 'Come aside by yourselves to a deserted place and rest a while.'"
Mark 6:30-31

One of the greatest things about having a mentor is that it is a relationship that provides true accountability. A mentor can speak into your life and address any areas that need to be brought into balance. When the apostles returned from ministering they gathered to Jesus and told Him everything that happened. As Jesus, the mentor, listened to the twelve He must have discerned something that needed to be addressed. Out of this conversation Jesus directed the twelve to take time to rest. This is the power of a mentoring relationship.

If the disciples had not received godly counsel from their mentor they most likely would have never thought to take time to rest after their recent kingdom activity. I have never met a person in the impartation phase who on their own, without the godly counsel of a mentor, understood that importance of taking time to rest from kingdom activity. This is because the glory of young men and young women in the faith is their strength. However, the splendor of the mature in faith is the wisdom they possess. (See Proverbs 20:29) The young in the faith always need to have their zeal and strength rightfully directed!

As a mentor, Jesus was able to help them navigate around potential burnout or spiritual harm that has happened to multitudes of believers through the years. This is just one example of the type of wisdom, redirection, and accountability a mentor will provide for your life. A mentor will be able to help guard you from potential pitfalls that would keep you from being able to continue in the good works you were created to perform.

"For My thoughts are not your thoughts, nor are your ways My ways,' says the Lord. 'For as the heavens are higher than the earth, so are My ways higher than your ways, and My thoughts than your thoughts.'"

Isaiah 55:9

There are many spiritual truths that will not initially make sense to you during this phase. This is because the ways and methods of the kingdom of God are so much higher than what you are naturally accustomed to. Having the wisdom of a mentor when facing crossroads as to what you should do is invaluable. Normally the way of the kingdom is always contrary to what will feel natural for you to do. A mentor relationship provides a person that can speak from godly experience and impart good judgment for you in times like this. Every believer needs a person that can look them in the eye and say, 'what are you doing.'

The most dangerous idea you could harbor during this phase is that you are above the need of accountability. It is a sad reality that many people reject the idea of having a mentor because of their underlying issues of self-will or rebellion. Self-will always feels natural to your flesh, but when followed will always lead you away from the power of the cross. (See Philippians 2:3) Submission and accountability is something that is learned behavior because it does not come natural. However, there is safety in submitting to godly counsel and the guidance of a spiritual mentor. (See Ephesians 5:21)

"Likewise you younger people, submit yourselves to your elders. Yes, all of you be submissive to one another, and be clothed with humility, for 'God resist the proud, but gives grace to the humble.'"

1 Peter 5:5

Every healthy spiritual mentor has themselves learned the lesson and power of submission. The flesh of each of us is like the unbroken horse running in the wild. A wild horse is full of strength and full of potential but still wild and self-directed. A broken horse has learned to come under the direction and power of another. This is the essence of becoming broken in the biblical sense. Brokenness is being in a position where you have become dependant on outside help. You then are in a position where you are able and willing to be taught, guided, and molded. A broken horse has become submitted and dependant on the direction from another source other than its self. A healthy spiritual mentor that has learned submission can also be used by God to help teach you.

"Obey those who rule (lead) over you, and be submissive, for they watch out for your souls, as those who must give account. Let them

do so with joy and not with grief, for that would be unprofitable for you."

    Hebrews 13:17 (Parenthesis Mine. NKJV Marginal Reference)

A spiritual mentor that is not a pastor or leader over the people of God in a local assembly must be submitted to the ones in place in order to be a healthy mentor. If they are not, then you should not submit yourselves to them. Mentors who have not learned to submit to others are not worthy of having other people submit to them. These unhealthy mentors are the types who distort what biblical submission is because they have never learned it themselves. They are wolves in sheep clothing. (See Acts 20:29-30) Remember this as a guide to discern the spiritual mentor(s) that God has truly connected you with.

Submission is not blind obedience. Therefore, you would never have to submit to anything that is contrary to Scripture. As a follower of Christ you are never to submit to anything that is contrary to His ways and Word. However, God will teach you submission by you learning to listen to and obey your mentor or pastor's godly advice. The idea that you can be a lone ranger and still fulfill your purpose in the kingdom of God is not biblical. You are to learn to obey and be submissive to those God has set in place to watch out for your soul. You have become a part of the body of Christ and have been placed under the leadership (or joint) that God has set in place. (See Ephesians 4:11-16)

For example, this means there are times when facing a decision you will feel like you should go left but God will speak through your mentor to go right. The difficulty of such a moment is that you probably will not perceive that God is speaking through your mentor. This is the lesson of submission. In something that is not contrary to Scripture, can you submit to the advice and counsel given to you by your mentor? To be submitted to a person means that you will obey what you are asked to do as long as it is not against the principles of Scripture.

The issues of submission and accountability deal with more than just your actions. The attitude you harbor is a vital aspect of walking in biblical submission. It is not submission when you do something in obedience to the leader over you while griping the entire time. Paul said, *"Do all things without complaining and disputing"* (Philippians 2:14). It is not wrong if you disagree with a decision of a leader. However, the attitude you possess towards the leader, the attitude in which you carry out what you were asked to perform, the words that you express, and the manner in which you express them, all determine if you are manifesting true submission. This is because it is always necessary to be clothed with humility in order to walk in biblical submission. (See 1 Peter 5:5)

Posture of Biblical Leadership

"But Jesus called them to Himself and said, 'You know that the rulers of the Gentiles lord it over them, and those who are great exercise authority over them. Yet it shall not be so among you; but whoever desires to become great among you, let him be your servant. And whoever desires to be first among you, let him be your slave- just as the Son of Man did not come to be served, but to serve."
Matthew 20:25-28a

The posture of biblical leadership is servanthood. Jesus, as the ultimate example for biblical leadership, said that He did not come to be served but to serve. This means that when Jesus entered into relationships with others it was to empower them with His serving. This is the difference between an attitude of 'what can I get' and one of 'what can I give.' The Lord contrasts the standard for godly leadership with the leadership mentalities, qualities, and techniques of the world. This makes it clear that not every successful leader in the marketplace would be successful in church leadership.

There is a great difference between lording over people and leading people. The later seeks to release people while the former seeks to control them. The leadership methods of the world are motivated by reaching the top in order to be "over" others. The leadership methods of the kingdom are motivated by the desire to serve others in reaching their dreams. The world leads by coercion and force while Christ led by example and love. Leadership motivated by love is *"to lay down your life for the brethren"* (1 John 3:16).

Biblical leadership is always about what is best for others, not what is best for me!

"Let no one despise your youth, but be an example to the believers in word, in conduct, in love, in spirit, in faith, in purity."
1 Timothy 4:12

Paul exhorted the young minister Timothy to be an example to the believers. This is the essence of any type of biblical leadership: lead by example. People will follow leaders that they know have a heart to serve and help them reach their potential in Christ. The only true way to assure the hearts of those you are leading is by your example. The old saying still applies, 'Your actions speak louder than your words.' Believers should want to follow leaders who manifest the biblical posture of servanthood. Therefore, if leaders have to seek to control or manipulate their followers, something is out of order.

"But I trust in the Lord Jesus to send Timothy to you shortly, that I also may be encouraged when I know your state. For I have no one like-minded, who will sincerely care for your state. For all seek their own, not the things which are of Christ Jesus. But you know his proven character, that as a son with his father he served with me in the gospel."
Philippians 2:19-22

Paul in this text reveals that he had become certain about the motives of Timothy. Timothy had assured the heart of his leader Paul by his serving. Notice that to have proven character is to have a heart of servanthood. Serving is not something you do for a while as you wait for a place of leadership in the church. Servanthood is the nature of godly leadership! Therefore, servanthood is the prerequisite as well as the continual requirement for being in a leadership role. Paul sent Timothy to help churches he planted because he was confident that he would sincerely care for their state. It was Timothy's proven character of serving that opened up the opportunity for him to serve in a leadership role. For that reason, servanthood is first the necessary posture for any and all types of leadership roles within the church.

People who want to be in a leadership role in the church but who have never demonstrated the posture of biblical leadership will never sincerely care for the state of the people. This type of believer is what Paul described as those who *"seek their own, not the things which are of Christ Jesus"* (Philippians 2:21). They see leadership as a chance to advance their agenda, seek their desires, and be in control. Such a mentality is what Jesus rebuked as the ways of the unbelieving world. A person who has not first learned to be a servant will never be a godly leader in the kingdom of God. Jesus said the greatest in the kingdom must learn to be a servant to all.

"But let these also first be tested; then let them serve as deacons, being found blameless."

1 Timothy 3:10

Paul instructed Timothy that even deacons must first be tested. Their character and behavior was to first be observed or tested by the light of Scripture before they could serve in a leadership role. Observe that even this role of leadership was described as serving as a deacon. Again, serving is always the method of the kingdom of God for your life.

For example, David first served Saul before he became the great King over Israel. Saul first served no one and later had the throne taken from him by God. Elisha first washed the hands of Elijah before he performed twice as many miracles as him. (See 1 Kings 3:11) Joshua first served as the assistant of Moses before he led the people into the promise land. The same is to be true for you. Follow the biblical path to leadership and find a place to serve! And then continue with a servant heart in leadership.

Chapter 20

Gifts of the Kingdom

"But to each one of us grace was given according to the measure of Christ's gift."

Ephesians 4:7

As a member of the body of Christ you have been given at least one gift. In this Scripture it is described as a gift that Christ has given you. From the Scriptures we are told that God will never regret that He has given you this gift. (See Romans 11:29) The gift you have received was given by grace. It is what the Scriptures refer to as a gift of grace. (See Ephesians 3:7) You did not earn this gift but were given it because of God's divine provision and grace.

The gift you have been given is a measure of the divine capabilities of Christ or also known as grace. It is a divine enablement. You have been given a grace gift that allows Christ to perform a supernatural function through you. The amount of divine capabilities you have been given determines the measure of the gift you were given. Every believer has been given one gift, but not every believer has been given a gift that has the same measure of Christ's ability. Also, some believers have been given a measure that includes several of Christ's gifts. The measure of grace you were given determines the type of gift you possess in Christ and the function that you are to perform in the body of Christ.

"For I say, through the grace given to me, to everyone who is among you, not to think of himself more highly than he ought to think, but to think soberly, as God has dealt to each one a measure of faith. For as we have many members in one body, but all the members do not have the same function."

Romans 12:3-4

Similar to a human body, the body of Christ has many members but still remains one body. Each member of the body does not have the same function as the others. Your function is determined by the measure of grace that God has dealt to you. Here Paul calls the measure of grace a *"measure of faith."* The gift you had been given comes with a measure of faith that allows you to operate in that gifting. It is because of this given measure of faith that it feels natural for you to use your gift and function in the ministry appointed for you. The differences of functions in this verse correlates to the differences of ministries and activities of 1 Corinthians 12:5-6.

Your opinion concerning your function in the body of Christ should be soberly or of a right estimation. How you view your function for the body of Christ is to be determined by the measure of faith or grace you have been given in your gifting. Every believer has a function or purpose in the body of Christ. However, not every believer has the same level of function or influence in the body. For example, a pinky is important in the body. Nevertheless, a pinky does not have the same level of function or influence as the heart in the body.

*"For we dare not class ourselves or compare ourselves with those who commend themselves. But they, measuring themselves by themselves, and comparing themselves among themselves, are not wise. We, however, will not boast beyond measure, but within the limits of the **sphere** which God appointed us - a **sphere** which especially includes you."*

2 Corinthians 10:12-13 (Bold Mine.)

The word translated as "sphere" in English is the Greek word *"metron"* (Strong's 3358). This is the exact Greek word that was translated as "measure" in the previous quoted verses. The gift of grace that you were given determines your God-appointed limit and sphere of ministry and activity in the kingdom of God. It is not wise to compare your gifts and measure to those of other believers. This has led many believers to become jealous, unsatisfied, and rebellious to what God had appointed for them to function as. In order for the body of Christ to perform in its full capacity, each individual member must accept and remain in their God appointed sphere of function that correlates to their gifting.

"But one and the same Spirit works all these things, distributing to each one individually as He wills."

1 Corinthians 12:11

In context, this Scripture refers to each believers gifting. Every believer must come to know and accept the measure of grace they have been given in their gifting. This is coming to rest in God's sovereignty on the topic. God, the Spirit, has distributed to each believer individually gifts as He wills. Notice your will did not come into play when you were given your gifting. God sovereignly chose to distribute to each believer as He desired and willed. Accepting what God has distributed is remaining in the fear of the Lord. It is submitting to God's divine order and design for your life in the body of Christ.

"But now God has set the members, each one of them, in the body just as He pleased."

1 Corinthians 12:18

This means that the ministry and activities or function that God has given for you in the body of Christ is also determined by Him. Your gifting is enablement for the function you have been called to perform. For example, you cannot be called to function as a prophet and not possess the gift of prophecy. Nevertheless, you may possess the gift of prophecy and not be called to function as a prophet. In order to be able to perform certain functions in the body of Christ you must have been given a certain gift or gifts. The gifts are the empowerment to fulfill the functions you have been given to perform.

311

"There are diversities of gifts, but the same Spirit."

1 Corinthians 12:4

Though there are many spiritual gifts, it is the same Spirit that manifests through them. Your fellowship with other believers is not based on you having the same gift as them but in partaking of the same Spirit.

The Bible lists numerous gifts that God has given to the body of Christ. These lists are not to be considered as containing every possible spiritual gift from Christ. (See 1 Corinthians 12:8-10, 28-30; Romans 12:6-8; Ephesians 4:11)

"Therefore, brethren, seek out from among you seven men of good reputation, full of the Holy Spirit and wisdom, whom we may appoint over this business."

Acts 6:3

In this text, the Apostles instructed the believers to seek out seven men who could oversee the business of distributing to the needs of the widows. They gave the requirements that those chosen were *"full of the Holy Spirit and wisdom."* The prerequisite that they were full of the Holy Spirit refers to being baptized with the Holy Spirit and remaining in a position of being completely yielded to Him. The Apostles knew that any work for God must be performed by the empowerment of the Holy Spirit. As the Scripture states, *"Not by might nor by power, but by My Spirit, says the Lord of hosts"* (Zechariah 4:6). Therefore, it was and still is a necessary requirement for those laboring in the work of the kingdom.

The second prerequisite was, that in addition to being full of the Holy Spirit, that they possessed wisdom. This means that it was necessary for those chosen to have demonstrated that they had been given the manifestation of the Spirit through the gift of wisdom. The seven men chosen were to have a good reputation of being full of the Holy Spirit and also of manifesting wisdom. First Corinthians 12:8 states, *"For one is given the word of wisdom through the Spirit."*

You will notice in the book of Acts a continual pattern that Luke uses. For example:

Acts 1:8 - *"you shall receive power when the Holy Spirit has come upon you"*

Acts 4:31 - *"they were all filled with the Holy Spirit, and they spoke the word of God with boldness"*

Acts 6:3 - *"seven men of good reputation, full of the Holy Spirit and wisdom"*

Acts 6:5 - *"And they chose Stephen, a man full of faith and the Holy Spirit"*

Acts 6:8 – *"And Stephen, full of faith and power, did great wonders and signs among the people"*

Acts 10:38 – *"how God anointed Jesus of Nazareth with the Holy Spirit and with power"*

All of these examples have a common factor; they speak of the Holy Spirit and some characteristic. The characteristic that is connected to the Holy Spirit refers to the specific manifestation or gift of the Spirit that was given and operating in the person's life. These Scriptures identify people with a diversity of gifts but yet of the same Spirit.

For example, the specific manifestation of the Holy Spirit that Jesus said the disciples would receive at Pentecost was power. This word translated power is the Greek word *"dunamis"* (Strong's # 1411). It is related to one of the manifestations or gifts of the Spirit. In 1 Corinthians 12:10 the gift is called the "working of miracles." The gift of "working of miracles" is a special ability given by God in order for a believer to activate *"dunamis"* power for the purpose of miracles. This is because the word translated "miracles" is the same Greek word *"dunamis."* Therefore, it is correct to say that a gift of the Spirit is the "working of *dunamis*." The apostles received power or the manifestation of the Spirit related to the working of miracles on the day of Pentecost.

We are told that Stephen had received the manifestation of the gift of faith and the gift of working of miracles. Remember the word translated power in these verses is the same Greek word used for the gift of working of miracles. Every believer has received *"dunamis"* power but not every believer has received the gift of the Spirit to work the "dunamis" power for miracles. (See 2 Timothy 1:7 &

1 Corinthians 12:10-11) Again each of these Scriptures identify the manifestation or gift of the Spirit in a believer's life who had been empowered for the kingdom.

"As each one has received a gift, minister it to one another, as good stewards of the manifold grace of God."

1 Peter 4:10

The gift you have been given is to be a blessing to those around you. You must purpose in your heart to impart to others the measure of grace you have received. The gift is for the building up and edifying of the body of Christ. You must never forget that it is not your gift but Christ's gift given to you. This means that you will have to give an account for your stewardship of this gift. (See Luke 12:42)

In order for you to accomplish the work and assignment that God has called you to perform, He has gifted you with His ability. This gifting or ability you possess is the anointing and empowerment for you to perform your work of ministry. Your gifting is the unique expression of Christ that God has empowered you to manifest. For example, I have never met a person with the gift of giving that did not love to give.

Your gifting allows you to do easily what it takes others time to develop. The gift God has given you is just that – a gift. God instantly, through His gift, provides you with a divine ability to perform your call. You can always grow in your understanding of your gifting. You can always grow in allowing your gifting to work through your life. There are areas in your soul that may need to be transformed so your gifting can be free to work. But the fact remains, you received a divine ability instantaneously when God imparted His gifting to you. Your gifting is a supernatural endowment from God. God's divine grace allows you to perform a function as if it has always been natural for you to accomplish such a task or action.

As you are faithful to minister your gift to others, it will release grace or divine influence upon them. This means that it will help them personally develop in the area of your gifting. For instance, not every believer has the gift of faith but every believer is to have faith. The gift of faith enables a person supernaturally to have strong faith. This means that for the ordinary believer, faith must be grown in and developed. However, to some who have been given the gift of faith, their faith has been granted to be instantaneously strong and developed. Why does God do this?

"According to the effective working by which every part does its share, causes growth of the body for the edifying of itself in love."
Ephesians 4:16b

Gifts were given to the members of the body of Christ in order for the body as a whole to be developed and reach maturity in Christ. The gifts given to the body of Christ are "the powers of the age to come" (Hebrews 6:5). The grace gift given to you is to be imparted for the development of other members in the body of Christ. When you operate in your gift it will effectively work to help other believers be developed in the area of your gifting. A person with the gift of faith is to encourage, stir up, and build up others both in their personal faith and in the exercise of their faith. Every gift is to cause growth in the body in its respective area because every gift is a manifestation of the person of Jesus Christ.

"Having then gifts differing according to the grace that is given to us, let us use them: if prophecy, let us prophesy in proportion to our faith; or ministry, let us use it in our ministering; he who teaches, in teaching; he who exhorts, in exhortation; he who gives, with liberality; he who leads, with diligence, he who shows mercy, with cheerfulness."
Romans 12:6-8

Notice that every gift mentioned is an aspect of the person of Christ that every mature believer is to develop in. Every mature believer is to be able to prophesy, to minister, to teach, to exhort, to give, to lead, and to show mercy. However, not every believer was given the gift of prophecy, the gift of ministry, the gift of teaching, the gift of exhortation, the gift of giving, the gift of leadership, and the gift of mercy. Your gifting is the unique expression of Christ that God has empowered you to manifest.

"But the manifestation of the Spirit is given to each one for the profit of all."

1 Corinthians 12:7

This makes it very clear that the gifting you have been given is to help the other members of the body of Christ develop that specific aspect of the person of Jesus Christ. Every manifestation of the Spirit is for the profit of all! What you are gifted in seems to come naturally for you because you have been empowered by the Holy Spirit for it. However, those without your gift do not find it natural for them to manifest the aspect of Christ that your gift allows you the grace to manifest. This means those who do not possess the gifting you have must develop, and have formed, that specific manifestation of Christ in their own life. You have been empowered by the Holy Spirit to demonstrate and help develop that area in the lives of other believers. The grace gift has enabled you to understand so much concerning the area your gift pertains to, and this knowledge needs to be imparted to others.

If you have been given the gift of giving then your life should demonstrate, teach, and stir up concerning giving in the life of other believers. If you have been given the gift of teaching then your life should demonstrate, teach, encourage, and stir up a passion in others for the Word of God. If you have the gift of exhortation your life should demonstrate and teach others how to be an encourager to those around them. If you have been given the gift of working of miracles then your life should help others learn to activate "dunamis" in their own life for the working of miracles. When you manifest your gifting you are manifesting an aspect of the person of Jesus Christ that needs to be developed in every believer.

"For He whom God has sent speaks the words of God, for God does not give the Spirit by measure."

John 3:34

This verse is talking about Jesus who was sent to this earth to speak the words of God. Jesus, as the divine Son of God, was given the Spirit without measure. Paul said, *"For in Him dwells all the fullness of the Godhead bodily"* (Colossians 2:9). You and I, on the other hand, have only received a measure of the Spirit through our gifting. This measure is the grace gift that we have been speaking about. Therefore, in order for you to reach maturity and the measure of the stature of Christ, you have to receive impartation from other believers who have been graced with a gift and aspect of Christ that you do not possess. By receiving this type of impartation it will enable you to be built up and developed in those areas of the person of Christ. This describes the reason for the healthy interdependence that you are to have with the other members of the body of Christ.

"There are diversities of ministries, but the same Lord."
1 Corinthians 12:5

There are many different ministries that the Lord has determined for people to perform. Every believer has been called into the fellowship of Jesus Christ and into the kingdom of God. (See 1 Corinthians 1:9 & 1 Thessalonians 2:12) However, not every believer has the same ministry to perform within the kingdom of God. The same gifting may be given to two believers yet they have different ministries.

Your ministry is the type of service you have been assigned to perform for the body of Christ. Your ministry refers to the specific manner of service that you execute in order to manifest your gifting and an aspect of the person of Christ. The ministry is the specific vehicle through which your gifting is expressed for the edifying of the body of Christ. The gifting is the empowerment of the Holy Spirit to accomplish the ministry.

For example, two people can have the gift of teaching but one's ministry or service of their gift is through pulpit ministry while the other's is through writing children's books. Two believers can have the gift of leading while one's service is to a committee in the local church and the other person's is in the maintenance of a building. Two believers can have the gift of prophecy while one is called to the ministry of a prophet and the other is called to be a teacher. These scenarios demonstrate the greatness of God and His manifold wisdom. (See Ephesians 3:10)

Discovering Your Gifting

"And He Himself gave some to be apostles, some prophets, some evangelists, and some pastors and teachers for the equipping of the saints for the work of ministry, for the edifying of the body of Christ, till we all come to the unity of the faith and of the knowledge of the Son of God, to a perfect man, to the measure of the stature of the fullness of Christ."

Ephesians 4:11-13

The ministries of an apostle, prophet, evangelist, pastor, and teacher are specifically for the equipping of the saints for the work of ministry. These five ministries are appointed to oversee and lead the rest of the body of Christ. Every overseer or leader of the body of Christ, by God's design, is to be one of these ministers. Those as staff in a local church make up the leadership or eldership. (See 1 Peter 5:1-4; Hebrews 13:17; 1 Timothy 4:14) These ministries have been particularly given to bring believers to maturity in Christ and enable the body to function in a healthy manner.

"From whom the whole body, joined and knit together by what every joint supplies."

Ephesians 4:16a

The body is joined and knit together by joints. This reference to "joints" pertains to the five overseeing ministries of apostle, prophet, evangelist, pastor, and teacher. It is these ministries that provide the structure for the body to stay connected and healthy. These "joints" have been empowered by the Holy Spirit to impart a supply of grace that equips the saints for the ministry that they have been assigned to perform. If you are not submitted to a local church and this type of "joint" leadership then you are disconnected from a necessary supply of the Spirit. Without receiving impartation from such a supply, you will not be able to grow up into the image of Christ, and not fulfill your purpose in the kingdom of God.

"According to the effective working by which every part does its share, causes growth of the body for the edifying of itself in love."
Ephesians 4:16b

The supply of the Spirit that comes through these ministries is in accordance to the divine energy that works through the measure given to every part or member of the body of Christ. These five ministries have been given to enable and empower every member of Christ to function in their given measure of gifting for the overall growth of the body in love. People who are not knit together with other believers and remain submitted under these leaders of the body of Christ are out of the divine order of God for their life. Such people are continually susceptible to attacks, hindrances, and entanglements. There is divine protection under God's divine order.

"Those who are planted in the house of the Lord shall flourish in the courts of our God. They shall still bear fruit in old age; they shall be fresh and flourishing."
Psalm 92:13-14

To be planted in the house of the Lord means that you have become connected and submitted to the local church and its leadership. When you are in such a position then you are able to flourish because you are able to receive the supply of the Spirit that God imparts through the local church leadership. To be planted means that you remain in a fixed position. You remain under authority and keep an attitude of submission and respect. This will cause you to continue to bear fruit for the kingdom of God. You will stay fresh and full of the oil of the Holy Spirit. You will continue to flourish in your assignment for God. Your ability to discover your gifting and fulfill your ministry for the kingdom is first determined by whether you are submitted to such leaders in your local church.

The leaders of a local assembly of believers have been placed by God to help you discover your gifts. As you remain planted and begin to flourish God often times uses the leadership above you to confirm the gifts you have been given. Also, as you remain submitted to the leadership, opportunities for you to serve will open up. These times of serving will provide an environment for your gift to be discovered, manifested, and then confirmed.

"Now in the church that was at Antioch there were certain prophets and teachers...As they ministered to the Lord and fasted, the Holy Spirit said, 'Now separate to Me Barnabas and Saul for the work to which I have called them.' Then having fasted and prayed, and laid hands of them, they sent them away."

Acts 13:2-3

Another way to discover your gifting while you remain planted is through times of fasting. Fasting is one of the ways to earnestly desire spiritual gifts. (See 1 Corinthians 12:31, 14:1) It was during a time of fasting and ministering to the Lord that Paul and Barnabas was set apart for a specific work. Notice both the Lord and the leadership around Paul confirmed his gift and the ministry that he was to perform. It was also after a season of fasting that Jesus *"returned in the power of the Spirit"* (Luke 4:14). He went full of the Holy Spirit into the season of fasting and came out both full and in the power of the Spirit. (See Luke 4:1) The specific manifestation of power related to the working of miracles was stirred in the Lord during this time of fasting.

Stay planted, connected, and under the leadership God has placed over you. Have a desire to know and operate in your gifting. Look for opportunities to serve. Spend time earnestly desiring to be used by God through fasting. Be willing to stay within the measure or sphere God has appointed for you. With such a heart and corresponding actions you will discover your gifting! (For more on this subject check out the author's other book on discipleship)

Rewards in the Kingdom

"For the Son of Man will come in the glory of His Father with His angels, and then he will reward each according to his works."
                                                                Matthew 16:27

God is so good. He forgives you, regenerates you, transforms you, lives through you and then will still reward you. When Jesus Christ returns, He will reward His followers for the good works they allow Him to perform through them. Every time you allow Christ to express Himself through you it will lay up a reward for you in the age to come. You will be rewarded in the millennium for each time you take up your cross in order for the life of Christ to manifest through you.

This is why impartation phase and multiplication phase are joined with the last pair of elementary teachings of Christ which are resurrection from the dead and eternal judgment. Your faithfulness now in ministering the gifting you have to others, and administering the kingdom of God, determines the amount of rewards you will receive at the judgment seat of Christ. It is an amazing fact that Christ will still reward us for what He alone accomplished through us. These rewards are given, because in order for Christ to live through you, you must have the cross applied daily to your soul.

Your current service for the body of Christ affects your future experience in the millennial reign of Christ. God notices and keeps record of every time you deny yourself for the cause of the kingdom. God keeps an account of every time you suffer for His name sake. Jesus said, *"Blessed are you when men hate you, and when they exclude you, and revile you, and cast out your name as evil, for the Son of Man's sake. Rejoice in that day and leap for joy! For indeed your reward is great in heaven* (Luke 6:22-23). You are to follow in the footsteps of our Lord who first embraced suffering while looking to the glories that would follow. (See 1 Peter 1:11)

"Now if anyone builds on this foundation with gold, silver, precious stones, wood, hay, straw, each one's work will declare it, because it will be revealed by fire; and the fire will test each one's work, of

what sort it is. If anyone's work which he has built on it endures, he will receive a reward. If anyone's work is burned, he will suffer loss; but he himself will be saved, yet so as through fire."

1 Corinthians 3:12-15

The reason transformation and formation phase are necessary to navigate through before you seek to fulfill your purpose in the kingdom of God is because your motives and character affects whether your service is worthy of rewards. All activity in the kingdom of God will be tested by the fire of God at the judgment seat of Christ. This judgment is not concerning heaven or hell but between rewards and loss of rewards. As a born again child of God you have already passed from death to life and escaped the eternal judgment for your sins. (See John 5:24)

The fact that you have escaped through faith in the finished work of the cross from an eternal hell does not mean you are to live without a law. You are still under the law of the kingdom, called to walk worthy of the kingdom, and called to walk in the good works that God prepared before hand for you to walk in. This is the essence of what the judgment seat of Christ is to evaluate. At the judgment seat of Christ, your obedience and faithfulness to Christ the King of the kingdom will be tested by fire. The fire will determine your life's work in the kingdom of God.

Only that which is of the character and life of Christ will be able to meet the standard of God. This is what the Scripture referred to as building with gold, silver, and precious stones. These elements represent that which is divine and of Christ. This is God's standard for the test to come. As a follower of Christ you know from the Word of God ahead of time the standard your life's work will be evaluated by. The wood, hay, and straw speak to that which is of the flesh and done with impure motives. The great news is that if you will allow Christ to live through you then those works will always stand the test. You will be rewarded for what Christ performs through you and you will suffer loss of rewards for that which is done in your own strength or impurely.

Having a perspective that your current situations provide potential future rewards is extremely important. All throughout

Scripture, the future blessings and rewards are put in front of God's people to strengthen, encourage, and keep them living for the eternal over the temporary. Jesus, numerous times, taught about people's potential to receive future rewards. It is biblical to receive motivation for your service to Christ because of the thought of future rewards. However, to perform services in the kingdom of God for men to see will cause you to suffer loss of rewards. Nevertheless, it remains true that to have a problem with such a thought of being motivated through the idea of rewards is to have a problem with the teachings and person of the Lord Himself. (See Matthew 10:41-42)

"By faith Moses, when he became of age, refused to be called the son of Pharaoh's daughter, choosing rather to suffer affliction with the people of God than to enjoy the passing pleasures of sin, esteeming the reproach of Christ greater riches than the treasures in Egypt; **for he looked to the reward.***"*

Hebrews 11:26 (Bold Mine.)

Understanding and looking to the potential rewards in the kingdom has great importance. Such a perspective enabled Moses to refuse the false labels of the world and the passing pleasures of sin. It strengthened Moses, not just to endure suffering for the sake of Christ, but to choose it rather than what the unbelieving world had to offer him. Moses acknowledged that, in the long run, the reproaches of Christ in his life were greater riches than the treasure in Egypt. The future rewards in the kingdom that were to come were of greater value and significance than what Egypt presented. It was only as he looked to the reward that he was able to have a right perception and receive strength to endure to temporary sufferings that we experience as children of God.

Resurrection of the Dead Key Points
(All KJV Scripture References)

1. The resurrection of the dead is known as the <u>hope</u> of believers.
    "But when Paul perceived that one part were Sadducees and the other Pharisees, he cried out in the council, "Men and brethren, I am a Pharisee, the son of a Pharisee; concerning the hope and resurrection of the dead I am being judged" (Acts 23:6)!

    "And have hope toward God, which they themselves also allow, that there shall be a resurrection of the dead, both of the just and unjust" (Acts 24:15).

    "And now I stand and am judged for the hope of the promise made by God to our fathers... Why should it be thought incredible by you that God raises the dead" (Acts 26:6,8)?

    "But I do not want you to be ignorant, brethren, concerning those who have fallen asleep (died), lest you sorrow as others who have no hope" (1 Thessalonians 4:13).

    "Looking for the blessed hope and glorious appearing of our great God and Savior Jesus Christ," (Titus 2:13).

2. The resurrection of the dead includes <u>all</u> people.
    "And have hope toward God, which they themselves also allow, that there shall be a resurrection of the dead, both of the just and unjust" (Acts 24:15).

3. The resurrection of the dead is divided into <u>two</u> parts. (See Acts 24:15)
    A) Resurrection of the just
    B) Resurrection of the unjust

4. The resurrection of the just is also called the resurrection of <u>life</u>.
   "And shall come forth; they that have done good, unto the resurrection of life" (John 5:29).

5. The resurrection of the unjust is also called the resurrection of <u>damnation</u>.
   "And shall come forth; they that have done good, unto the resurrection of life; and they that have done evil, unto the resurrection of damnation" (John 5:29).

6. The resurrection of life from the dead has an <u>order</u>.
   "For as in Adam all die, even so in Christ all shall be made alive. But each one in his own order..." (1 Corinthians 15:22-23).

7. Christ was the <u>firstfruits</u> of the resurrection of life.
   "For as in Adam all die, even so in Christ all shall be made alive. But each one in his own order: Christ the firstfruits," (1 Corinthians 15:22-23).

   A) Christ was the first to be resurrected never to die again.
      "Therefore, having obtained help from God, to this day I stand, witnessing both to small and great, saying no other things than those which the prophets and Moses said would come— [23]"that the Christ would suffer, that He would be the first to rise from the dead, and would proclaim light to the Jewish people and to the Gentiles" (Acts 26:22-23).

   B) Christ was the first to rise because He is the resurrection and the life.
      "Jesus said to her, "I am the resurrection and the life. He who believes in Me, though he may die, he shall live" (John 11:25).

8. Many Old Testament saints were raised <u>after</u> Jesus' resurrection.
   "And Jesus cried out again with a loud voice, and yielded up His spirit. Then, behold, the veil of the temple was torn in two

from top to bottom; and the earth quaked, and the rocks were split, and the graves were opened; and many bodies of the saints who had fallen asleep were raised; and coming out of the graves after His resurrection, they went into the holy city and appeared to many" (Matthew 27:50-52).

9. The resurrection of the dead preached to New Testament believers will be in the <u>future</u>.
   "Who concerning the truth have erred, saying that the resurrection is past already; and overthrow the faith of some" (2 Timothy 2:18).

10. The resurrection of the dead for believers will take place at the <u>end</u> of time.
    "Martha said unto him, I know that he shall rise again in the resurrection at the last day" (John 11:24).

11. The rest of believers shall be resurrected at Christ's <u>coming</u>.
    "For as in Adam all die, even so in Christ all shall be made alive. But each one in his own order: Christ the firstfruits, afterward those who are Christ's at His coming" (1 Corinthians 15:22-23).

    A) First those who have died as believers in Christ.
    B) Second those believers who are alive and remain at the time of His coming.

    "For if we believe that Jesus died and rose again, even so God will bring with Him those who sleep (died) in Jesus. For this we say to you by the word of the Lord, that we who are alive and remain until the coming of the Lord will by no means precede those who are asleep (dead). For the Lord Himself will descend from heaven with a shout, with the voice of an archangel, and with the trumpet of God. And the dead in Christ will rise first. Then we who are alive and remain shall be caught up together with them in the clouds to meet the Lord in the air. And thus we shall always be with

the Lord. Therefore comfort one another with these words"
(1 Thessalonians 4:14-18).

12. The resurrection of Jesus Christ was the <u>evidence</u> that He was
the Son of God.
*"And declared to be the Son of God with power, according to the
spirit of holiness, by the resurrection from the dead" (Romans
1:4).*

13. The resurrection of Jesus Christ is the <u>assurance</u> of the fact that
we shall be raised from the dead.
*"Now if Christ be preached that he rose from the dead, how say
some among you that there is no resurrection of the dead? But if
there be no resurrection of the dead, then is Christ not risen:" (1
Corinthians 15:12-13).*

14. Our resurrection shall be in the <u>likeness</u> of Christ's resurrection.
*"For if we have been planted together in the likeness of his death,
we shall be also in the likeness of his resurrection" (Romans
6:5).*

A) Our resurrection body shall bear the image of the heavenly
Man. (1 Cor. 15:47-49)
B) Our resurrection body will be raised in incorruption. (1 Cor.
15:42)
C) Our resurrection body will be raised in glory. (1 Cor. 15:43)
D) Our resurrection body will be raised in power. (1 Cor.
15:43)
E) Our resurrection body will be raised a spiritual body. (1 Cor.
15:44)

15. The resurrection comes <u>before</u> the eternal judgment.
*"And many of those who sleep in the dust of the earth shall
awake, Some to everlasting life, Some to shame and everlasting
contempt" (Daniel 12:2).*

Eternal Judgment Key Points (All KJV Scripture References)

1. Eternal judgment is certain for all <u>mankind</u>.
   "And as it is appointed for men to die once, but after this the judgment" (Hebrews 9:27).

   "Therefore, as through one man's offense judgment came to all men, resulting in condemnation, even so through one Man's righteous act the free gift came to all men, resulting in justification of life" (Romans 5:18).

2. The eternal judgment takes place <u>after</u> the resurrection of the dead.
   "Now as he reasoned about righteousness, self-control, and the judgment to come, Felix was afraid and answered, "Go away for now; when I have a convenient time I will call for you" (Acts 24:25).

   "Of the doctrine of baptisms, of laying on of hands, of resurrection of the dead, and of eternal judgment" (Hebrews 6:2).

3. The future judgment is <u>eternal</u> in nature.
   "Of the doctrine of baptisms, of laying on of hands, of resurrection of the dead, and of eternal judgment" (Hebrews 6:2).

   "Then He will also say to those on the left hand, 'Depart from Me, you cursed, into the everlasting fire prepared for the devil and his angels:…And these will go away into everlasting punishment, but the righteous into eternal life" (Matthew 25:41,46).

   "The devil, who deceived them, was cast into the lake of fire and brimstone where the beast and the false prophet are. And they will be tormented day and night forever and ever" (Revelation 20:20).

4. The eternal judgment is through <u>Jesus Christ</u>.
   "For the Father judges no one, but has committed all judgment to the Son" (John 5:22).

   "And has given Him authority to execute judgment also, because He is the Son of Man" (John 5:27).

   "And He commanded us to preach to the people, and to testify that it is He who was ordained by God to be Judge of the living and the dead" (Acts 10:42).

   "Truly, these times of ignorance God overlooked, but now commands all men everywhere to repent, because He has appointed a day on which He will judge the world in righteousness by the Man whom He has ordained. He has given assurance of this to all by raising Him from the dead" (Acts 17:30-31).

5. The eternal judgment of God is <u>righteous</u> and true.
   "The fear of the LORD is clean, enduring for ever: the judgments of the LORD are true and righteous altogether" (Psalm 19:9).

   "Behold, the days come, saith the LORD, that I will raise unto David a righteous Branch, and a King shall reign and prosper, and shall execute judgment and justice in the earth" (Jeremiah 23:5).

   "I can of Myself do nothing. As I hear, I judge; and My judgment is righteous, because I do not seek My own will but the will of the Father who sent Me" (John 5:30).

   "And yet if I do judge, My judgment is true; for I am not alone, but I am with the Father who sent Me" (John 8:16).

   "Who, knowing the righteous judgment of God, that those who practice such things are deserving of death, not only do the same but also approve of those who practice them" (Romans 1:32).

"But we know that the judgment of God is according to truth against those who practice such things" (Romans 2:2).

"But in accordance with your hardness and your impenitent heart you are treasuring up for yourself wrath in the day of wrath and revelation of the righteous judgment of God" (Romans 2:5).

6. The eternal judgment will bring everything of man, including his works and the <u>secrets</u> of his heart, to light.
   "For God will bring every work into judgment, including every secret thing, whether good or evil" (Ecclesiastes 12:14).

   "Therefore judge nothing before the time, until the Lord comes, who will both bring to light the hidden things of darkness and reveal the counsels of the hearts. Then each one's praise will come from God" (1 Corinthians 4:5).

   "Some men's sins are clearly evident, preceding them to judgment, but those of some men follow later" (1 Timothy 5:24).

7. The standard for the eternal judgment is God's <u>Word</u> and Law revealed to man.
   "He who rejects Me, and does not receive My words, has that which judges him- the word that I have spoken will judge him in the last day" (John 12:48).

   "For the word of God is living and powerful, and sharper than any two-edged sword, piercing even to the division of soul and spirit, and of joints and marrow, and is a discerner of the thoughts and intents of the heart. And there is no creature hidden from His sight, but all things are naked and open to the eyes of Him to whom we must give account" (Hebrews 4:12-13).

   Also See Rom 2:11-16

8. The eternal judgment of God separates people based on whether one has received Christ and their name is written in the <u>Book of Life</u>.

   "He who believes in Him is not condemned; but he who does not believe is condemned already, because he has not believed in the name of the only begotten Son of God" (John 3:18).

   "Most assuredly, I say to you, he who hears My word and believes in Him who sent Me has everlasting life, and shall not come into judgment, but has passed from death into life" (John 5:24).

   "And this is the testimony: that God has given us eternal life, and this life is in His Son. He who has the Son has life; he who does not have the Son of God does not have life" (1 John 5:11-12).

   "And I saw the dead, small and great, standing before God, and books were opened. And another book was opened, which is the Book of Life. And the dead were judged according to their works, by the things which were written in the books. And anyone not found written in the Book of Life was cast into the lake of fire" (Revelation 20:12,15).

9. After the current separation of unbelievers and believers then comes the future judgment based on each one's <u>deeds</u>.

   "But in accordance with your hardness and your unrepentant heart you are treasuring up for yourself wrath in the day of wrath and revelation of the righteous judgment of God, who "will render to each one according to his deeds" (Romans 2:5-6).

   <u>*Rev 20:12, 15*</u> *"And I saw the dead, small and great, standing before God, and books were opened. And another book was opened, which is the Book of Life. And the dead were judged according to their works, by the things which were written in the books. And anyone not found written in the Book of Life was cast into the lake of fire" (Revelation 20:12,15).*

10. The judgment seat of Christ for believers involves <u>rewards</u> or loss of rewards.

    "If anyone's work which he has built on it endures, he will receive a reward. If anyone's work is burned, he will suffer loss; but he himself will be saved, yet so as through fire" (1 Corinthians 3:14-15).

    "For we must all appear before the judgment seat of Christ, that each one may receive the things done in the body, according to what he has done, whether good or bad" (2 Corinthians 5:10).

    "The seventh angel sounded his trumpet, And their were loud voices in heaven, saying, "The kingdom of the world has become the kingdom of our Lord and of His Christ, and He will reign for ever and ever!" The nations were angry, and Your wrath has come, And the time of the dead, that they should be judged, And that You should reward Your servants the prophets and the saints. And those who fear Your name, small and great, And should destroy those who destroy the earth" (Revelation 11:15, 18).

    "And you will be blessed, because they cannot repay you; for you shall be repaid at the resurrection of the just" (Luke 14:14).

11. The judgment of unbelievers involves their level of <u>punishment</u>.

    "And that servant who knew his master's will, and did not prepare himself or do according to his will, shall be beaten with many stripes. But he who did not know, yet committed things deserving of stripes, shall be beaten with few..." (Luke 12:47-48).

    "Since it is a righteous thing with God to repay with tribulation those who trouble you, and to give you who are troubled rest with us when the Lord Jesus is revealed from heaven with His mighty angels, in flaming fire taking vengeance on those who do not know God, and on those who do not obey the gospel of our Lord Jesus Christ" (2 Thessalonians 1:6-8).

    "Who devour widows' houses, and for a pretense make long prayers. These will receive greater condemnation" (Luke 20:47).

Section IV.

Multiplication Phase –
Christ in You the Hope of Glory

Phase
Introduction

As believers continue to fulfill their purpose in the kingdom of God, they are to mature to the spiritual growth stage of being a father or mother in the faith and enter into the multiplication phase for discipleship. Therefore, multiplication phase is connected to the last pair of the elementary teachings of Christ as a believer continues through his or her service to lay up rewards for the age to come. Multiplication phase deals with the entire person, the whole counsel of Scripture, and all four of the primary methods that facilitate spiritual growth as the father or mother in the faith reproduces what God has accomplished in them in the lives of others. Observe the full chart on the next page!

Three Ages Elementary Teachings of Christ Represent	Spiritual Growth Stages	Phases for Discipleship	Primary Division of Truth	Primary "M" Facilitates Growth for Phase
Age 1 Transferring Kingdoms *Repentance from Dead Works and Faith toward God*	Babes	I. Foundation 1 Cor.3:11 (Spirit)	Gospel of Jesus Christ, Elementary Teachings of Christ Overview	Ministry of the Word
	Little Children		Gospel of Grace, Paul's Gospel, Word Of Righteousness	
Age 2 Life in God's Kingdom *Doctrine of Baptisms and Laying on of Hands*	Little Children	II.Transformation Rom. 12:2 (Soul)	Revelation of the Mystery	My Role
	Children			
	Children	III.Formation Gal.4:19 (Soul)	Revelation of the Mystery	Modeling Community
	Young Men			
	Young Men	IV.Impartation Matt.10:7-8 (Body)	Gospel of the Kingdom	Mentoring
Age 3 Life in the Millennium *Rewards for Resurrection and Judgment*	Father	V.Multiplication John17:6-8,20 (Entire Person)	Whole Counsel of Scripture	All the M's

Chapter 21

What's Next?

*"You therefore, beloved, since you know **this** beforehand, beware lest you also fall from your own steadfastness, being led away with the error of the wicked; but grow in the grace and knowledge of our Lord and Savior Jesus Christ. To Him be the glory both now and forever. Amen."*

2 Peter 3:17-18 (Bold Mine.)

As a spiritual father or mother you must continue to grow as you fulfill your purpose in the kingdom of God. For you to stop growing in your intimacy with the Lord is to become more vulnerable of falling from your steadfastness. You must continue to pursue the Lord and grow in both grace and knowledge. To grow only in knowledge will cause you to become prideful and religious. (See 1 Corinthians 8:1) However, to grow only in grace will cause you to be zealous but not according to knowledge. (See Romans 10:2)

The "this" in the verse above that the Apostle Peter is referring to is the fact that there are people who distort and twist Scripture. The way to guard your life against such error is to continue to grow in the grace and knowledge of our Lord. To stop growing means you have stopped experiencing intimacy with the Lord. You must continue to remember that everything is to flow out of your relationship with the

Lord. You have been called to a relationship with a living Savior and this must always be your first priority.

You will never reach a place where you no longer need to spend time in the presence of the Lord. It was because you remained yielded to the Lord that you have reached such a place of being conformed into the image of Christ. You have been faithful to position yourself in a place so God could *"work in you both to will and to do for His good pleasure"* (Philippians 2:13). You must continue to keep your eyes on the author and finisher of your faith. Christ must always remain the center of your life.

"I have fought the good fight, I have finished the race, I have kept the faith."

2 Timothy 4:7

You, like the Apostle Paul, must continue to fight, run, and keep the faith. You are to finish your race and you are to finish with obedience to what you have already learned and received through impartation. You are to do what you know to do. That is what is next for you. You are to continue to be faithful. You are to continue to walk in the light. You are to continue to stand against the enemy. You are to continue to grow in your spiritual understanding of the whole counsel of Scripture. You are to continue to be engaging in the four M's that primarily facilitate spiritual growth. You are to finish *"strong in the Lord and in the power of His might"* (Ephesians 6:10).

You are to continue to reproduce in others what God has accomplished in you. God expects what He has sown in you to be multiplied as you minister it to others. This means multiplication phase is about you mentoring others. You are to be a vessel of God's Spirit to help other believers navigate through the phases. As a father or mother in the faith, you should be able to discern where any believer is in their spiritual development. Therefore, once you have determined the phase, you are then able to impart to them the relevant teachings that are connected to that phase. You are to lead others through the divine design for discipleship that you yourself have gone through.

"I have manifested Your name to the men whom You have given Me out of the world. They were Yours, You gave them to Me, and they have kept Your word. Now they have known that all things which You have given Me are from You. For I have given to them the words which You have given Me; and they have received them, and have known surely that I came forth from You; and they have believed that You sent Me...I do not pray for these alone, but also for those who will believe in me through their word."

John 17:6-8, 20

This prayer of Jesus' gives us great insight into what the Father had sent Him to accomplish. He was to impart spiritual reality into the lives of a few. Jesus manifested the name or character of the Father to the disciples that He was given. He taught them the word of God and how to keep it. He developed and equipped them with intent. Jesus did not want what He started to stop with them, but through them to multiply in the lives of others. Notice that Jesus prayed not just for His disciples but also for those who would come to believe through their ministry. It is clear that Jesus expected what He sowed into the lives of the disciples to cause a multiplication of disciples around the world. This is the essence of multiplication phase.

"Imitate me, just as I also imitate Christ."

1 Corinthians 11:1

You are not Jesus Christ; nevertheless, Christ should be living through you to the extent that you model His character, ways, and ministry to those around you. As God connects you with other believers who are younger in the faith, be purposeful in leading them through the divine design for discipleship. Let your life be an example for them to follow as you remain connected to Christ. (Colossians 2:18-19) Mentor those that God has entrusted to you with expectancy for multiplication; that those you mentor will grow to become a father or mother in the faith and then will, in turn, mentor others.

"And the things that you have heard from me among many witnesses, commit these to faithful men who will be able to teach others also."

2 Timothy 2:2

I encourage you to read the author's other book on discipleship that deals specifically with topics pertaining to the multiplication phase!

Chapter 22

Dokimos?

"Be diligent to present yourself approved to God, a worker who does not need to be ashamed, rightly dividing the word of truth."
2 Timothy 2:15

With a great responsibility comes the need for great and continual preparation. As a mentor or leader to other believers, you must be diligent to continually present yourself approved to God. The word "approved" is the Greek word *"dokimos"* (Strong's # 1384). The use of this word is extremely interesting. During the time of the early church all currency was made from metal and not from paper. The minting process consisted of melting the metal into liquid and pouring them into molds. When the metal cooled, the edges of the coin needed to be shaved smooth. Due to the metal's softer quality, many people would shave the coins smaller and lighter than what was deemed as the standard for circulation. The extra shavings would enable them to keep more metal to make more money.

However, there were money makers who were men of integrity who would not accept money that did not meet the determined standard. These money changers only allowed the full weighted money to be put into circulation. It was these men who were called *"dokimos"* or "approved" according to (Donald Barnhouse). God demands for His workers to be approved. Such workers are those who are faithful to uphold the standard of God and His Word. Notice, an approved workman must rightly divide the Word of God. They are genuine men and women of God, who fear God and stand on the authority of His word. An approved worker has been examined and tested by God to be genuine and faithful.

"Blessed is the man who endures temptation; for when he has been approved, he will receive the crown of life which the Lord has promised to those who love Him."

James 1:12

Enduring temptation enables you to be approved. Jesus said, *"If anyone loves Me, he will keep My word"* (John 14:23). Temptation tries you. It tests your heart and your faithfulness toward the Lord. An approved worker is a person who is Christ-like. An approved worker has experienced genuine transformation and formation in their character and maintains it through continual intimacy with the Lord.

"For our exhortation did not come from error or uncleanness, nor was it in deceit. But as we have been approved by God to be entrusted with the gospel, even so we speak, not as pleasing men, but God who tests our hearts. For neither at any time did we use flattering words, as you know, nor a clock for covetousness- God is witness. Nor did we seek glory from men, either from you or from others."

1 Thessalonians 2:3-6

An approved workman does not use the word of God for flattery, covetousness, or to circulate error or deceit. Your heart determines if you are an approved workman. You must understand that error or deception is a fruit of the condition of the heart. Not rightly dividing the Word of God is a matter of the heart. When workers in the kingdom have perversion, impure motives, and self-seeking in their hearts, it will eventually be revealed through their service or teaching. Paul was approved by God; therefore, his exhortation did not come from error, uncleanness, or deceit. He did not use flattering words for self gain or covetousness nor was he after the praise and glory of men.

"For there must also be factions among you, that those who are approved may be recognized among you."

1 Corinthians 11:19

The Apostle Paul viewed factions or divisions in a positive light. He understood that any divisions that were created would cause those who are approved, as well as those who were unapproved, to be recognized by believers. Jesus said, *"Therefore by their fruits you will know them"* (Matthew 7:20). A person who causes division and factions in the body of Christ is not approved by God. The Bible says a person who devises evil and sows discord has perversity in his heart. (See Proverbs 6:14) Such a believer needs to repent and be restored in order to become an approved workman. (See Galatians 6:1 & 1 Corinthians 5)

You must continually guard your heart. You have navigated through the phases of spiritual development, but you still need to be diligent to remain an approved workman. Doing so will keep you from having to experience any shame. Paul said, *"I discipline my body and bring it into subjection, lest, when I have preached to others, I myself should become disqualified"* (1 Corinthians 9:27). The word "disqualified" is translated from the Greek word *"adokimos"* (Strong's # 96). This is the exact opposite of a "dokimos" or an approved workman.

Safe guard your life by continuing to walk in the light and be faithful to do what you know to do. Keep the formation spiritual disciplines active in your life as a way to fellowship with the Spirit of the Lord. Stay in the word and continue to grow in the grace and knowledge of the Lord. As you grow in spiritual knowledge, continue to rightly divide the Word of God. Discipline your body and keep it in subjection to your inner man. Continue to major on character and yet still hunger for the gifts of the kingdom. Above all stay clothed with love as you keep your relationship with Christ as first priority!

"But seek first the kingdom of God and His righteousness, and all these things shall be added to you."

Matthew 6:33

Again, I want to encourage you to read the author's other book that focuses specifically on truths that pertain and will equip you further for the multiplication phase!

I want to end with a prayer for you:

I pray that God will continue to empower you to walk in the good works that He has prepared for you before the foundation of the earth. I ask that you would be surrounded with the favor of God. I ask that God would send the right mentors into your life and the right people for you to mentor. I ask that the word of God would multiply through your life in the days to come. May His kingdom come into your heart each day. May the Lord keep your spirit, soul, and body blameless until His coming. May you be preserved for His kingdom. May you hear and follow His voice. May a fresh anointing of the Holy Spirit come upon you! May you always walk worthy of His kingdom all the days of your life and may you stand fast in the liberty by which He has set you free. I ask that you would abide in His love and reach your potential in Christ Jesus. May you be conformed into the image of Jesus Christ. I pray that you would continue to grow in the grace and knowledge of Christ. May you flourish where you are planted. And it is in the name of Jesus I pray. Amen!

Appendix

Baptism into Christ

- Baptism into the Body of Christ
- Holy Spirit is the baptizer/ The element is the body of Christ
- Occurs when a person is born again
    - o Ephesians 4:5, Galatians 3:27, Colossians 2:11-13, Galatians 2:20, 1 Corinthians 6:17, 1 Corinthians 10:2

Some Results of Baptism:
- *Born into the Kingdom* - Romans 14:17, Luke 12:32, John 14:27/ *Receive the seed or nature of God* - 1 John 3:9, Galatians 3:16, Galatians 4:19, John 4:14 (well of life)

Aspect 1: **Water Baptism**	Aspect 2: **Holy Spirit Baptism**

- Command by Jesus
- Water baptism in the name of the Father, the Son, and the Holy Spirit or water baptism in the name of the Lord Jesus
- A minister is the baptizer/ The element is water
   o Matthew 28:19
   o Acts 8:35-38
   o Acts 9:18
   o Acts 10:47-48
   o Acts 16:15
   o Acts 16:33
   o Acts 19:5
   o 1 Corinthians 10:1-2
 	
Water baptism is a rite of identification by which new believers become associated with Jesus and His followers; symbolizes our identification with Jesus' death, burial and resurrection.
 	
This baptism is an outward expression of an inward reality.
 	
A result: Witnesses to our righteousness (1 John 5:8)
	- The Promise of the Father
	- Being Baptized with the Holy Spirit
	- When the Holy Spirit has come upon you
	- Gift of the Holy Spirit
	- Receiving the Holy Spirit (in full NT ministry & role)
	- Jesus is the baptizer/ The element is the Holy Spirit
	   o John 1:33
	   o Matthew 3:11
	   o Luke 3:16
	   o Acts 1:4-5,8
	   o Acts 2:1-4
	   o Acts 8:14-17
	   o Acts 10:44-47
	   o Acts 11:15-17
	   o Acts 19:6
	   o John 7:38-39 (rivers of life)
	- Initial evidence – speaking with other tongues
	   o Acts 2:4,11
	   o Acts 10:44-47
	   o Acts 19:6
	   o Matthew 12:34
	   o OT types
	A result: Empowerment for Kingdom purpose (Acts 1:8)